A masterpiece in the genre of spiritu
gently and fearlessly speaks to ot
weaving together into a luminous whoιε ....
psychological, mythic, historical, and spiritual dimensions of
embodied experience. In this magnificent exposition of the
emerging Deep Feminine, the reader will find clarity, compassion
and a tender reflection of his or her own soul. *Servants of the
Sacred Dream* not only describes a healing process but evokes it.

Melanie Reinhart, author of *Chiron and the Healing Journey*

In *Servants of the Sacred Dream*, Linda Hartley has undertaken
the timeless quest of wrestling meaning from psycho-spiritual
crisis. Using her own descent into the dark night of the soul, she
shows how this *nekyia*, as the Greeks called it, brings forth
treasures, the gifts of the underworld journey. She brings a new
depth and perspective to the feminine face of God, and reaffirms
how the loss of the feminine spirit leads us to lopsidedness and
catastrophe. This is a book that affirms the human ability to grow
from suffering and walk the ancient shamanic paths once more,
with beauty and dignity.

Stephen Larsen, author of *The Shaman's Doorway*, and co-
author with Robin Larsen of *A Fire in the Mind: The Life of
Joseph Campbell*, and *The Fashioning of Angels: Partnership as
Spiritual Practice*

With generosity and brave truthfulness, Linda Hartley guides us
through a comprehensive and timely exploration of the terrible
and essential steps towards wholeness within the great challenges
of the development of the feminine in our contemporary world.

Janet Adler, author of *Arching Backward: The Mystical
Initiation of a Contemporary Woman*

Linda Hartley is author of *Wisdom of the Body Moving*, and works as a body-oriented therapist, teacher, and trainer. She currently runs training programmes in Integrative Bodywork and Movement Therapy in England and Germany, and a series of workshops and retreats for women – Woman, Body, Earth and Spirit – which explore the 'deep feminine' through movement, bodywork, and myth. At home in England, she runs a private practice offering body-oriented therapy and Authentic Movement to individuals and groups.

Servants
of the
Sacred Dream

Rebirthing the Deep Feminine:
Psycho-spiritual
Crisis and Healing

Linda Hartley

ELMDON
BOOKS

Copyright © Linda Hartley 2001
First published in 2001 by Elmdon Books
9 The Green
Saffron Walden
Essex CB10 2DS

Distributed by Gazelle Book Services Limited
Falcon House, Queen Square
Lancaster, England LA1 1RN

British Library Cataloguing in Publication Data
A catalogue record for this book is available from the British Library

ISBN 0-9540117-0-8

Typeset by Amolibros, Watchet, Somerset
This book production has been managed by Amolibros
Printed and bound by T J International Ltd, Padstow, Cornwall, UK

Contents

For Dave—
his living and his dying,
which brought me to my path

Acknowledgements

In a journey such as this book reflects, there is some mysterious power that must first be acknowledged. I give my humble thanks to that which guided, held, and refused to allow me to give up, even through the most difficult moments. This power came to me in many different ways. Most importantly, through the gift of friendship, it would arrive with a timely word of wisdom or encouragement, a simple act of kindness, a gesture that implied something had been witnessed and understood. It arrived in the form of a book that needed to be read just then, a supportive voice on the end of the phone, a gift or letter that needed to be received, a moment of intimacy, an unexpected visit that would lift my spirit and connect me once again to the unpredictable and magical flow of life.

These gifts of friendship flowed through many people. Some passed through my life briefly, and were there at the most critical moments; others were constant companions on the way, keeping me connected to life. Among them were Jane Orton, Carole Bruce, Jay Ramsay, Denise McCormac, Katya Bloom, Teresa Marlar, Susanne and Joel Hartley, Shelagh and Alasdair McGeagh, Beverley Ferguson, Helga Frensel, Claudia Grange-Taylor, Varsha Lighthill, Patrice Heber, and Maryshka Bigos. My students and colleagues were also a source of deep inspiration, support, love, and affirmation of the path I had undertaken, which held me during the writing of this book. To all of these friends, I offer my heartfelt thanks for the shared moments, the acts of kindness, love, and support.

For their healing, I am especially indebted to the late Lizzy Bingley, Robert Lever, and Stephen Silver. They showed me that healing is a journey of love, respect, the deepest care for the mysterious processes of life, and an ever-unfolding understanding of myself and my path on this earth. For their skill, sensitivity, knowledge, and wisdom, I am deeply grateful. Without this, I could not have found the power within me to grow and heal.

I am also grateful to Judith Meikle who helped me to understand the nature of abuse of power in therapy. She constantly showed through her own example how genuine care, compassion, honesty, and humility are the essential foundations of any healing or therapeutic relationship, and she restored hope when all hope had been lost.

My thanks go also to Christine Murdock, John Firman, and Annie Morgan for their insightful comments on the manuscript in its earlier stages, and to Amy Corzine for her editorial help.

The therapist who led me into the crisis which forms the raw bones of this book must also be acknowledged, for without him the book would most certainly not have been written in the form it now appears. So, as the 'ally' who precipitated the encounter with the depths of my being, which led eventually to much learning, deepening, and embracing of lost parts of myself, I acknowledge his crucial role in this story.

The person who, more than any other, constantly brought me back from the edge of the abyss, was my spiritual teacher, the Venerable Lama Chime Rinpoche. His kindness and compassion opened my heart to the preciousness of all life. Through him, the mysterious power that kept my heart open to life worked most strongly and clearly, ever insisting I grow, strengthen, and discover who I truly am. To him I truly owe my life, and will be ever grateful.

And finally, I pay my respects to the earth which held me, witnessed me, received me when I fell, inspired me when my spirit was ready to fly, and revealed to me the meaning of the wilderness. The garden and the cottage which were my home whilst I wrote this book provided the safe space, the cocoon, for the process of writing and healing to take place. And the leafy lane, which I walked daily during the periods of writing, became sacred ground. Here, as I trod my half-formed thoughts and feelings into the muddy track, or sang my songs to the earth and sky as I walked, this book came into being. Thank you mother earth, for the beauty and the healing that is there to be witnessed and received always.

Acknowledgment of Sources

Introduction

The re-emergence of the *deep feminine* into individual and collective consciousness is at the heart of a transformation we are being challenged to make today. To connect to the source of the feminine we must journey deep within ourselves, a journey which often entails suffering crises of body, soul, and spirit as we seek the ground of our inner being.

This path is most fully embodied in the lives of women. It is also travelled by mystics and shamans in their initiatory and healing journeys, and through the creative process of the artist. Crises on the path are challenges of the deepest order whereby we are called to realign our psychological and spiritual core to a new way of being. Attitudes prevailing in modern culture generally misunderstand, reject, or pathologise those experiences that herald the return of the conscious feminine.

For about five thousand years, the world has been dominated by patriarchal consciousness and its social orders, religions, and values. Today we are recognising that this age is reaching an end, must end. We are being forced to look at the values we are living by, the world we are creating according to those values, and to question the choices we are making, for they may be crucial to the well-being and survival of humanity far into the future.

Beleaguered by social conflicts, wars, famines, environmental pollution, and the threat of annihilation through weapons of mass destruction or ecological breakdown, our world is changing at a pace so rapid that the individual human being struggles to keep up. The human intellect seems to have an unlimited capacity to invent, create, and dominate, but our bodies and our feelings do not so quickly adapt to the pace of technological progress which our minds have initiated. The cost of progress to our physical and psychological health has been high. Something has been left behind in this race, and we desperately need to reclaim it.

Crisis and Renewal

When something has outlived its usefulness it must give way and allow in new influences. If it does not, it grows excessive and its potential good qualities become distorted, repressive, and abusive, instead of life-affirming and supportive. Patriarchal dominance has reached such a point. Patriarchy is not, of itself, bad, and has clearly served a necessary purpose in the evolution of human society. But it has now become unbalanced and distorted, and to follow on this path any longer will lead us into very real disaster.

When the old does give way, the process of change itself invariably brings with it a period of chaos and suffering, but suffering of a different nature from that inflicted by an abusive system holding on to power. We are, collectively, at such an edge and faced with the choice of welcoming change and the emergence of new values and consciousness, or resisting the inevitable and continuing to suffer the distortions of a system grown rigid, insensitive, and often brutal.

Britain during the last decades of the twentieth century had a particular significance in this process. We witnessed the dying days of a once great empire, an empire that was the pinnacle of patriarchal achievement. History has shown us that all great empires turn barbaric in their fall. The sophisticated form of barbarism which we experienced towards the end of the last century was couched in euphemisms like 'economic growth', 'free enterprise' and 'technological progress', which so readily degenerate into the abuse of human and natural resources, ecological crisis, and exploitation of the vulnerable. Instead of conservation, 'conservatism' came to mean something closer to ever-increasing 'consumerism', and political choices were largely dictated by fear and greed, so closely linked in a society that feels itself to be living insecurely at the edge. This country was depressed, as it struggled between the need for radical change and a resistance to accepting this need.

However, living at the edge also brings a growing awareness of both the plight and the changes that are necessary and potentially immanent. New awareness is bringing new concern. At the edge, we see how precarious and painfully vulnerable life is – human life, the life of the earth, all sentient life. With this realisation, we also begin to feel how precious life is. And, as cracks in the old structures begin to appear, new life quickly begins to take root there.

Of course, Britain is not alone in these trends. Other 'empires' are dying, and all countries of the modern world are faced with the same issues and concerns today. In any country facing the demise of an historical greatness and power, a particularly difficult struggle may be experienced between the tendency to cling to the old order, and the need to embrace the new awareness and values that are attempting to emerge into our collective consciousness. The emergence of something new brings with it a reactionary swing towards the old and familiar, about to slip out of reach forever, as we try to cling to safety and certainty. Much of the pain, struggle, and fear of times of change come as a result of the conflict between the wish for everything to stay as it is, the need to move on, and futile attempts to avoid the pain of the chaos and confusion that change often brings with it.

At such an edge, we also experience a heightened awareness of all that is wrong with the old state of affairs, all that has failed or gone amiss, the injustices and abuses formerly unrecognised or denied, and the 'unfinished business' that calls to be resolved before we can move beyond it to something new. So we enter the new millennium with an enormous agenda for positive change in areas such as the care of children, education, health, human rights, protection of the natural environment and endangered communities, and much more.

Individuals who are sensitive to the undercurrents of the collective process may feel this conflict acutely, and in a personal way. With the breakdown of communities and the family, loss of religious values, and the threatened collapse of once stable institutions, economies, and ecological balance, many people inevitably suffer great personal misfortune. But not only as a result of the external changes taking place in the world; the crisis we are going through is, at its heart, a crisis of consciousness, and it is the consciousness of the individual which is being challenged to grow through these times. Faced with personal and global crisis, we are being challenged to open our awareness to both the risks that confront us today, and the potential for cultivating a new, creative, and more compassionate approach towards life and living.

The challenge of opening to new awareness, though a collective issue, can only be done by the individual. The struggle to become free of an outmoded system of beliefs and values, and open to embrace a new way of being, perceiving, and acting in the world, can only be felt in the hearts and minds of individual people. Through personal experience, many today are suffering the birth pains of collective transformation, the awakening of new consciousness. As individuals, we each embody, in the personal details of our unfolding lives, the collective process.

A person going through a process of profound inner change is often viewed by society as mentally ill, suffering a pathological condition that needs to be treated or cured. But such a condition may be not only pathological in nature. Breakdown or mental illness may be caused by the awakening of new awareness and the struggle to be free of the power of old mechanisms of control, both internal and external; it may hold the potential for real and deep healing and change to take place. In such a healing crisis the individual, like the collective, is faced with the pain of past hurts and fears, deepened awareness of present predicaments, and the need to resolve conflicts which keep her bound within the old power dynamics. She is also confronted with the challenge to embrace new consciousness, open to a deepened sense of who she is, and through this, to accept more fully her purpose and responsibility in life.

Within the healing crisis lies the potential for growth and change, a psychological and spiritual rebirth, but it is a delicate process and one that can easily be aborted. The attitudes of family, friends, professional helpers, and society towards the individual's experience are crucial in providing a positive context of meaning. Although the distress experienced must be acknowledged and appropriate care given, if the process is viewed and treated as *purely* a regressive and pathological breakdown, then it may become so; the healing potential may not be able to unfold in such an environment. The meaning and value that is given to the crisis is crucial; as more and more individuals are being confronted, or are confronting themselves through journeys of deepening consciousness, there is an urgent need to develop a better understanding of the processes involved, and the kind of support that is required.

Returning to the Source

This book will explore some of the issues often hidden behind labels of psychopathology, and attempt to offer some alternative perspectives from which to evaluate our suffering and ordeals. It will address both the pathology of body, soul, and spirit, and the potential for deeper meaning –

the ways we may get lost, and the possibilities for growth and healing that may be found within the crisis – placing the individual's experience in both a cultural and a spiritual context.

The crisis I am speaking of is psycho-spiritual in essence; it occurs when the psyche is burnt by the light of spirit, when the ego is overwhelmed by a too-sudden opening of consciousness which it is not yet ready to embrace. Many things may act as catalysts for such crises. Traumatic life experiences such as bereavement, the loss of an important relationship or job, a serious illness or accident, for example, can plunge us into the 'dark night of the soul' and a profound search within our own depths for meaning and new life. The opening of consciousness may also be stimulated by hallucinogenic drugs, deep psychological work, or intensive meditation practice. Christina and Stanislav Grof, who have researched and worked extensively in this field, have named such crises 'spiritual emergencies'. In their book of that name, they describe some of the many causes and varieties of experience encountered 'when personal transformation becomes a crisis'. [1]

As we midwife ourselves through these times of collective change, we need to develop an understanding of the process of regeneration, and the needs of the person going through its critical stages. With the necessity of a change in consciousness facing us today, more and more people are being called to make the journey into the depths and heights of their being. It is not surprising that, along with a growing need, a rich variety of teachings and methods for awakening consciousness have now become available to us. We have access to ancient teachings from both eastern and western spiritual and healing traditions, which are finding a new home in the lost and searching souls of modern men and women. Great teachers from distant lands now visit our own home towns, so that we no longer need to make arduous journeys in order to hear profound teachings that were once secret and hard to find. And with the understanding of human nature that western psychology has developed, a great array of new methods for healing, personal development, and transformation has also emerged in recent years. As with any birth, this brings with it unimagined possibilities as well as risk and danger, for we are treading a precarious path between worlds.

Those worlds are the realms of psyche and spirit, of the known and the barely knowable, of life and death, of matter and mystery. We are attempting to create, or perhaps remember, and cross the bridge between these worlds in order to return to what has been lost, forgotten, left behind. It is our soul and our spiritual values that we have all but lost in the mad race for material progress. Through our personal and collective crises, we are being called upon to return to our source, and redeem what has been cast out, wounded, or forgotten. Many of us are being called to descend, on the journey of soul-making, into the underworld, the dark side of life, and there undergo the initiatory ordeals of death and rebirth.

This journey has been described in many different and poetic ways through the religious and mythological writings of every culture in history. There are common themes underlying these varied descriptions of the process which point to its universality, despite the fact that each culture has dressed the story in the garb of its own cosmology and symbolism. In *Rebel in the Soul*, a commentary on an ancient Egyptian mystical text that prepares the initiate for spiritual transformation and rebirth, Bika Reed describes the Egyptian view:

'The "Book of the Gates" depicts the progression of the sun through the night. The twelve hours of the Dark Night are depicted as regions of the Underworld. Each region is an 'hour' of the Night and has its gate. To pass the gate, one has to know the name of its Guardian.

'The consciousness moves through the Underworld from gate to gate in a process of slow animation. For Egypt, life and consciousness are synonymous. To be dead meant to be unawakened and inert, moved like a leaf by the wind. 'To be dead', for Egypt, is a state of inanimation, preceding consciousness or life. The process of animation, depicted in the "Book of the Gates" was called "Coming Forth Into Day".'[2]

In the process of travelling this dark path into life, or consciousness, we need guidance; without proper guidance, we may become lost in the dark regions, prey to madness and despair. Yet modern western culture has, by and large, lost touch with a spiritual tradition and philosophical context that might embrace such experiences, and guide the traveller through them.

There is no appropriate guidance because an understanding of the universal journey through the underworld, and acceptance of the natural cycles of life, death, and rebirth, have been lost and denied by our modern western culture. Patriarchal consciousness is turned towards defying and overcoming the powers of nature, darkness, death and decay, and is focussed on a linear concept of progress that denies the cyclical processes of nature. Even many 'new age' approaches to healing and growth tend to deny or dissociate from the dark side of life. And so the traveller through the dark night of the soul all too often becomes the mad-woman and may find herself incarcerated in a mental hospital – or exiled in other ways from home, family, and community – because there is no rightful place for her misunderstood experience within our society.

Without an understanding of the potential meaning of the crisis, proper guidance and support cannot be given. Understanding in this context also means personal experience, for if we have not gone through and survived the experience of the underworld ourselves, fear may prevent us from being able to support another who is undergoing the ordeal. What we don't know always makes us fearful, and the powerful emotions encountered in this process can be particularly threatening to a culture that has denied and repressed their expression for many centuries. Psychiatry has drugged them into silence, but today we must learn to listen again to the inner voices that are crying out to be heard, for they may hold the seeds of healing that the world so desperately needs.

Embracing the Feminine

The perspective that is offered here has evolved out of my personal experience of a crisis which occurred whilst I was undergoing psychotherapy training. During a process that was potentially transformative and healing, I was plunged into a deep, psycho-spiritual crisis that was drawn out into a long period of psychosomatic illness and depression. This crisis was precipitated by therapeutic work that was seriously misguided, and which left me abandoned in a deep process that I could find no completion for. My wish in writing about this experience, and the long path to recovery and healing, is an attempt to share with others who may find themselves in crisis, or those helping them, some of the things I have learnt through it. My hope is to share the knowledge that there *is* a way through, as we face our fear and our aloneness. Knowing that, individually, we may come through such ordeals, deepened, enriched, and empowered, gives me hope that humanity, poised on the brink of its own breakdown, also holds the potential to grow and become enriched through such a process.

This perspective has come first out of my own experience and reflection, and has been supported by many stories I have heard from friends, clients, students, teachers all around me, and in the works of other writers. Their stories have shown me that there are issues within my own story that are widespread, cultural, and of this time. I am grateful to all of those who have shared their own experiences with me, either directly or through their writing, as their insights and courage have supported, encouraged, and affirmed my own growing understanding.

The central issue that emerged from my own crisis concerned the repression and abuse of the feminine by a domineering and distorted masculine. This was played out in my experience of therapy with a male therapist, a dynamic that also reflected wider issues of gender within our society. Abuse of power was occurring, but instead of it being addressed therapeutically, I was subtly revictimised, in much the same way that women have been victimised for centuries by men in positions of power over them. Recognition and understanding of abuse of the oppressed feminine, and the emergence of the re-empowered creative feminine spirit is one of the central issues of the crisis of our present age. It is crucial to both personal and collective healing.

It may be naïve to say that women's greater involvement will save the world, but I do believe that we will not be able to grow in creative and life-affirming ways unless the values and principles of the feminine, and the women who give voice and action to them, are honoured and heeded as truly equal to the masculine way. One of the most important developments of the last century was the social and political emancipation of women. In the coming century, the values of the feminine must return to consciousness so that all of our lives may be spiritually enriched and empowered by this creative source.

Throughout history, many great races and empires have flourished and died; so too have cultural ages evolved and passed to make way for something new and different to emerge. The 'death of an age' that we are now experiencing is not a new phenomenon, but another turn in the greater cycle of the evolution of humanity. At each stage in human history, a new aspect of culture and consciousness has emerged with the dying of the old. An essential element of what we are witnessing and experiencing now is the return of the feminine principle into consciousness, and the emergence of a spirituality which places the Goddess, feminine aspect of divinity, once again in her rightful place at its heart.

The terms masculine and feminine are used here in the way that they are usually understood in psychological language – not to mean male and female gender, but as symbols for certain principles, values, qualities, aspects of being and consciousness. Men and women alike embody both principles, but women are by nature generally more attuned to the qualities of the feminine. Connection with the earth, the cycles of nature and the body, feelings and instincts, inclusiveness, relatedness, intelligence born out of intuition, insight and natural wisdom, and the creative processes of birth, death and rebirth are a woman's natural realm. With the repression of feminine consciousness by the patriarchy, it is the feminine, feeling, wise, instinctual, and cyclical nature of both men and women that has been denied, though historically it is women who have suffered most obviously from the oppression and abuses caused by this repression.

Today it is women who are resonating most strongly with the stirrings of this reawakening consciousness, and women who are called to descend first on the journey to the underworld in search of the banished Dark Goddess. The story of *Woman* and the re-emerging feminine principle is, therefore, at the heart of this book. [1]

Likewise, God and Goddess refer here to masculine and feminine aspects of spirit, symbolic expressions of complementary spiritual qualities, accessible to all of us. Although we may talk about masculine and feminine aspects as if they were distinct and separate, they are only separated through our own conception. But, in order to move beyond this fundamental duality in our thinking, we first need to address the distortion and imbalance we have created between the discernibly different qualities and values that the terms masculine and feminine represent. This means re-evaluating both masculine and feminine, and their relationship to each other, within the

---

1 For this reason, and also because I am speaking of personal experiences as a woman, I have chosen to use the feminine pronoun throughout; in places, I talk about experiences that pertain more specifically to women, though they may be relevant to processes of the feminine in men too. In other parts of the book the feminine pronoun is intended to refer equally to both men and women, and is used alone for the sake of simplicity.

personal, social, political, and spiritual areas of life. Within the spiritual sphere, it demands the re-inclusion of the Goddess into our concept and our experience of the divine.

For many modern women, the Goddess has become, once again, a potent symbol of feminine wholeness, power, wisdom, and creativity, which can give women the strength and confidence to be and to act in the world from an empowered, authentic source. For some, the Goddess may be a felt sense of a nurturing, containing, grounding, and empowering wise presence in the universe; an experience of space, or the universe, as innately intelligent, conscious awareness; a sense of the creative and beneficent presence of God-the-Mother. Respecting the differing experiences and conceptions of the Goddess that we may have, I invite them all to be embraced here.[3]

The feminine, and the Goddess, have been feared by western patriarchy as dark, abysmal, chaotic, destructive, unconscious; because of this fear the feminine principle has been denied, repressed, and pushed further into unconsciousness. The challenge today is to awaken conscious feminine awareness, and to choose to live by the values of that creative consciousness; it is a challenge of surrender to the Goddess within, and a challenge of the heart. We take up that challenge when we begin to look into our own hearts and feel the pain of the wounds we carry within us; and as we do so, we begin to listen again to our own truth, and learn to express that truth in the world. Many women today, and men too, are beginning to express through their creative work, their relationships, and the quality of their lives, the truth that is the voice of the feminine spirit, the Goddess. When we find her spirit within us, we find an inner strength and support for our lives, but we must remember that we also have a responsibility to give voice to that spirit, to let her speak through us; without us, the Goddess in exile will not be heard and cannot return. As Chani Smith writes in *The Absent Mother*:

> 'The Shekhinah calls us to return…she knows the route to her salvation, and can direct us and give us inspiration, but we must not forget that she too is in the wilderness and needs our help.'[4]

Travellers between the Worlds

In making the journey of return to the source of the feminine spirit, we engage with our healing and creative powers, evoking the healer and artist within us. The journeys of descent or ascent into 'other worlds' have been understood by cultures world-wide, and since the recording of history began, as the journey of initiation of the shaman or wounded healer. People today are still experiencing these initiatory journeys but without the support of a cultural context which gives meaning to them. A crisis of physical illness or mental breakdown may be a potential opening to 'other worlds' which can awaken us to gifts of healing, creativity, knowledge, and wisdom.

The initiatory journeys of the shaman and the artist offer a context for the crises we are encountering in the modern world, and in our individual lives. Both the shaman and the artist are travellers between the worlds. Their art is that of travelling the bridge between the known and unknown, in order to bring back the knowledge, power, inspiration, and healing that their communities are in need of. The need for the experience of the artist, healer, and mystic, always closely linked in former times, is urgent today.

In her book *Psychic Energy*, Esther Harding states:

'The unmediated experience of spirit, in all its numinous power, came to only a few isolated individuals.... Many experiences are recorded, so that we can read how it was with the saints and mystics whose visions and dreams produced ecstasy or terror. It was only later that these experiences were organised under fixed symbolic and ritual forms to make a church in which the many could find a solution of life's problems and rest for their souls. The fact that this could happen is evidence that the original experiences, while occurring to a few only, had yet a general validity; the few had the necessary vision to perceive the psychic reality that was present, unseen and unrecognized, in the unconscious of the large majority of their contemporaries. This is the function that the artist and the seer have performed in all ages.'[5]

Today it is not only to the few that such experiences may occur. The awakening of consciousness to the fire of spirit is becoming a possibility, and maybe, in the emerging age, a necessity for not only the especially gifted or fortunate few, but for the many. We are all being called upon to be artist and seer unto ourselves, to learn to make the journeys within the depths and heights of our own being where we may contact the source of the healing and creative powers which can renew our lives. In the era that we are now entering, we are being called upon more and more to seek guidance and conscience within ourselves, from our own conscious feeling and awareness, rather than from some external authority.

When the individual psyche becomes sensitised and attuned to the stirrings of collective psychic process, our personal journeys seem to reflect very precisely the outer events we witness in the world. Listening to our own personal experience, to the issues which confront us in our relationships, our dreams, our body symptoms, our visions, and the feelings of our hearts, we learn about the underlying forces that are shaping our collective experience, and what the world is in need of today. Those individuals, institutions, and nations most sensitive, vulnerable, and perhaps aware of the issues facing humanity may be those who experience most intensely the chaos and destruction that heralds in change; those who are most sensitive and vulnerable may be the first to let go of their fragile hold on security, and make the descent into the womb of the Dark Goddess, the place of destruction and death which is also the place of transformation and rebirth.

This book is a weaving together of many different, often paradoxical, strands of experience. Weaving has traditionally been considered a woman's craft and the work of the Goddess. Women weave the disparate things of the world into relationship – connecting, bringing together, embracing the whole. The masculine invents and creates the new, forging a direct path into the future; the feminine works with what is, creating a meaningful present.

The voice of the feminine is heard through the specific, the immanent, the real and personal, rather than the abstract and theoretical. As we tell our stories we begin to weave meaning into the confusion of events that seem to be our lives, and make sacred through this meaning the suffering and loss that has been our experience. In the act of creating out of our suffering comes healing. Like the shaman and the artist, we must return from our journeyings with a gift for the world; this, my own gift, is an attempt to bring meaning to the suffering and the darkness we go through as we seek consciousness and the true life of spirit, and again make sacred our sacrifices. I offer it to all fellow travellers, and to those great souls who have gone before us, who, in their wisdom and kindness, hold the thread along which we may tread – over the chasm between the worlds.

I will begin by telling a part of my own story.

Part One

Body, Soul and Spirit in Crisis

So cold here. And still

Silence. And the rush of waves
pounds within my skull, deep
in the old recess of memory. You drowned here
in this silent deep.
While the foam noiselessly churned the sky above,
your thoughts fled into nothingness.

I die for you again, this day.
Holy terror floods my veins and pours
into the ocean, weeping.
Dry is the air where your own blood may have run beside
me, standing, gazing to your grave
far out in the northern seas.

It is so cold here. And still.
My face against the wind is numbed and motionless.
Waves turn, only to be caught like stone
and petrified; the tide retreats to leave them
mounded, naked, blackened chars piled—death upon death—
along the wide white shores.

Let the ocean waters flood my grieving lungs,
fill my empty places, sorrowing.
But my heart cannot be filled
by mortal nor by elemental cause. It seeks,
over and again it seeks the groundless ground of dying
where it may be freed.

Face to face with nothing, buried in the silence
that engulfs the roaring waves—
like stone I turn and turn, but cannot move.

1 The Wastelands of the Heart

Some years ago, I was present at the birth of my sister's child. It was the first time I had witnessed a birth. I thought I was prepared for the pain and bloodshed that it would entail, but I was not prepared for the possible complications of a 'difficult' birth. The first stages of the birth, which took place at my sister's home, seemed to be going well and quite normally; but, on arriving at the hospital, we were informed that the baby was in distress. Hospital procedures quickly turned what began as a natural birth into an emergency. As the labour reached its crucial stage, I anxiously watched the flickerings on the screen that were monitoring his heartbeats. The air in the room was heavy with tension and the pain of my sister and her baby as they struggled in the battle between life and death. Eventually his head emerged, and, for what seemed like an eternity, I looked on helplessly as the young nurse tried to cut the cord that was wrapped tightly twice around his neck.

Finally he was freed and pulled out. It was an indescribable moment. I cannot remember having ever before felt such a pure, spontaneous, and unconditional love as I experienced then between this little being and myself. I saw his wholeness, completeness, nakedness, as if there was nothing he had ever been or would become that was not present in him and visible at that moment of his birth. Perhaps we never so fully embody our power and love as in the act of birth; the birthing child can touch our souls and awaken our hearts. His heart was full and open, and it opened mine in response.

The next moment I was overwhelmed by an unbearable pain; I thought that he was dead – that the struggling to be born had gone on just too long, and he had drowned in his birth fluids as the cord was cut. As the midwife

4

held up his body for the first time it looked heavy and lifeless, the skin bluish and swollen with fluid; no movement or sound stirred in him.

Something wrenched inside of me, like a great chasm opening up, and a flood of memories and feelings of all the loss and grief I had ever known rushed up. And with that it seemed came the grief of the world, of every mother's loss, and the pain of every child that had died, young or old, was there in my own broken heart.

The doctor quickly took him and laid him down; he gently sucked the water from the baby's drowned lungs, and breathed new life into him with his own breath. Some minutes later as this tiny new being lay quiet, resting from his ordeal, he opened his eyes and looked for a moment into mine. It was a wise and knowing look. I knew that he would be all right. He grew to be a healthy and happy little boy, bright, full of energy and mischief; a child who would shout and cry as easily as he laughed and loved. I have, as always, a very special love for him.

This event had a deep impact on me, and marked something of a turning point in my own life, the beginning of a journey of giving birth to my self, of opening to my heart through the darkness and death that had surrounded it for so long. For me the story of my little nephew's 'birth and death and rebirth' symbolically spoke to, and vividly reflects the painful but vital process of becoming truly alive – the universal search to discover our true nature, to touch our souls and free our hearts from the bonds we have tied them in. It is a rite of passage, a journey through the crack between the worlds, through death and the underworld to a rebirth in new life. My own experience of his birth was like a premonition of the passage I had unknowingly embarked upon.

The chasm that this experience opened up in me was an old memory and an endless well of grief. A few days after my seventeenth birthday, my boyfriend had died. He had been my dearest friend and soul-mate; with him I felt a joy I had not felt before, and an awareness of my own emerging womanhood and beauty. Our love held that exquisite blend of passion and innocence that we may find only in our first true love. We had talked of marrying, but were both young and knew that we would wait. With him, my life had been filled with light and colour and possibility.

His death was sudden and unexpected. He drowned while swimming in the sea. The newspaper said the next day that he had died a 'hero'; he was helping to save a friend in difficulties who couldn't swim, when he was pulled down himself by strong undercurrents. I felt that at some unconscious level, as with many 'accidental' deaths, he had died of a broken heart. I can never know for sure if that was true, but I had previously tried to leave him, and had betrayed both him and myself in that. I imagined the wound had opened up his soul. Our wounds are like gateways into deeper levels of our being, where we may touch on not just this one hurt or loss, but all the pain we have accumulated through our lifetimes. The gateway may be an opening into the healing of old wounds, but sometimes the flood overwhelms us and we die; we may die physically, through accident, illness, or suicide, as if mistaking the level of the wounding and making real the inner psychological death; or we may die to our own soul, close off our broken heart whose pain we cannot bear to feel.

When Dave died, I died too. I felt as if my soul was split in two and went with him into the darkness of death. There was nothing but blackness in my mind – no colours, no light anymore. I lived in hell, in a living death. And my loss, my grief was all I had left. I was nothing but this grief and had to centre my still growing identity around the tragedy. The shock had also opened up awareness of the pains of my early life, and I felt like an infant mourning for the loss of her mother's comfort and security. Yet I felt old; a knowledge had come too suddenly that I was not ready to embrace, a knowledge that should not come until the later years of life, and I was an old woman before I had even grown up.

Nine months later my father died of cancer. He had been ill for some time before my friend's accident, and I had ended the relationship at my father's request that I was needed at home to help my mother and family through the difficult period of his illness. At that time I couldn't see how to conform with the wishes of both these men that I loved most, and had to choose. As a daughter still tied to my father, a father who was dying, I had weighty chains of fear and duty around me. I still needed the love and protection of my father and family, and felt bound to try to save them. In my ignorance, I betrayed myself, my own emerging womanhood, and my first love, in trying to fill my father's place in the family. I had acted like a true 'father's daughter' and it led, so I felt, through a series of circumstances to the death of the one I loved. I felt responsible for my friend's death, though it was many years before this guilt became truly conscious.

I grieved deeply over Dave's death, and was filled with horror, obsessed with images and fantasies of his dying which I had not been there to witness.

I wished that it had been me that had died, not him. At nights I would talk to him, trying to bring him back, at least for a moment. I could not contain so much pain and the shock eventually froze some corner of my heart, enclosed it in a dark and icy cage with only his image to keep it alive. When my father died I was numbed and could hardly feel the pain, only a terrible feeling of loss, confusion, and emptiness at being a daughter without a father. I was left with nothing that would fill the empty place inside that Dave and my father had left.

One of the most difficult things to bear was the isolation I felt. Death is so feared in our culture that we don't know how to approach the bereaved in their time of greatest need. We try to hide death from our view, so that when it does touch our lives we are at a loss as to how to face it. Nobody but Dave's parents, who shared the loss most deeply, ever mentioned even his name in my presence. I felt there was no one to whom I could talk about my feelings, and that my experience had cast me into another dimension of life where there was only a darkness that others feared to come into contact with. I began to feel as if I carried within me an evil that would hurt and destroy others if they came too close. Demons were taking possession of me, taking up their residence in the dark empty space that was inside me. I felt terribly alone in my grief, with only my own dark fears and fantasies to keep me company.

I know now that death offers an opportunity to open our hearts and share at a depth that we rarely share in the normal course of life. Death cuts through our small concerns and opens us to a deeper level of feeling through which we may touch the love that is at the heart of our experience. More than anything I needed to be in the company of my friend's parents, for with them my grief was allowed, and I could feel a little of this meeting of hearts through our shared pain. But eventually I had to leave school and home and learn to make my way, fatherless, in the world. It was then that something in me closed off. I hid the dark secret that was at the heart of my life, and with it I hid myself.

I learnt not to feel the pain too much, so that I could get on with the business of life, though this denial cost me greatly. It seemed I must try to forget what I knew in order to survive in an unsympathetic world, although hardly a day went by when I did not think about the loss of Dave and my father. It was hard to find any deep and lasting satisfaction or happiness in my life, although I did follow a creative and challenging career in which I had some success. I had other relationships, but none of them worked out; I feel my heart was not free to love fully and my soul was still tied to the image and the memory of Dave. But when my nephew was born, the powerful energy of birth broke open the shell around my heart, and once again I felt my body tremble with the weight of grief and the love it opened me to.

Shortly after his birth, I had another encounter with death. A friend of mine had suffered a breakdown, and on leaving hospital I offered her a room in the house where I was living, not realising in my naïveté that she still needed a degree of care that I was unable to give at that time. One morning I found her close to death, having taken an overdose. I saw a battle going on within her between the forces of life and death, as if two souls had inhabited her body and were fighting to claim it for their own. A level of her mind appeared to be semi-conscious and was gesturing to me for help, trying to show me what she had done. But the will that had driven her to take her life was wreaking its destruction on her body, and overwhelming her control. It was shocking to witness. Fortunately, she arrived in hospital in time to be saved.

Breaking the Heart Open to Love

It was also around this time that I first met my spiritual teacher, Lama Chime Rinpoche. My own life was in a painful turmoil that had drawn me into my friend's illness, attracted to something I must have recognised unconsciously in myself. I was in need of help, and becoming aware enough of my own suffering to be ready to open to it.

Every experience of life may be attempting to guide us towards the discovery of our inner good nature and our hearts, if we but knew how to listen to the messages. However, it may be a long time before we are ready to heed this call. Readiness comes out of an inner necessity when we begin to recognise the extent and depth of the suffering and confusion of our life. We each experience the necessity in our own way; it may come through grief, despair, discontent and longing, feelings of hopelessness or mental confusion. We finally know we must surrender. There really is no other way.

I was drawn to the Buddhist teaching because it spoke to my real inner experience in a way that the conventional teaching of the Christian church that I had grown up with did not. With Dave's death, I also experienced the 'death of God' within me. I felt betrayed and abandoned – if there was a God it was a cruel God, and there was nothing of comfort to be found anywhere to hold my pain. The one I loved had been taken away forever, and I found nothing and no one there to help me in that, as seemed to be promised in the Christian doctrine. No wisdom was offered that might help me find meaning in, or acceptance of, his untimely death; the only sense the teaching of the church seemed to offer was that we had been punished for some sin we did not even know we had committed. In hurt and anger, I, in turn, abandoned God. I stopped believing and in place of God's image, Dave became the spirit who was my connection to the divine. At the time of his death, I had long since grown out of my childhood belief in 'God-the-Father in the Sky'; but in deep mourning we regress to states of awareness experienced in early infancy and childhood, and our early concept of 'God-the-Father' may loom back into consciousness, with all its undertones of parental authority, judgement, and punishment.

The first truth of Buddhism tells us that life as we know it, samsara, is suffering. In that simple truth, I felt my own experience embraced and validated, rather than denied as I had felt it to be in a society that admonishes us to hide our pain, put it aside and get on with life – a society which tries to deny death itself. Until we really feel the truth of suffering within ourselves we may feel no incentive at all to develop and grow spiritually. If life has been relatively kind to us, we may manage to maintain a comfortable status quo within its little ups and downs. Or we may have blinded ourselves to the reality within and around us. But as we open our hearts and minds a little, or have them opened by those misfortunes that are also our opportunities to grow, we have to accept that human existence involves deep pain, suffering, and an acute vulnerability to the inevitable tragedies of living and dying, from which none of us are free. Buddhism bases its path towards liberation upon acceptance of this existential suffering.

Like many westerners today, I found it more acceptable to look within myself for the path towards freedom and happiness than to a God who had already died to me. Looking outside for what we lack and need is an aspect of the old patriarchal mode of heroic journeying; it is the way of crusading and conquering in order to possess that which is longed for – 'the other' – be it wealth, power, love, or spiritual grace. Today, as the old rule of the patriarchy loses its hold, we are being called to embark upon another kind of journey which seeks the wisdom of the inner heart through inclusion of feminine, receptive values and process, and through acceptance of our human suffering and woundedness. It is a way of opening to what is within, rather than seeking to possess, or be possessed by, what is without.

Our wounds can be doorways into deeper dimensions of reality, deeper experiences of being, if we can bear to step through them. The deaths of the two people I most loved offered such an opening, and it was to an indescribable depth of pain that I opened, too deep to fathom at the time. But if I was truly to live my life I had to face this death that was within my soul. When the necessity and the readiness to look is there, so too does the opportunity come. It first came for me in meeting with my spiritual teacher, whose love held me through the most frightening and painful part of my journey.

At about the same time I began sessions in psychosynthesis counselling, and later went on to begin a course of training in this therapy. It was through my process in therapy that I finally came to explore more consciously my woundedness, and to search in my heart for the meaning it might hold for me. It was there too where I was finally overwhelmed by the pain I carried within me and witnessed all around me in the world and the lives of others. The therapeutic work was breaking down my boundaries and my psyche began to disintegrate. Unable to contain the depth of consciousness and feeling that I had been opened to too quickly, I was laid wide open to the energies of the collective unconscious. Never had I been able to see so clearly, but never had I been so unable to function in the world or communicate what I saw and felt, and my outer world fell apart too. It took more than five years to recover enough from the experience, for my broken mind to heal enough for me to feel that I was living in the world again, but there are levels of the crisis which will take much longer to fully heal.

One of the many things I have learnt through this painful healing process is that, when we lose a loved one, it is the death of something within us that we grieve most deeply. It is hard for most of us to own fully the goodness and beauty within as our own special qualities. We project the qualities of our inner self onto those we love most dearly, as if they could carry them for us uncontaminated by the inadequacies of our own personality, with its human weaknesses and limitations, its dark shadow and suffering. As carriers of the darkness, we need the light in the eye of our beloved to give our life joy and meaning, to keep our hearts alive with love. It is the loss of this reflection of some part of our inner-most divine self that throws us

into the abyss of sorrow, that opens us to the dark empty space within ou
hearts which the loved one once filled. We feel deeply the sense of loss at
the untimely ending of a loved one's life, and grief at the waste of a unique
potential that was not allowed to reach fulfilment; we feel sadness at the
thought of the wonderful experiences of life that they will never taste, the
loss of the gifts they had to offer to the world; we may also feel anger or
guilt at their death. There is the deep ache of loneliness, and all the pain
and difficulties of adapting to life without the one we loved and with whom
we shared our intimate moments. But the deep and enduring loss is that of
our own true and beautiful nature that we bury with the beloved one, loss
of the joy in our heart that their presence evoked. Our own joy. If we can
go through our grieving to the heart of our unbearable pain, then we can
reclaim our heart, and live with the love that we shared with them eternally,
both deepened and enriched. When the pain at the centre of the heart is
touched, it feels clear, clean, burning, like a fine knife going in; the heart is
broken, but it breaks open to love in a deeper way.

Stephen Levine beautifully expresses this in his book, *Who Dies*:

'This is perhaps the most difficult of the balancing acts we come
to learn: to trust the pain as well as the light, to allow the grief to
penetrate as it will while keeping open to the perfection of the
universe.

'When we speak of loving someone, what we mean is that that
person acts as a mirror for the place within us which is love. That
being becomes our contact with ourself. When that mirror is
shattered, the grief that we feel is the loss of contact with that
place within us which is love. Thinking of that person as other
than ourself, we mourn our loss, we re-experience our sense of
separateness and isolation that originally motivated us to look
outside of ourselves for that essential unity we call love.

'Examining the loss of our reflected love we come back in contact
with ourselves, with love itself, in the formless connection that
was always present between us. In touching love, we touch the
other. In touching what was shared, the grief burns its way to
the center of the heart.

is our essential love that we experience when the grieving
nks into the ever-present heart. Grief of the loss of the
. Grief for the lost reflection of the place within where all
originates.' [1]

When the heart is torn apart, it breaks open to love. When it cannot break, we live in darkness and despair, like stone people, the living dead. I wondered whether my father died of an unbroken heart. I felt he suffered deeply and locked his pain within him. A series of disappointments and misfortunes in his professional life, and the stress of continuing to support a family under the burden of that inner pressure may have led him to despair and give up the struggle. The cancer eventually consumed him. My deepest sadness was that the love of his family was not enough to enable him to continue living through the difficulties. Giving up is not an alternative to letting go, to surrendering to another level of being. Without truly feeling and acknowledging the love that holds us together, life becomes sterile and meaningless. Why go on with the struggle to survive in such a harsh and unjust world? Why bother to fight for life when life is so painful and cruel?

At some point in life, many people may ask themselves such questions. How is it that some manage to come through, while others give up, give in to the despair? It is an important question in our godless age of existential despair and confusion – an age when we wander homeless, seeking the roots within us that we have lost touch with, unsure if there really is meaning in our experience and suffering, or not. Faith that there is some meaning and purpose in our lives may bring us through, keep us persevering against all odds. Loss of faith that there is some greater meaning, some value and purpose to our lives, and loss of connection to the spirit of love that gives meaning and holds the disparate things of life together is at the heart of the sickness which faces modern society. When love is lost, life falls apart, we fall apart.

My father died not alone, but isolated, cut off from meaningful contact with those who loved him, and from his own truth, for we had all been sworn to secrecy about his impending death. We lived a lie. No one must let him know that he was dying, and he too upheld the lie, for I am sure that he knew the truth about his condition. But no one spoke of it with him, and it must have left him utterly and terribly isolated. For nearly eighteen months, he lay slowly dying in his lonely world. At night, I would lie awake listening to the long silences between his rasping breaths, wondering through each pause if he had breathed his last. In my frustration at the lie and the distance between us, I would try to 'talk' with him silently, with my mind, about death and dying. He had no religion, no God – he called himself an atheist, though I always felt he was a spiritual person in his own way. Yet he had never found a map for his own way, or a community to share it with, and so I suspected he found no guidance or consolation to help him through his dying. I innocently and naïvely tried to tell him that death may not be so frightening, nor so final, through sending him positive feelings about it. But I did not have the courage to defy the authority that told me to keep silent. So much was left unsaid, so much potential for the healing of our relationships left untouched, and I mourn that deeply. We all lost one of the greatest opportunities of our lives, and I, in my youthful ignorance and insecurity, allowed it to be that way.

All personal stories begin somewhere with our parents and our ancestors. What I felt to be my father's despair takes a central place in my own story, along with the passion, rage, and creativity that were locked in behind the despair. As a sensitive child, I felt those energies acutely; having a strong attachment to my father, his feelings had a profound effect upon me. I have carried, as children do, the unacknowledged suffering of the beloved parent. I took it upon myself to fulfil his incomplete life after he died, to bear the fruits of the dreams that he had been unable to ripen in his own life. Having witnessed his life cut short mid-way, I wanted to do it differently, yet I had no idea what that meant. So I went out into my own life with no guidance and no clear models to follow.

The Crack between the Worlds

After meeting with my spiritual teacher, my life began to improve, to become more workable. Something was opening inside of me and I began to feel love and joy in my heart again. There had been other openings before this. During the course of a bodywork training my boundaries had become more permeable as I explored and let go of many of my body's holding patterns. As old defences began to loosen, I found I was opening to the collective pain; I could feel the broken heart of the world, a limitless depth of suffering, and in that suffering I could feel myself connected to humanity. Yet at that time I felt helpless to do anything about it. I knew I had to reach somehow for a feeling of connectedness through love and joy as well, or I would become lost in a sea of darkness.

With my teacher and spiritual community, I was beginning to sense this possibility of deep and joyful communication. At that time most of my energy was taken up in laying good foundations for my life, finding my place on the earth. For most of my life I had been a 'spiritual seeker', but I had never laid the good foundations that would secure me well and lovingly in the world – foundations that are necessary if we are to follow the spiritual path. In his teaching, Chime Rinpoche would often remind us that we cannot build a golden roof on our house until we have first laid the foundations and constructed walls to support it. I realised that I had been trying to do just this, in an attempt to make bearable the pain that was buried within me. A golden roof would arch over it all and make life just so beautiful again. But, of course, that is impossible and the roof would have to collapse even in the attempt to build it. So I was learning to live in the world, on the earth, with care.

Yet something else was stirring through my unconscious mind, and began to break through in small flashes into consciousness. Or maybe it was that my conscious mind delved for a moment into unknown realms beyond. I began to experience something that was like a momentary opening in my normal perception, a glimpse into another world. The first was like the tiniest blinking of the eye, the inner eye, except that my eye blinked open and just as swiftly blinked closed again. I will call what I saw light, but it wasn't like any light I'd ever seen before. It was like looking beyond magical veils to another universe that was nothing but brilliant, startling light. So startling was this light that I could barely look – it opened to me, and in the surprise of it, I closed.

I began to experience similar glimpses, like a blinking-open of the eye, but this time into a terrifying vision of darkness. Again not like any darkness I had known – not like the darkness of night, or even the absolute blackness of a deep underground cave. It's hard to describe the frightening quality of this dark – I felt I was looking through the fabric of the world as it disintegrated into a chaos of pain and terror. I felt sure that if the vision stayed any longer I would go insane with the pain it inflicted on my mind. It seemed to be a vast world beyond worlds, a lost universe, a chaos of darkness and formless forms, sharp-edged and dangerous. I was relieved these openings were fleeting, but disturbed by them – were they something to be avoided at all costs, or something I would inevitably have to face?

Then I began to experience this vision in a physical way, as if the substance of my own body was becoming insubstantial, returning to the specks of atoms floating within the vastness of space that was me. The earth too was shifting, dissolving under my feet, like wet sand on the shoreline dragged back by the undertow of the waves. I was travelling in America when I first began to experience this sensation, near to the heart of the continent. In a moment of anxiety, I decided to catch the first Greyhound back to the East Coast, and set off at five o'clock the next morning. In the middle of this vast and foreign landmass, I felt as if all boundaries and definitions were beginning to fade. I needed to get home, or at least to the nearest coastline whose natural boundary might give me some sense of security.

These glimpses passed, and my life carried on as usual. I was enjoying my life and work, and had begun my therapy training. Through the therapy I was embarking upon a journey through the landscapes of the psyche, into the depths and unknown worlds within, as real in our experience as those without – to be ignored at our peril, to be explored at our risk and potentially great reward. I found myself travelling a fine thread of a path that spanned between the relatively known worlds of the psychological, and the unknown territories of the realm of spirit. En-route is what feels like a chasm, a deep void or crack between the worlds. It may be so terrifying for us to step out into that space that only a deep-felt sense of the necessity and meaning of such an act may be sufficient to lead us to it. At some level of my being, I consciously made this choice, and chose with it the path of woundedness and suffering. My frightened ego fought and struggled all the way, but deeper in my heart I trusted the wisdom of necessity.

At the beginning of her book *The Chasm of Fire*, Sufi teacher Irina Tweedie writes:

> 'The Path of Love
> is like a bridge of hair
> across a chasm of fire.'[2]

This book is a remarkable and moving account of a woman's journey towards spiritual realisation, through surrender to the power of Love. Her opening statement speaks of the worlds of courage she possessed, which took her so far through and beyond the breaking open of the heart. Her story has sustained me through many moments of weakness, and I am grateful for her telling of it. But before I could find this story, and others which gave some sense of validation to what I was experiencing, I had to walk a long time in darkness, unsure of the rightness of what I was enduring. Faith is being tested in those dark times, and we are not immediately given comfort and confirmation by others.

If we choose this difficult path, it is likely we will get burnt on the way; perhaps it is impossible to cross this chasm without being touched by the flames within its depths. The burning, if we can endure it, purges away that which obscures the vision of the heart; it is the burning-up of illusions by the light of consciousness, of spirit, as we begin to open to that light. As with the refining of gold, the spirit is purified through ordeals of fire. It is by continuing to walk the 'bridge of hair', even as we burn, that we may develop real spiritual strength. But being human and limited, and having nothing in our education, our modern culture, or religion to prepare us for such a journey, we may falter and fall as we tread the burning path. This experience, and that which helps us to come through it, is the story at the heart of this book. It is in the burning, the fall, the death and return, that we have to confront our most difficult inner obstacles, and through them that we are given the opportunity to go deeper and to learn our most important lessons.

I felt I had faltered, been burnt, and had a deep taste of the surrounding dark void, but I finally came to accept that even the falling, the disintegration and death could be part of the path, and maybe even an inevitable part. A Zen teacher once said that we have to die at least four times on the spiritual path; it is not the dying itself, but how we die and what meaning we make of it, that will determine its value as an experience of growth and learning. Spiritual practice teaches us how to die in a conscious and creative way.

I had begun to open again to the loss of Dave and my father, to feel again the depth of grief I had been unable to integrate at the time of their deaths. Having found a guide to help me, it was time to open and feel the whole of my heart again. The psyche is wise, if allowed to follow its own process without interference; we are given such opportunities when we have gained enough strength to look again at our unresolved pain and conflicts. So often we feel that we are doing well, finally making a good life, when suddenly we are hit by another blow. 'It's so unfair', rails our little mind, 'just when my life was going so well.' But we can only look into our depths when we have enough strength to face what we will find there. So life seems to swing us round the roller-coaster of experience. But if we can step back a little, create some space between ourselves and our immediate experience, we may see the design that is working itself out in our lives, and the opportunities for growth and change that life presents us with.

I found that meditation practice was gently and gradually reawakening the buried feelings that needed to be felt, and at the same time I was becoming stronger, happier, more confident in myself. But together with this, the therapeutic work began to dig at ever-increasing speed into deeper and deeper levels of my psyche. I had not been able to let go fully of the two men whom I loved, and a whole life experience and identity had been built around their presence within me. They had come to represent some unowned and essential aspects of my own being, and in that they held me at the deepest levels of my psyche. I was unprepared for the too-sudden cutting of these ties which the therapy led me to, and the structure of my inner world began to collapse.

In this, the therapeutic work was seriously misguided. I can see with hindsight that the natural course and rhythm of my own psychic process had been disturbed by the therapist's mistaken interpretations and interventions, and by the dynamics of our relationship. At the time I did not have enough understanding of the process I was involved in, and had put my trust in his guidance. Unfortunately he also did not properly understand the grieving process, the reactivation of trauma, or the important function that my father and my friend still held within my inner world, and what was needed before I could safely let go of them. If the psyche persists in holding onto something or someone it means that trauma connected with the relationship or situation has not been fully processed; we keep recreating similar situations and relationships in an unconscious attempt to re-experience the original event so that we may complete and resolve it. Holding onto someone from the past means that the person still holds some essential meaning for us, carries the image that connects us to some essential aspect of our being. This function needs to be recognised and reclaimed before we can fully and safely cut the ties to the personal level of attachment.

When a loved one dies we can experience a deepening of the spiritual connection we have with them, as if, no longer restricted by physical form and personality, their essence is more present to our awareness. Freed of earthly life, we can sense their consciousness expand into the unboundaried universe; when we feel a deep soul connection to the person, we find our own consciousness drawn with them into this expanded state of awareness. The person in death may take on a spiritual meaning for us that they might not hold whilst still living. Ancestor worship, which is a feature of many old religions and cultures, acknowledges the psychological and spiritual importance of this bond for the individual and the community. In Dante's *Inferno*, the pilgrim's deceased lover, Beatrice, serves as his guide along the last steps of his journey to heaven. This expansion of consciousness which we feel with a loved one's death potentially opens us to both the glory and the terror of the infinite unknown, to the reaches of both heaven and hell; *how* we each experience it depends on many personal circumstances. (This will be explored further in Chapter Three.)

I had been encouraged in my therapeutic work to cut the ties that still bound me to my father. At first, I was filled with a deep sense of emptiness, of life as grey, meaningless and futile. I became deeply depressed after this work. I have since understood that my creativity was symbolically rooted in my connection to my father, and with the cutting of the tie to him, through a process of guided visualisation, I also cut myself off from my own creative source and spirit.

Marion Woodman describes how images relating to our mother and father complexes often symbolise 'our connection with our richest source of creativity'.[3] Jung writes that such images symbolise 'union with one's own being'.[4] If this connection is carelessly cut, the connection to self and the inner psychic process is brutally disrupted. Through allowing myself to be wrongly guided into doing just this, I lost connection with my creative ground. My Godless state had returned. God's 'absence' began to haunt me like a palpable presence, and all of life felt empty and meaningless.

We never open to the light or dark alone. Opening to one opens us to the other, for we can't have light without shadow, or darkness without light. There began an escalation of spirals into ever-increasing heights and depths, precipitated by the therapeutic work, and in particular its use of imagery and powerful evocative techniques. I touched heights of joy and euphoria, felt my heart opening in great blazes of love, saw wonderful visions and listened to the wisdom of my own soul's voice, felt a deep nurturing connection to Mother Earth, to the Goddess within, and to my community of friends. I also touched the deepest sense of loneliness I had ever known, the terrible pain of being separated from my own spiritual source, of being so far from truly living the life of love I longed for, and I felt painfully alone and helpless.

When I first entered the therapeutic process, I loved the world of imagery, the treasures the imagination can reveal. Now I view it with a great deal of caution, for I have learnt through painful experience that there are dangers. Making such bold forays into that world unleashed a flood of energy from the unconscious that my ego was not able to contain. I was travelling to the heart of my pain, to the real grief of losing Dave, and I found I had 'married' myself to him in death. In my deep unconscious, he was still with me, and I with him. I didn't realise I still needed it to be that way, for he still held the mirror of my own inner being. He was the reflection of my spirit, the beloved of my soul. In trying to say finally farewell to him, and bury the old love and grief, I lost my connection to spirit, and my will to live.

There is in us a soul-energy that wills to live, and a soul-energy that wills to die. I have always known my will to die, but now it took possession of me, was devouring me. My boundaries were breaking open, and in touch with this deep layer of pain and darkness within myself, I was again opening deeply to the suffering of others, where it touches mine. Without boundaries, I was opened to the flood of collective psychic energies, and the fathomless pain of human life. Stanley Keleman describes how the deaths of others that we witness or experience shape our own fears and concepts of our own death.[5] For me, my father's was isolated, secret, unspoken, dark, unknown, unlived. Dave's death was sudden, tragic, horrifying, meaningless – overwhelmed by the depths of the ocean. Both shaped my experience of the death that I was opening to within myself.

It was another experience in my therapeutic work that finally broke me. This journey was to my mother, and to the Great Mother, inwards to the deep source of nurturing – to feel myself held, lovingly held in a way that no human ever had, or maybe could hold me; to feel the pain of the lack throughout my life of that great boundless and unconditional Love, and be touched to my very depths as I opened to it now. I cried deeply like a child, and, out of my tears, the Mother spontaneously gave me a gift, a crystal of light, of radiant, numinous power. I trembled as I held it, feeling its powerful energy. At that moment, and I think quite significantly, my therapist had to leave the office for a few minutes to attend to some business; I was left alone with this numinous feeling that shook me to my core, and my uncertainty as to how to contain it. The crystal informed me that it was dangerous, but that it also held within it the power to guide me through the danger. I trembled so much I feared my hands could not hold it. I imagined placing it in my heart, for I felt that was the place where it belonged. I wasn't ready to show it to the world; I didn't know how to *be* this radiant light, how to live it; I felt it needed protecting, holding. I also sensed that I needed protection from its power. The whole experience felt profound, but it was not grounded or integrated into ordinary reality and personal relationships, and so it was potentially dangerous, as the symbol itself had revealed. Without such grounding, the world of the imaginal can take on a power and a reality of its own, which can be dangerous.

I left this therapy session feeling deeply moved, my heart tender but unprotected, too vulnerable for life, and tried to continue with my day of work. As I went to bed that night, still feeling raw and deeply sad, I tried to reconnect to the nurturing feeling of holding that I had experienced. There was a deep letting-go, surrendering to being held, and as I let go into it, I cried. I cried to a depth I had rarely cried before, my whole body sobbing like a new-born child. I cried for hours, endlessly, deep into the early hours of the morning, and couldn't stop. Images of my life flashed before my eyes. I cried through all the pain of my life, the losses, the humiliations and failures, the hurts and betrayals, the guilt, anger, frustrations and fear. I cried right back into my early infancy, my life unfolding backwards as I fell through all the suffering and darkness I had known. I felt I was dying.

I fell back into the suffering before birth, of the baby trapped in the womb, and back beyond to other lives and deaths it seemed. My own lives, or other people's – they all became one as the pain and suffering of the ages flowed through me, through my tears. I was burning up. The light of the crystal in my heart illuminated all the darkness surrounding it, and I could not bear the sight of the suffering and wastelands of my life. I felt I could never redeem the darkness or recreate myself out of the inadequacies and failure that I saw before me. I had to begin again. The old had died, been burnt to ashes. I saw the light in my heart surrounded by a black charred corpse, all that was left of the person I had known as me. And I didn't yet know how to live as this radiant numinous light that was my heart. It was too new and vulnerable, still a seed needing to be held within and gently nurtured, and all that might hold it had been burnt away. I was not ready, like an infant cast out of the womb too soon. And so I found myself hurled into the underside of life, the world of death, with no way to return.

The visions and experiences we encounter in inner work are not immediately or necessarily realised in ordinary life. I would echo the words of Steve Smith in his introduction to the work of American Zen teacher, Charlotte Joko Beck, when he says that 'powerful spiritual openings that are artificially induced do not insure an orderly and compassionate life (and may even be harmful)'.[6] This is one of the limitations and dangers of some therapeutic techniques which, if they are used in a way that is overly directive or suggestive rather than receptive to the client's natural process, may artificially evoke spiritual energies and experiences which cannot be properly responded to and integrated. Changes have to be worked for if they are to be real and lasting, and the experiences lived through and integrated into the personality and everyday life. Such openings may give insight or a sense of the direction in which we need to go; but they can also be extremely destructive if not handled with great care and skill. My experience in therapy had evoked powerful psychic energies that, once unleashed from the unconscious, then became my living reality.

Into the Abyss

A threshold had been crossed, and at that twilight edge I had fallen – out of life, out of time – to the shadow side of life. In this 'other world', many levels of feeling and experience were occurring simultaneously. At one level, I sensed the potential for deep healing and transformation. From another perspective, I was breaking down. My boundaries had gone, my mind broken so that it had no means to contain the overwhelming energies and feelings that I was opened to. I was at the mercy of a chaos of powerful emotions that were quite visibly destroying me. I struggled with the will to die that seemed to rise from some deep place inside of me, and break my spirit, my essential connection with heaven and earth. I tried to trust the wisdom of the process I was in as my inner and outer worlds fell apart, tried to hold the rightness of both the levels I was experiencing – that of *soul-making* and of *ego-breaking*.

With my psychic boundaries lost, my perceptions were radically altered; I could see through things, into other levels of reality. I knew there was light at the heart of the experience, but before I could touch it I had to face the wall of darkness that surrounded it. I had slipped through the crack between the worlds.

It was as if the walls of my home, which had been before a safe and sacred space, became transparent and substanceless, and the dark energy of the city flooded into my unprotected being. I was falling, falling, deep to the icy core of the earth, at the heart of her fires. I was also floating in the endless dark universe, a tiny, helpless bundle of fear, so incredibly vulnerable, insignificant, unheld, and alone. My body ached to be held, grew thin, emaciated, every fibre strained with the wrench of endless tears. The grief and pain were unbearable. My heart felt like a dark abyss through which I was endlessly falling. There was no comfort anywhere, nothing to hold.

All the solid forms around me were dissolving, and only the minutest parts hanging together loosely gave a semblance of structure. A crack in the corner of a wall, the grey of the asphalt, the way that long row of cars was parked, the railway line stretching into a horizon of rooftops and telegraph poles – the most ordinary sight would bring a sudden feeling of fear and dread in the pit of my stomach, my head would reel and my body, wanting to flee to safety, would be paralysed.

I was awed at the centuries of labour that had gone into piecing together all the bricks, stones, wires, pillars, metal sheets, glass, paint, wooden planks, nuts and bolts that made up the city of London. I perceived them all hanging there in space, unconnected, unsupported, without that essential something that holds the universe together. The view of this crazy complex of stuff brought panic. It was as if I could feel the lives of all the millions of people who had built and lived in this city, and the whole thing felt so desperately futile and meaningless. I could see through the veils of identity people were wearing, through the addictions to their work, fine and fashionable clothes, being respectable, being drunk, being sad, being 'really fine, OK', having a profession, having wealth or power or families to take care of. And what I saw behind the veils was a depth of suffering, despair, and fear so overwhelmingly painful to witness. I was seeing them as they were, beneath the veils that hid them from their truth, but I knew I was also seeing the reflection of where I had come to in myself.

No longer was I able to pursue the everyday activities which, I now saw, used to protect me from feeling the pain too closely. I could not work or engage in normal social life, and had to abandon the training course I had begun, leaving the support of the community of friends I had made there at the time when I most needed them. I could barely take care of myself. I experienced the people around me withdrawing as if in fear of the spectre I was holding up, as I had done after Dave's death, and many friendships were lost. To read a newspaper or watch the television reduced me to floods of tears, as the suffering I witnessed in the world touched my raw and bleeding heart. If I tried to read a book it was the same, and my fragmented mind could not concentrate on the words for long enough to find some solace there. There were moments when, in the midst of feeling the deepest pain, I would simultaneously be touched deeply by the beauty of nature around me, by the preciousness and fragility of life, or moved to tears by a small act of kindness. But these moments of a gentler kind of opening were hard to sustain amidst the turbulent anguish of emotion. My life was a void and I cried for hours, sometimes days and nights on end, with no relief, sobbing from my deepest depths, not even knowing the cause of my tears. The pain and grief felt ageless and without end. Crying in this way was further breaking down my boundaries, and exhausting my strength, but I could not hold the flood. A negative spiral of destruction had set in and I felt I did not have the resources within to turn the tide. I had no choice but to surrender my will to this great Will of unknown force that was changing my life, and my very being, even if it devoured me completely.

I was aware of standing on a very fine borderline between sanity and insanity—not the sanity of the ego successfully adapting and conforming to external reality, for that boundary had already been crossed, but the border between a sense of the basic sanity within, the wisdom of the heart which illumines reality in a new way, and the insanity of psychosis. I seemed to be in the depths of psychotic process, but still in contact with that place of basic sanity. Rather than a loss of consciousness, it was a deepening and intensification of consciousness, a level of awareness beyond the ordinary concrete mind, where I could see through things with a deep and intuitive knowingness very hard to express in words. It is a knowing that is felt and expressed as being, rather than through actions or words, a subtle knowing, but with the loss of ego boundaries I had no means to communicate what I saw, felt, or knew. I needed only to be allowed to be, just be. I could do nothing. But it felt unbearable to be able to do nothing, whilst feeling so alone in this void.

The rhythm and pace of these dark lands is much slower and deeper than that which we are accustomed to, and I fell out of rhythm with the tides of life around me. I balanced precariously on that fine line between basic sanity and insanity, one foot in each land, one eye on each of these realms, and my heart torn between the two. It felt like not the border between the known and the unknown, for I was already deeply in unknown territory; but further out, between the unknown and the unknowable, the untouchable, the uncontainable.

Eventually a book came my way that I could read, a story of one man's travels in the mountains and monasteries of Ladakh, rich in the teachings of the Buddhist tradition, and told in the easy style of story. I feared I was well and truly fallen from my path by now, but I found some reassurance of the necessity of my experience, however extreme I then felt it to be. The Rinpoche tells the author:

> 'The heart and understanding need winter also. They need desolation, unhappiness, even sometimes death. Milarepa said, "A man who is aware finds a friend in desolation and a master in winter." That is why spring does not dominate the whole of the life tapestry.... . The spirit needs spring and winter, beauty and terror, meeting and parting, needs every experience and every energy to achieve wholeness. Milarepa said, "Contemplate all energies without fear and disgust; find their essence, for that is the stone that turns everything to gold." '[7]

The tapestry of my life at that time felt entirely dominated by cold icy winter, the hells of Tantaros, furthest reaches of the underworld. I was in that 'pneumatic region of air and wind…a region of dense cold air without light (where) the dead are clad like birds'.[8] The cold winds blew right through me like knives of ice, and I was as insubstantial as the wind itself. It felt like an initiation into death, into the formless realms of the Bardo, which, the Tibetan Book of the Dead teaches us, we must learn to embrace in life in order that we may die consciously, with wisdom, clarity, and an open heart – that we may die into the Light.

I believed, even at the time of the initial crisis, that I was undergoing a process that was potentially meaningful and deeply healing. But as a result of failures and misguidance in the therapeutic work, I suffered a crisis of disintegration which I did not have the resources to resolve.

When the transformatory work of profound inner change is underway, the depths touched sometimes reveal forgotten trauma. Events from earlier life, which were too distressing or life-threatening for the ego to be able to assimilate at the time, are stored in the body as areas of numbness, tension, or dissociation, or in the unconscious psyche as images.[9] When the techniques of bodywork or image work touch, manipulate, or interfere with these resurfaced bodily and symbolic memories, without due respect and care, the risk of re-traumatisation in therapy is great. If re-traumatisation should occur during a process of deep psychological transformation, the trauma *must* be dealt with as such. To override it, and treat the crisis purely as a process of spiritual emergence, may result in symptoms of post-traumatic stress disorder or complete psychic breakdown.

The pathological aspect of the breakdown I suffered came about by opening to *too much* consciousness too quickly through the therapeutic work; this was compounded by a lack of proper care, support, and understanding of the process I was in by the therapist and trainers who were guiding me. Although the essence of this process was of potentially great value, even necessity, I was unable to find resolution at the time because I was in effect abandoned in the midst of the crisis.

External abandonment usually occurs when the therapist has already abandoned the client internally, or perhaps was never truly there for her in the first place. Abandonment occurs internally through the attitudes, beliefs, expectations, misunderstandings, and feelings of the therapist towards the client, and will be inevitable if the therapist is unconsciously serving his or her own personal or professional needs over those of the client. Being abandoned in such a condition is virtually a death sentence. Because the process I was going through had been theoretically addressed in my training, I assumed that it was understood and would be supported experientially, but, in practice, this was not the case. My situation was not properly recognised or understood, and I felt little real care or concern about what happened to me; the primary concern of those responsible seemed to be to maintain their own good reputation. I had to leave the training and the people who had been my friends there, and the incident was successfully swept under the carpet. Nor was I alone; there were other 'casualties' of this training programme at that time who suffered a similar fate.

At first, my therapist tried to deny what was happening. Then he was unavailable for several weeks, and did not respond to telephone calls. When we did eventually meet, he seemed more concerned with finding a meaning that would justify his own actions than in offering help or trying to understand what was happening to me. I felt as if I was being led across a raging river, deep and turbulent waters, leaping across stepping stones, when my guide let go of my hand and I fell. He threw a rope, but in his attempt to pull me quickly out, the one I had trusted to hold the lifeline tugged too strongly and it broke. He pulled too strongly because he was afraid to deal with the raging waters, and could not take the time to safely hold me there. I was lost in the swirling waters. The containment of the therapeutic vessel had been broken, and I felt completely alone and shattered with grief, despair, and overwhelming fear.

And yet the transference that the therapeutic work had evoked was by now so deep that I was unable to acknowledge the abandonment fully and turn for help elsewhere. When I began this course of therapy, as part of my training, I was in good health, happy and content with my life, successful in my work as a movement therapist and bodywork practitioner, and had many friends. After fifteen months of therapy with this man, I was on the verge of suicide or hospitalisation, and hopelessly dependent upon him to help me survive the ordeal. Because he had guided me into this situation, I believed he was the only one who would be able to see or understand where I was, and so help me through the process. I was sorely mistaken, for he was the one who could neither see nor understand. He admitted to me, much later on, that at the time he had had 'much more important things to deal with in his life than my process'. A therapist who is not able, for whatever reason, to support a client through a depth process should be extremely careful not to evoke such depths, or at the very least to ensure that other help is available when necessary. This therapist neither acknowledged the limitations of his own experience, skills, time, and attention, nor found alternative support when he was unable or unavailable to offer it himself.

Once in this place of deep despair we need to be held there; no amount of will can get us through it quickly, and any attempts to pull us out lead only to greater suffering and feelings of isolation. Our soul experience is denied in this, and we are laid open to the preying madness of doubt in our own deep integrity and wisdom. When the lifeline which the therapist holds is broken, a potential breakthrough can turn into a pathological breakdown. As Hillman says:

> 'And the more this despair can be held, the less the suicide will 'just happen'. To hope for nothing, to expect nothing, to demand nothing. This is analytical despair. To entertain no false hopes, not even that hope for relief which brings one into analysis in the first place. This is an emptiness of soul will.... Upon this moment of truth the whole work depends, because this is the dying away from the false life and wrong hopes out of which the complaint has come. As it is the moment of truth, it is also the moment of despair, because there is no hope.'[10]

Hillman claims that if a therapist abandons a client in this place of deepest despair, if the client becomes a burden, a case the therapist would like to shelve away, he is effectively killing the client.[11] This may well be the cause of some suicides that happen during the course of therapy. During depth processes, the therapist serves as the client's essential link to life, and when this link does not serve, suicide or psychosis may be the result. Jung has warned that a person should not embark upon the process of individuation through depth therapy or analysis unless he or she is willing to see it through to the end; how much worse it may be when the client makes the commitment to see the process through, but the therapist does not. To get only halfway in this work leaves us abandoned, lost in the underworld, in the chaos of hell, with no way out. And this is a truly terrible fate. It leaves us vulnerable to being taken over by the powerful archetypal energies of the unconscious which have been evoked by the work.

In the face of such pain, consciousness might seek its escape in the oblivion of death or psychosis – might attempt to leap out of the suffering mind and body altogether. So long as there is a remnant of integration of the inner core of the psyche, so long as our internal witness remains tentatively present, we can still make a choice to stay with the pain in its intensity, and the burning; without this, we may become lost in the realms of oblivious waste. Marion Woodman observes that:

'Psychosis resides in the identification with an archetype. So long as there is resistance, which is to say pain or illness, the individual is able to maintain a precarious differentiation. Pain protects us from psychosis.'[12]

We might also say that psychosis shields us from fully and consciously feeling the pain – the pain that surrounds the heart, that must be felt if the heart is to be opened and freed. But sometimes, when the pain becomes too great, we cannot safely feel it without the loving and supportive presence of another human being to bear witness to our suffering. The consistent presence of another person who can witness us, with love, compassion, and acceptance, is essential to the containment of such deep inner work. Pain can burn through to the core of the psyche when there is no inner or outer witness to help contain it, and may destroy us.

For a long time I could not acknowledge the destructiveness of the therapeutic relationship I was in. Later, when I began to break through the denial, I was at first in such a vulnerable state that I could not leave it. For several years after the initial crisis, I suffered periods of deep depression and complex psychosomatic symptoms, continually on the edge of breaking down again, my mind still fragmented, struggling always on the slippery edge of the abyss. The treasure that seemed to have been a promise of this work had not yet been claimed and I had to face some very painful realities. The whole process began to feel like a failure, and a terrible waste of years of my life.

All through the succession of crises that the therapeutic work had precipitated, I tried to maintain a sense that there was some purpose in the loss and suffering, that even the feelings of meaninglessness were a necessary part of the process I was enduring. I persisted in this, even in the moments of deepest despair. But despair means loss of hope, and I had to finally acknowledge complete loss of hope. Despair will not let go of us until it is fully allowed. But loss of hope can lead to loss of faith, and faith is needed to bring us through the darkest times. Without it, we face our most dangerous edge. I was losing faith that there was some meaning or purpose in the process I was going through, and with that I was losing faith in myself and all that had sustained me.

The painful reality that brought me to this edge was, with the ending in failure of the therapy, the final acknowledgement of how I had been used and abused in the therapeutic relationship. At first, I had denied it. Then I began to see it, but for a long time tried to 'work through it' within the therapy itself, believing that this was necessary in order to free myself from the damaging relationship. But it was not possible. Finally, I had to accept fully the extent of the misguidance I had received, and the failure of the therapy. I realised that throughout all the years of work I had not been truly seen; my essential dilemma had been misunderstood by the therapist, my truth denied, and I had been subtly manipulated in a direction that was counter to the wisdom of my own psyche. Professional boundaries had been violated, and the therapist's own personal and professional needs had become active ingredients in the work. All of this denied my own process, and effectively tore me apart.

A wise part of me had known this all along, and this part of me suffered deeply, but another part of me had persistently denied the truth. Denial is of course one of the characteristics of abusive relationships. That part of us which is dependent on the relationship can make us blind to common sense until, if we are lucky, we come to the critical end of the road where we know we will not survive if we don't face up to the awful reality.

Surviving this experience has been perhaps the most difficult thing I have ever done in my life, and the road to recovery has been long, painful, confusing, and very lonely. Writing this book has helped me to make some sense of the many levels of experience and feeling, the apparently conflicting perspectives and attitudes, the ambiguities, contradictions, and paradoxes that have marked the years of struggle to recover and heal. I may never fully heal the damage caused by this relationship, but I do feel deepened and enriched by the healing journey I have gone through because of it. Again I am able to work and participate in life, whilst acknowledging that healing is an ongoing process and not an end to be achieved.

My experience has also convinced me that the dreams, visions, insights, and experiences encountered in such extreme states are often sensitively attuned to the stirrings of the collective soul, and may shed light upon the processes the world is going through today. I believe that each individual who survives his or her own inner holocaust, and grows through the experience of personal dissolution, can help to shed light on the way for others who are suffering, so providing a ray of hope for the healing and renewal, in our times, of the spirit of humanity.

My experience in therapy with a man who, inadvertently, oppressed the deeper stirrings of my feminine being, abused the power he held over me, and consistently abandoned me in my moments of greatest need, awakened in me a conscious concern with issues of the oppression, neglect, abuse, and violation of the feminine by the masculine throughout generations of patriarchal civilisation. The reclaiming and conscious embodiment of the deep feminine, of the inner creative spirit of woman, and of the transformatory cycles of life, death, and rebirth, became my path. This is the gift that I received through my inner journeyings, and I am grateful now for this lesson in the depths of life.

The Dying

In death the elements dissolve, one into the other.

Earth dissolves into Water:

First a subtle trembling of the ground, like shifting sand
  — no sureness underfoot, a giddiness.
A chasm opens in the earth and I am falling,
circling, rising, flying, up and down are all the same.
The path is lost. No light here. No hand to hold,
no ground.
The dancers movements spiral outwards as she falls and
caught in space are torn from her frail body,
tatters of a dance disintegrating into dark.

Water dissolves into Fire:

Weep, weep. My heart is breaking.
Tears of grief, a wound so deep.
It bleeds and bleeds. The ocean red with my heart's tears.
The dancer drowning in her grief sheds her last blood,
cries her life dry.

Fire dissolves into Air:

There is a green light, crystal fire in my heart.
It burns and cleanses — its bright life illuminating
all the pain and suffering of the ages,
burning, burning, burning.
Down and down through pain and darkness burns the fire;
till everything is black and charred.
The fire dies. There is no more to be consumed.

Air dissolves into Space:

A wind, cold wind stabs through my heart.
It has no home, no life, no warmth.
There is no kind protecting love to hold it close.
A dark deep void of pain and grief
into which the sharp ice winds are drawn
and lost in endless space.

2 Breaking Down and Breaking Through

'Who, if I cried out, might hear me – among the ranked Angels?
Even if One suddenly clasped me to his heart
I would die of the force of his being. For Beauty is only
the infant of scarcely endurable Terror, and we
are amazed when it casually spares us.'

Rainer Maria Rilke, Duino Elegies

Our world today is in a crisis perhaps deeper and more widespread than any we have known throughout recorded history. Not only is the survival of the human race under threat, but we have created the potential for the devastation of our home, the earth, and all her inhabitants too. We perch precariously on the brink of catastrophic breakdown as the insubstantial structures of our society groan under the weight of ever-increasing pressures from within and without. We begin to see that the trusty foundations of social order are not the permanent and invincible systems we once believed them to be, and the ground on which they have been built no longer seems so sure, but threatens to crumble.

The sciences born of the rationalistic, materialistic, linear, and heroic mode of thinking, which helped create the modern world and define its values, are now disproving those very theories which they first proposed, and upon which our whole world view was built. New physics has discovered that the world of matter is not the solid, inanimate, and predictable machine that modern technology and society has based its modus operandi upon. In fact the new paradigm affirms the view of reality which has been held by Buddhist philosophy for many centuries – that of the nature of reality as being ultimately empty, not inherently self-existent. The very scientific thinking that led us into the age of industrial and technological progress is now pulling the philosophical and intellectual ground from under our feet. In recent history, along with man's growing belief in the power of his own intellect and his ability to dominate nature, came a widespread loss of faith in traditional religion and the cultural and spiritual ground which once sustained us. Now, with this new-found ground also being swept away by the very science which first fostered its growth, and cut off from the roots of tradition, we grasp at any passing debris as we free-float through our anxiety, hoping for something in which to place our faith again.

Collectively we are in the throes of great upheaval, clutching at whatever semblance of the old order can still be grasped as we sense its structure crumbling. In times of change – personal, social, or political – old patterns tend to rigidify as we seek to cling onto the dying remnants, trying to maintain a sense of safety and certainty in an uncertain world. If it slips away, we clutch at something else, and so our loyalties may shift from here to there in an attempt to appease the anxiety and convince ourselves that things really can go on the way they have been doing. It is hard for us to accept that this may not be possible and that we may have to change our lives and our values in a deep and fundamental way if we are to survive, and beyond that, to live – to live a life that is meaningful and rewarding, and not just a continual battle for existence.

Loss of spiritual and philosophical roots, and anxiety about our own survival and that of our way of life, has helped create the symptoms of a collective crisis. Not one corner of the world has been left untouched for we have taken something of our mechanistic, materialistic view to almost every race and tribe around the globe, and the effects of our technological expansion can be felt world-wide. Evolution cannot and should not be stopped – there is a natural process of development at work – but with growing awareness and skill comes greater responsibility, and up to now we of the modern world have not shown enough responsibility or sensitivity towards the earth and all of its inhabitants in our handling of the powerful means now in our minds and in our hands.

Violence, crime, and war continue to increase, motivated by fear, greed or poverty, uncontrolled aggression, and lack of respect for the needs, rights, and values of others. In a world of abundant proliferation and wealth, children starve and old people die of cold and neglect. In our cities, temples of civilisation, there is mass unemployment, homelessness, loneliness, despair, and violence; the stress of modern life makes people angry, frustrated, uncaring towards each other, and contributes to all manner of physical and mental illness. We pollute the earth, the air, the rivers and sea, the dome of sky that protects us from above, all in the name of progress, when all the time it is leading us into greater global danger. We all participate in this, though we may try for the most part to ignore this fact; the enormity of the crisis too often fills us with feelings of despair and helplessness so that we numb ourselves to it. Unless of course disaster comes too close and hits our personal lives directly.

We have been conditioned to consider this state of affairs 'normality', and educated to perpetuate this reality. At home we battle daily with traffic jams and unhealthy levels of noise, communicate with machines instead of the hearts of our fellow human beings, in order to carry out the soul-less work of making a living. We make money, power, possessions, and reputation our gods, whilst denying the gods and goddesses of the earth, and the needs of our own feeling hearts. And if we can mange this battle well, we are respected as healthy, sane, and well-adjusted people, even though we may do it through violation to ourselves and others.

Hillman describes this as the manic-defensive phase of humanity's breakdown.[1] He claims that in order for humanity to stop murdering the planet and all those living upon it, it needs to feel its real despair, pain, grief, and rage. Only by acknowledging and living through this experience can the despair itself be transformed into positive and creative attitudes and actions. Many individuals are beginning to face consciously the crisis we are collectively in, born out of the need for humanity to awaken from the spiritual and psychological wasteland it has created. However, their work and their courage are often misunderstood and undervalued, or marginalised, by mainstream society. Because collective resistance to change is so stubborn, only real disaster may be enough to usher in the needed changes in attitude, values, and behaviour. In fact, it is very often disasters, created by either human or natural forces, that herald in the necessary changes in both society and individual lives.

A crisis always offers an opportunity for growth. We reach crisis point when the old ways are no longer serving us, are restricting us or failing to serve their former useful function, when we need to let go of them and create new ways. As we grow and evolve, so the structures that we formerly used to order and contain our experience must also grow and change. Change involves a death and rebirth. This is a natural phenomenon of nature; perhaps it is only in the affairs of humankind that we have crises, for we tend to resist natural change and stubbornly push on until we can push no further, when the old way is then forced to give way, to break. Such resistance causes pain and heartache, anxiety and fear. It is hard to imagine the caterpillar resisting its transformation into a butterfly, pulling back in fear from the process of dissolution that it must undergo during its chrysalis phase. Its whole nature is oriented towards accepting this inevitable event. The word chrysalis stems from the Greek *khrusos,* which means gold; this suggests the great value that the process of transmutation itself held for the ancient Greeks. *Psyche*, or soul, also means butterfly; it is the soul that is renewed and transformed through the process of disintegration and dissolution.

It seems that we are facing such disintegration and upheaval on a global scale, where we cannot continue along the soul-less path we have been treading and assume that we will necessarily survive; we must seek radical change. Such breakdown and change invariably involves great confusion and suffering, for when old structures die away we are opened to the fundamental chaos of nature that underlies them, and which they served to contain. Because of our need for the structure and order that will protect us from chaos, we frequently hold on too long to outmoded systems of personal, social, and political organisation, or try to grasp too quickly at new ones. We need instead to learn to live more comfortably with chaos, which is essentially a creative source, for it is out of the waiting and the 'being with what is' that truly innovative and appropriate new directions can emerge. This seems hard for us to do, and chaos, rather than being accepted as a creative and ever-changing flow, pregnant with potential, expresses itself instead in needless destruction, violence, and war.

The Face of Global Change

Just before we entered the last decade of the twentieth century, we witnessed the literal breaking-down of a structure that had held the world in a precariously maintained peace since the end of the second World War. The

Berlin Wall was opened, quite suddenly and unexpectedly. After the initial euphoria came a tidal wave of social and political unrest and upheaval which swept through the communist countries of Eastern Europe, and struck at the heart of Soviet Russia itself. Many people suffered and died in the ensuing chaos. The world witnessed both the joyful promise and the harsh realities inherent in such dramatic change, and the whole balance of international politics and power shifted as a result of this event. A similar process occurs when an individual suffers the breaking down of internal psychological structures, for which she is unprepared; chaos and conflict are likely to follow the initial joyful opening of boundaries.

Symbolically Berlin represented a story of our times, a story of healing and reunification, both personal and global. The way was opened for success in negotiations between the east-west superpowers, bringing to an end the Cold War. But during the 1990s we witnessed the Gulf War, the collapse of the USSR, conflict in many countries of Eastern Europe, and a drawn-out war in former Yugoslavia which has torn it apart. It seems that collectively we were not ready to forsake our dualistic 'us and them' stance – not ready for such a radical change of heart as this. From a psychological perspective, it also appears almost inevitable that other enemies and dictators would emerge, once the Soviet aggressor had been 'tamed' or befriended; the psychological pressure within the collective psyche could not be contained, and war continues to proliferate around our planet.

Repeatedly we witness how greed for power, control, or wealth motivates dictators, warlords, and leaders of oppressive regimes to act with blatant cruelty, brutality, disregard for the rights of others, and lack of care for human life and suffering. Of course it takes a certain personality to commit the kinds of atrocities we have witnessed in recent decades, but a Hitler or Saddam Hussein, for example, is not an individual isolated from the soul of humanity. The aggression that they express is a phenomenon of the collective psyche, of the extremes of cruelty and violence which most of us would like to deny having any part in.

Psychologically, humanity is like an organism with a life and soul of its own, with each individual member expressing some part and function of that whole. While the violence and war within our own hearts and minds is denied, collective aggression will be projected and played out by those whose personalities most readily lend them to such behaviour. This can only happen because we all participate in the process, lend our unconscious, projected energy to it; such individual dictators could not exist without some level of participation from the collective. We might think of the personality of someone like Hitler or Saddam as a crack in the structure of collective psychic order, a crack through which the darkest aspects of the human psyche can erupt. The earth itself provides a fitting analogy here, where a volcano erupts at the place in the earth's crust where the resistance to inner pressure is weakest. In a similar way the powerful forces of collective unconscious energies may push through the respectable and ordered structure of human culture at the points where there is least resistance to them.

The Gulf War was a vivid example of the quest for power and control over wealth and resources, and from the perspective of archetypal psychology, it offers a potent symbol for much of the violence and exploitation we are experiencing today. Saddam himself talked about 'The Mother of all Battles', and viewed from the archetypal perspective he was quite accurate in this description. This war was to do with the Mother, the Goddess, in her wrathful aspect. This ancient land, of which Baghdad is now the capital, once gave birth to and nurtured western civilisation; now the young civilisation turns against its Mother, attempting to destroy her with all the devilry that its technology and intellect could invent. Mankind has raped and robbed pieces of earth like this with no concern for the earth herself, and she has bled. Oil is a potent symbol for the blood of Mother Earth. This quest to bleed the earth of her oil is one of the many examples of our use and abuse of natural resources that we have long plundered with little thought for the consequences. But we must consider that the earth herself may have a soul, and suffers from this disregard and wounding; the earth-soul also rages at the violation.

The ravaged earth is both an example of and a symbol for the abuse of the feminine. In this symbol we see reflected the way that feminine power and creativity has been repressed, exploited, and abused, not honoured, but denied for centuries of patriarchal rule. Women, in particular, have experienced through their own bodies and spirits the way that the earth and its nature have been raped, plundered, and thrown aside when no longer useful. But the Goddess denied does not rest; she becomes wrathful and will destroy indiscriminately in her quest for justice and respect. It is this indiscriminate and chaotic fury of the feminine, of the Goddess, and of the unleashed and uncurbed forces of nature, that mankind so fears and tries to control.

The Goddess has long been associated with nature, the endless processes of birth, death, and rebirth, with the instinctual, feeling life of the body, as well as an inherent wisdom and pristine intelligence expressed through the needs and impulses which drive us. Through centuries of patriarchal rule, this natural life and wisdom have been denied, but in our attempts to deny and control, the outrage of the repressed feminine grows and becomes more dangerously potent. The negative feminine is experienced as chaos, the dark hell-womb of the unconscious. As the feminine begins to re-emerge from the dark tomb she has been banished to, she does not come at first with love and sweetness; her return is marked by rage and fury at her oppression. We have seen this in the militancy of the women's movement of the last century, when the feminine voice had to shout out in anger her will to survive, and more than that, her need to be heard, honoured, and respected. When the Goddess's fury erupts, it devours and destroys; nothing escapes her wrath.

The wars we witness seem to be truly battles of the Mother, but it is through the most lethal weapons of the patriarchy that her revenge is wreaked. The will of the repressed feminine is carried out by the products of a distorted masculine power that has become destructive and brutal, the very power that has suppressed her. So we face a battle waged by both the Mother and the Father, colluding in their negative and destructive aspects. How much more abandoned could we be? Yet both Mother and Father are within us too. Both the destructive and chaotic aspects of nature that are inherent in repression, and the distorted and brutal means of controlling it are ours, and together these powers destroy the freedom of the soul-child within.

Discussing the internalised figures of the Mother and Father, Marion Woodman writes:

'We unconsciously introject the power inherent in these archetypal figures which, in the absence of the individuation process, remain intact at an infantile level. So long as they remain intact, uninterrupted by the consciousness that can disempower them, the inner dictators enslave more cruelly than the outer.

'In my understanding of patriarchy, these outworn parental images wield the power that inhibits personal growth. So long as they are in control, conscious masculinity and conscious femininity are merely words. Men and women who are unconsciously trapped in power drives have no individual freedom, nor can they allow freedom to others. Women can be worse patriarchs than men. The myth of the sun hero fighting the dragon and winning his way to consciousness has suffered from overkill. The energies of that myth have been exhausted and we are now struggling with the abuses of its excess. In killing the dragon, we are now in danger of killing nature herself on whom we depend for life. *Moreover, the tunnel vision that has been so focused on conquering the unconscious mother has been blind to her conquering through the back door: the effort of centuries to kill the dragon has ended in the worship of mother in concrete materialism.* The sons and daughters of patriarchy are, in fact, mother-bound.' (Original italics)[2]

In the wars and exploitation of people and resources which we witness today, we see the explicit effects of this worship of the Mother as concrete materialism. The son-hero slays the mother-dragon; but, as Woodman points out, this myth has outgrown its usefulness, and we are desperately in need of a new myth to guide us through the crisis of rebirth which we are now experiencing. The new myths we are seeking, the stories which will contain the meaning of the drama of our present times, will reveal themselves, are revealing themselves, through the inner experiences of those individuals who are seeking to free themselves from the old power-bound dynamics of their own psyche. The growth of individual consciousness determines the evolution of collective consciousness. It is only through inner change within each of us that there will be real change in outer reality. And only through discovering a mutually enhancing and enlivening relationship between the masculine and feminine within can the soul-child, who holds the heart and hope of the future, be born into consciousness. Essential to this is the awakening of the conscious feminine, which enables us to come into a better relationship with our inner self, each other, and the earth. When this happens, we will no longer need to seek to dominate nature, or control and mindlessly plunder the resources of the earth, but will learn to feel respect, humility, and wonder again.

Humanity has evolved through the age of matriarchal rule with its magical and mythic mode of thinking, and patriarchal rule dominated by rational and mechanistic ideology. The new ways of being, of experiencing and perceiving life, in the age that is struggling to be born may not be like those of either of the previous ages. We cannot accurately predict what the new consciousness will be, for predictions can only be based on what we already have some conception of. But the hope is that the new consciousness will include the positive values learned through both the matriarchal and patriarchal ages in a marriage of feeling and knowledge, of wisdom and skilful action; that the wise and intelligent heart, and a personal authority based on feeling values and authentic experience, will be our guides into new ways of living and relating. Our present age is being called to step beyond the known bounds and open to an unknown future – to open awareness to experience new ways of being. Through the suffering of change, destruction, and death, the birth pains are being felt.

Pathology and Meaning – Redefining Basic Sanity

'And the nosing beasts soon scent
how insecurely we're housed in this signposted world',

writes Rilke. And the walls will inevitably crumble sooner or later. Personal, social, and political breakdown is an inevitable fact of life, and epidemic in these times of unprecedented change. But whether the breakdown leads us only deeper into sickness, desperation, and despair, or offers an opportunity to be born into a richer and more rewarding life, will depend on the value and meaning we give to it. To help us to understand the greater picture, we need to listen to the inner experience of the individual in crisis, for the individual creates and reflects the undercurrents of our social fabric. But it is also important, as Keith Thompson describes, that the individual not take their 'extraordinary' experiences too *personally*, or the greater cultural and universal implications may be lost.[3] We need to stay open to the greater story that is attempting to unfold through our own local, personal story.

Although modern technology and medicine have given us increased comfort and extended our life expectancy, more and more people in the modern world are suffering from mental illness and breakdown. Such experiences can teach us about our collective situation. The personality that breaks under the stresses of modern life reveals another crack in the collective armouring, a doorway through which unconscious forces of the collective psyche can flood through. Some people are especially sensitive to the tides of collective unconscious experience. In Jung's terminology, this would be described as the introverted intuitive type. Marie-Louise von Franz states:

> 'On a primitive level, he is the shaman who knows what the gods and the ghosts and the ancestral spirits are planning, and who conveys their messages to the tribe. In psychological language we should say that he knows about the slow processes which go on in the collective unconscious, the archetypal changes, and he communicates them to society... . The people generally did not enjoy hearing these messages. Many introverted intuitives are to be found among artists and poets.'[4]

The person sensitive to the collective unconscious may be especially susceptible to what we call psychological illness, particularly in a time when society itself is suffering from a great sickness of soul. Such people may carry the sickness and suffering of their community, when there is no cultural framework within which their vision and experience can be understood and responded to. Through the inner experiences of the sensitive soul, the messages of the 'gods and ancestral spirits' are heard. But western religion and society have denied the existence of these gods for many centuries, and we are too proud of our own achievements to want to heed the wisdom of the spirits of deceased ancestors. Also, as von Franz points out, people don't like to hear these messages. Today it is often the sensitive person, the one with creative or prophetic vision and intuitive insight into how things are, who becomes the one labelled by society as mentally ill and insane. It is easy for society to look down on such people as inferior, failures in the human race, when in reality they are often some of the most gifted, intelligent, and creative of people.

Arnold Mindell writes:

> '...[T]he existence of the universal dreambody means that we are a reflection of the greater world. Our dreams are world dreams with personal imagery associated to them, and which speak especially to us. Our body problems are also problems of the

world around us, we suffer in the way the whole world suffers. Our illness is a dream, it's a symptom of the incongruity of the world we live in. We can be our family's unconscious sensitivity, for example, or the world's unconscious suffering.

'…(For the individual)…transforming himself means coming up against interiorized cultural edges. If this transformation is to occur, he will have to disturb the status quo of the world around him as well.'[5]

Sanity is usually defined as the ability to adapt and conform to society, an alignment of the inner self with external reality. But when we begin to look at this reality through our hearts, we have to admit that the values of the modern world are, themselves, often quite insane. And how then can we say that those who cannot adapt to or cope with this reality are ill? Are we not all ill and suffering, to have created and be resigned to living in a crazy world? And might not the so-called sick person who 'disturbs the status quo of the world around him' have something of value to tell that world?

In his book *Narcissism – Denial of the True Self*, Alexander Lowen describes narcissism as a predominant trend of our culture, and it is the narcissistic individual who is often deemed to be the best adapted and most successful – and hence the more 'sane' – member of society. In describing the narcissistic condition Lowen begins by saying:

'Narcissism describes both a psychological and a cultural condition. On the individual level, it denotes a personality disturbance characterized by an exaggerated investment in one's image at the expense of the self. Narcissists are more concerned with how they appear than what they feel. Indeed, they deny feelings that contradict the image they seek. Acting without feeling, they tend to be seductive and manipulative, striving for power and control. They are egotists, focussed on their own interests but lacking the true values of the self – namely, self-expression, self-possession, dignity, and integrity. Narcissists lack a sense of self derived from body feelings. Without a solid sense of self, they experience life as meaningless. It is a desolate state.

'On the cultural level, narcissism can be seen in a loss of human values – in a lack of concern for the environment, for the quality of life, for one's fellow human beings. A society that sacrifices the natural environment for profit and power betrays its insensitivity to human needs. The proliferation of material things becomes the measure of progress in living, and man is pitted against woman, worker against employer, individual against community. When wealth occupies a higher position than wisdom, when notoriety is admired more than dignity, when success is more important than self-respect, the culture itself overvalues 'image' and must be regarded as narcissistic.... .

'Narcissists can be identified by their lack of humanness. They don't feel the tragedy of a world threatened by a nuclear holocaust, nor do they feel the tragedy of a life spent trying to prove their worth to an uncaring world.'[6]

The narcissistic individual has developed a 'facade of superiority and specialness' to hide the authentic feeling self within; this facade masks feelings of deep-rooted insecurity engendered by lack of connection to the true self. If the true self was never fully seen, accepted, and understood, there has been no place in which it could be nurtured and could grow. As a child, the person's own feelings and reality were consistently denied or found to be unacceptable by parents and those in authority. Hence the false self, the image of who one is, takes the place of the authentic feeling self in order to protect the integrity of the child in a world which denies her reality and her own truth.[7] The false self enables the child to appear acceptable to those on whom she depends for her very existence, or to become tough enough to survive in an untrustworthy environment; behind the false facade she can hide all that society would deem 'crazy' – that is, her authentic and spontaneous feeling life. In order to appear 'normal' and find a place for herself within the social reality, the child must grow into an adult cut off from genuine feelings, spontaneity, and authenticity; or, in other words, she must sacrifice her own reality for that of others. She is often doomed to a life of trying to prove her existence by proving her worth through ever more success, achievement, power, or perfection. In effect she must act insanely in order to appear sane in a crazy world! Lowen goes on to say:

'In general, insanity is seen as the mark of an individual who is out of touch with the reality of his or her culture. By that criterion (which has its validity), the successful narcissist is far from insane. Unless…unless, of course, there is some insanity in the culture. Personally, I see the frenzied activity of people in our large cities – people who are trying to make more money, gain more power, get ahead – as a little crazy. Isn't frenzy a sign of madness?'[8]

If we are to unravel the craziness in which we have become embedded, and generally accept as being normal, then should we not begin to listen to those who have not adapted and coped so well with this state of affairs? In the voice of insanity and mental illness, there may be wisdom, and even the seeds of healing for our collective ills. To hear this voice we don't have to spend our lives in mental hospitals listening to those 'certified insane' – although we might learn much from doing this also – but only to listen to that part of ourselves which perceives the meaninglessness, suffering, and insanity of our world and our own lives. In that way we may begin to see through the illusions we have created, and by which we live, to another level of reality and experience. The world of the authentic feeling life, of psyche or soul, of the visions and the 'messages of the gods' can show us the way. We need to create a little space in our lives, and in our minds, in order to open our awareness to the reality behind the illusions.

We are in the habit of viewing the breakdown and failure of the ego to cope with, adapt, and relate to external reality, as pathological. The sick person's behaviour is considered abnormal, maladapted, crazy, and their perspective on life distorted. There is a level of truth in this, but the breakdown or failure of defensive psychological structures can also reveal truths other than this conventional one. It is the way in which society views the condition that may determine whether such a state actually becomes a pathological or a meaningful experience. Most cultures of the past held the view that such altered states of consciousness were meaningful, potentially revealing wisdom, value, and healing for both the individual and the collective; they considered such experiences necessary to both social and cultural well-being and the health of the members of the community. An important place in such communities was held by those who were masters of altered states of consciousness – the shaman, the prophet or seer, the mystic, the priest, and the artist. This acknowledgement gave meaning to out-of-the-ordinary experiences and visionary states of mind. We have lost belief in such meaning, and instead would throw our potential visionaries and mystics into the garbage pail of mental institutions, out of sight, where their dreams might not disturb our sleep. It was fear of such powers that led the Inquisition to persecute thousands of ordinary women as witches, along with the healers and visionaries of the time.

Jung was the first of the modern psychologists to give credence to the voice behind pathology, to value it and recognise the basic sanity that underlay the madness. Others, such as R D Laing, Stanislav and Christina Grof, John Weir Perry, and Arnold Mindell to name but a few, have sought to do the same, but still society at large shuns those in crisis, outcasts them like modern-day lepers. The fear of what they represent and what they are trying to tell us runs deep. And it is not only the chronically ill who are treated in this way. The 'normally healthy' individual going through a crisis of profound change may suffer severe anxiety, depression, and other symptoms; she may fail to cope with life as she had done before, and risks being sentenced to the label of mentally ill. These people are often intelligent and successful, no more ill or unstable than the average person, but often acutely sensitive to the tides of collective feeling and the necessity for inner change that is confronting us. Many express the conviction that, through their 'illness' and the process of recovery, they are helping to effect change and healing not only for themselves but also for their families, communities, or humanity as a whole.

Alex Pirani writes of such depressive illness:

> '...[T]hey are ordeals that are fundamental to the life-cycle, to the death and rebirth of identity at different stages in the life process. Severe depressions often precede "creative breakthrough". What makes them so hard for us to bear in our Western world is that we lack acceptance of their inevitability and have no rituals, as more primitive societies do, to help us through these transitions. When we are in "the valley of the shadow of death" our distress and depression will be shunned, tranquillised, misread, silenced. Many are thrust into the dark sea-chest of an unenlightened mental hospital. Some go under; others survive. Faith, and a sense that there must be a meaning to the experience, will bring a person through.'[9]

It is important that we do come through such ordeals, not only for our own sake, but for the healing process of humanity, in which our own healing plays a part. But if we merely survive the experience, and don't transform the suffering and pain, we may be left with only bitterness, anger, and resentment towards the people or circumstances which we feel have failed us. We might remain victim to our own suffering, angry and fearful of further pain, still not truly alive to our own heart and our true creative self. To get beyond the anger, resentment, and despair we need to find the way back, to touch again our own heart and the source of creative life, wisdom, and love within. Until we can do this, our energy follows the line of attachment which keeps us tied to the suffering, or to those who have hurt and betrayed us, in a negative cycle of regret and misery. To make this transformation we need to rediscover faith and confidence, essentially in ourselves, and trust in the basic goodness and wisdom of our own true nature.

Living the Fear

Without a sense of faith in something that contains and gives meaning to such experiences, the death-rebirth crisis can be a terrifying ordeal, as everything we have known, including our most cherished beliefs, disintegrates within and around us. Our oldest, deepest fears are reawakened in this process – memories of our original death-birth crisis and our earliest experiences of disintegration states may be evoked. We feel again the agonies of the infant unheld and unprotected. Writing on the work of Winnicott, Davis and Wallbridge state:

> 'Trauma at the beginning of life…"relates to the threat of annihilation". The concept of annihilation is expanded in Winnicott's list of what he called the "primitive agonies" or "unthinkable anxieties":
>
> 1   Going to pieces.
> 2   Falling forever.
> 3   Having no relation to the body.
> 4   Having no orientation.
> 5   Complete isolation because of there being no means of communication.'[10]

These experiences are at the root of psychosis, and they can also be present during stages of the individuation process; it is these 'primitive agonies', first experienced in early life, that we re-experience during the death-rebirth crisis. The process reaches this substratum of the unconscious psyche, and may lead to psychotic episodes if not properly contained and guided.[11] The psychoid depths of the psyche are common to all of us, not just the 'psychotic', and can be evoked in and experienced by 'normally healthy' individuals in extreme situations. What we are becoming aware of today, as the means to access deeper levels of the psyche are becoming more readily available, and the cultural mind begins to open, is that we are all more deeply wounded than we may have previously realised; beneath the facade of normality, we all suffer deeply, and when we touch beneath the surface we realise there is a deep and pervading fear. Even a 'normally healthy' person can become temporarily borderline or psychotic when the deepest wounds are opened up, either through life events or through the consciousness-expanding processes of therapy, spiritual practice, drugs, and so on. Psychotic process is in fact very often an integral part of the process of individuation. Such crises also reflect the journey of shamanic wounding and initiation, as we will explore later.

Through my own crisis, what I found myself most intensely confronted with was a great fear, an unabatable terror. What lies behind the 'primitive agonies' and 'unthinkable anxieties' is a deep and pervading, raw, existential fear. It manifests as fear of abandonment, of being unheld, unprotected, ultimately of death or annihilation. We remember early experiences of abandonment or trauma as infants, and this personal level of the process needs to be held therapeutically. But the fear also relates to our present situation, our dive through the nets of illusory security into the universe beyond. It is fear of the void, the fundamental emptiness that underlies existence, with which we are ultimately confronted at such times.

It can be so terrifying to the ego-mind to confront this reality and face the naked fear, that it will create all manner of phenomena into the spaciousness, in order to preserve some reference point for its own existence. Ego needs reference points, and to the ego even faulty ones are better than none at all. This resistance on the part of the ego-mind to accept the reality of existence as insubstantial and impermanent causes endless secondary sufferings; it creates the symptoms of pathology by which we attempt to avoid confrontation with that reality. But at the heart of the experience what we are touching upon is sane and wise. Both levels can be felt in the crisis of undoing.

Although modern western psychology has generally located psychopathology and mental illness within the unconscious, this is not the view of some. M Scott Peck describes the collective unconscious as God, and the conscious, as man or woman, as individual. In his vision, the personal unconscious is the interface between them, and as such, it is a place of conflict and struggle between the will of God and the conscious will of the individual. For this reason, the unconscious has been seen as the seat of psychopathology and mental illness. However, it is consciousness that is disordered, Peck claims, not the unconscious; and because consciousness is disordered, it is in conflict with the source of unconscious wisdom that would seek to heal it. Illness occurs when the conscious self resists the individual's unconscious will, or the will of God.[12]

Peck claims that it is our relationship to the unconscious and its wisdom that is at fault, not the unconscious itself. Contact with it is necessary, and healing lies within it. This view is in many ways similar to the Buddhist perspective, which sees the clinging of the ego to be the cause of suffering and illness. Beyond this clinging, wisdom is realised, and this brings freedom from suffering and the dualistic thinking which creates it. The path is to see through the surface layers of disordered consciousness in order to discover the Buddha-nature within, not to dig out the demons until the basement is clean. However, we can be very unaware of much of what goes on at this level of clinging ego-mind, so it is also valid to talk of our unconscious habits and patterns of thought and behaviour; or of projecting our unconscious individual or collective fears, desires, and aggressions, all of which are expressions of ego, onto others. In Buddhist psychology, *all* phenomena are the product of ego, and most of the processes of ego go on beneath the threshold of our conscious awareness.

During a crisis of undoing, we experience the breakdown of roles, relationships, belief systems, psychological structures – in fact everything that once supported and sustained us in a familiar identification and lifestyle. As they dissolve, we are confronted with the fact that these seemingly trustworthy supports are, in fact, insubstantial and illusory. Until we can find a new identification, we feel lost and rootless. If we feel our very self to be disintegrating, we may begin to sense that it too is illusory, and here the deepest fear may enter. But when we feel that we have lost all, we might be compelled to seek for a sense of reality that is beyond the limited ego-identification with which we are familiar.

The view of Buddhism can be helpful to us in learning to encounter and work with such depths. The understanding that emptiness is the ultimate basis of reality gives a philosophical context within which to hold the process. Buddhism teaches that 'bliss and emptiness' are the natural state of the enlightened mind, and we must recognise that our view of self as something inherently real and substantial is an illusion, in order to realise this deeper reality.[13] This doesn't mean we are to throw out or destroy the ego. It is our attachment to self or ego, and our belief in its ultimate reality, not ego itself, which is the obstacle to spiritual realisation. We cannot live in the world without a stable enough ego, for it is the function through which we relate meaningfully with external reality, the interface between ourselves and the world around us. The importance of a healthy ego can be appreciated by those who have experienced its disintegration.

A stable enough ego and sense of self is also necessary to spiritual practice; only when we are in contact with our authentic inner self can we safely let go to something deeper. To practise meditation from the standpoint of the false or narcissistic self can lead to traps such as inflation or denial; or, if an integrated sense of self has not developed, we may be overwhelmed by psychic content. But there are times when spiritual growth evokes and even necessitates a 'loss of self' or 'ego-death', as we have seen. Faced with the experience of the existential void, the ego feels that it is dying; and in a sense this must be so, for if a more embracing awareness is to enter consciousness, the ego must change to accommodate this. We experience such processes as death or annihilation of our deepest self, as the concept of self with which we are most deeply identified is changing. If we are able to let go of this limited identification we can connect more deeply to our essential nature; and the more we can let go of identification with personal self, the more we can endure the ultimate emptiness of reality, rather than fear it as a dark and threatening, or meaningless, void. Through many such small deaths we might eventually grow beyond the fear and come to realise, as Chime Rinpoche would say, that 'there is no death because there is no self'.

A philosophical system based on dualistic thinking may be unable to provide a holding structure for the kind of awareness encountered in these depths. Dualistic thinking tends to view the experience of 'I' as something of enduring substance, and creates separation between 'I' and 'other'. In such a system, there is no place for the awareness of emptiness, beyond duality, which may be encountered in depth experiences. When we begin to approach the experience of emptiness from the perspective of the materialistic and dualistic thought structures of the western mind, we find there is nothing to contain our experience within this intellectual system. The visions and archetypal forces, the powerful emotions and out-of-the-ordinary experiences, the gods and demons we encounter on this path, take on a too-concrete reality, an 'otherness', which threatens to overwhelm the limited conscious mind.

We could also say that the void is so threatening to the ego that the moment it appears we immediately fill it with phenomena – perceptions, thoughts, emotions, images, concepts, beliefs, and so on – to avoid experiencing the reality. The more we open to it, the more tightly does the ego-mind hang onto the contents of consciousness as if they were real, circling them round and round endlessly. These are the 'demons' which we observe when we sit and watch our minds in meditation, and which we must face when we begin to open to deeper levels of awareness, and reality comes too close. The ego-mind fills the natural spaciousness of awareness with these gods and demons, be they fascinating or frightening, rather than lose its own sense of reality in the experience of emptiness. When we begin to open to what is *beyond* the ego in the mystical sense, from a mental basis that has been conditioned by dualistic and materialistic thinking, we may instead be opened to the psychotic strata of the mind that lies *beneath* the ego.

Buddhist teaching offers a training for the mind which enables us to encounter these deeper levels of consciousness. Through specific meditation practices, the gods and demons of our mind – the thoughts, fears, passions, and conflicts which haunt and consume us – are understood to have no inherent reality of their own, and when this is truly realised they cease to obsess or threaten us. The inability to realise truly that our visions and inner experiences are without any real and concrete existence external to our own minds, are essentially empty in nature, may lead to psychosis instead of enlightenment. In psychological language, we would say that the personality has been possessed by an archetype – or, in other words, a god or demon. The conscious mind becomes overwhelmed by and identified with the god or demon, and the emotional force that it represents. We can avoid this only when the integrity of the inner core self remains sufficiently intact.

If we open too suddenly to depths we have not been prepared to encounter, we can see how deeply we actually fear the enlightenment that we also seek. From the perspective of the small and limited ego-mind, the vision is too vast and terrifying to be embraced, and the responsibility of embracing it too awesome. When we are identified too tightly with the person that we believe ourselves to be, our potential wholeness seems impossibly large and magnificent for us to contain and express in a world that knows us in our smallness only. We often try to stifle the emergence of our spiritual being in order to maintain our familiar place in the world. In transpersonal psychology this phenomenon has been termed 'repression of the sublime'. We have to die to the old identification, and all the relative securities it may afford us, if we are to allow space for genuine realisation to emerge within us. And if we begin to allow that, or when, as often happens, the emergence comes uncalled for, we may also experience the terror of the ego which feels the growth as a threat to its very existence.

Perry describes how it is not the ego which is dying, although the term 'ego-death' is one often used to describe such crises. He believes that what is dying is the image of the archetypal centre, or 'higher Self':

> 'The archetypal center abides, but the image representing it is what needs cyclic renewal, with all that it implies about the outlook, lifestyle, and value system by which one lives.

> 'We are capable of apprehending the center only through its embodiment in images, and these are periodically transformed in the psyche's development; no form that it takes is static... .

> 'From time to time, then, a form of the Self is designated by a certain symbolic or mythic image, which captures the dynamic essence of that phase of a person's life, until it has done its work and its hour has come to be dissolved. The ego does sense that something is dying, and changes only secondarily to the demise of the image of the Self, the center. What happens to the ego reflects the dynamisms in the archetypal psyche. Of the two levels of the self-image, the archetypal one effects in-depth

transformations, while the personal one in the conscious personality reflects those more superficial changes. Then the reorganization of the self occurs on both these levels.'[14]

This also appears to happen at a collective and cultural level; when a particular phase of cultural life ends, both the symbolic images through which it expresses itself, for example in art and religion, and the lifestyle and values of the culture undergo profound changes. The more superficial changes occurring in society reflect those going on in the depths of the collective psyche. The ordination of women into the church is one current example of this, and one that is relevant to the central themes of this book. This change of form, and the difficulties women have encountered in bringing it about, are reflections of the re-emergence of feminine consciousness and spirituality into collective awareness.

If we have no system of belief or understanding which can give context and meaning to such experiences, we fear that our very being is being annihilated, and the fear of this can overwhelm. When we lack understanding and faith in the meaning and purpose of the experience, the fear can create pathology, though even with faith it is a tenuous thread of a path we follow. With faith in the process the fear can be experienced and contained, and even recognised as an essential part of the process of growth. But along with our own faith, it is also the love and support of another human being who understands and believes in what we are going through which will enable the transformation and renewal to be fulfilled. When we are involved in a process deeply affecting the *transpersonal* level of the psyche we need *personal* relationship in order to ground and bring it to completion; without this we can easily become lost. This is the dangerous edge, for in such states most people find themselves either at the mercy of inappropriate and non-comprehending psychiatric intervention, or hopelessly alone and isolated.

Facing the fear is a crucial part of the process. In *Shambhala — The Sacred Path of the Warrior*, Tibetan teacher Chogyam Trungpa writes:

'In order to experience fearlessness, it is necessary to experience fear. The essence of cowardice is not acknowledging the reality of fear.... Acknowledging fear is not a cause for depression or discouragement. Because we possess such fear, we also are

potentially entitled to experience fearlessness. True fearlessness
is not the reduction of fear; but going beyond fear.'[15]

According to Buddhist teaching, if we can fully experience and go
beyond the fear, we may begin to embrace the experience of emptiness, the
essential nature of existence and of our own enlightened mind. So long as
we are trapped by the fear, we are bound to identification with the ego.
When we can face our uncertainty and fear of the unknown beyond the
dying, then we begin to contact the wisdom of the ever-present heart. But
fear keeps us held in the memory of the past, and brings the past into the
present and future, so long as we cannot open our awareness to the
spaciousness of the present moment.

Were it an easy task to embrace and live the truth of our genuine heart
and enlightened mind, then surely we would do it. But our minds, full of
fear of the great unknown, full of the pride that makes us believe that little-
me knows best, and full of the desires and passions that drive us to seek out
ever more experience in the phenomenal world, stubbornly resist. Forever
busy seeking temporary happiness and pleasure in an attempt to fill the
void we feel within, we lose sight of the spaciousness that is our true home.
We spend our lives attempting to build strong walls of security to house
ourselves in, and to keep out the too great visions of reality. But these walls
are the illusory creations of a fearful mind, a mind afraid to know its own
depth, beauty, magnificence, and power.

What has been created must always offer itself up again in decay and
death, become the dust that will eventually nourish new life. All that we are
and have created is forever being sacrificed to the ever-unfolding creativeness
of Life. It is in our fear of, and resistance to, this natural process of change
and impermanence that we suffer most deeply, trying to halt nature herself
in her cycles. Without acceptance of death, we cannot truly live. We die to
ourselves when we attempt to hold still the wheels of change, for this is not
security, but a stasis that goes against nature and curtails our growth.

During these crises we experience fear at the dissolving of forms and
structures; this is a response of the solar plexus, of the ego which feels it
must control and hold everything together, like Atlas holding up the whole
world. The ego feels fear when it all falls apart. But at the same time, the
heart is opening, and in our heart we may feel the pain of a suffering that is
greater than our own personal loss, and compassion for the vulnerability

and fragility of all life. Experience may swing between these two responses, as the centre of identification is beginning to shift from the solar plexus, seat of the ego, to the heart. This movement may be felt as physical sensations shifting between these two centres, and sometimes associated bodily symptoms and illness accompany the process.

When we travel to the further reaches of our heights and depths it becomes at times impossible, and even meaningless, to maintain our normal functioning in the world. We drop out of life, and may be burdened with the stigma our society places on that which is unknown, misunderstood, and feared. Like death, for it is a kind of death, society shuns, even scorns those who have succumbed. As soon as we label experience as some 'thing' – an illness, a breakdown – it is boxed, categorised, and put safely away out of sight. The experience itself is denied in this, and with it soul; the meaning and potential value are lost.

Our modern culture has evolved a soul-less psychology that considers progress to be a linear development, an accumulation of successes which gives no valued place to the failures and 'deaths' of the ego caused by the stirrings of the soul, or the upheavals caused by the reawakening of spirit within us. Within this goal-oriented and masculine approach to growth, which attempts to deny or control the cycles and spirallings of human life, nature, and death, we find little that offers understanding, meaning, or acceptance of experiences of disintegration. They are feared or viewed as only maladaptive and pathological, and in this the potential value is denied.

Freeing the Heart

Every breakdown is a potential breakthrough, though it may not necessarily be so. To what exactly we break through is an individual issue; each discovers what she needs for her next step towards wholeness. But there is always the promise of new life with every death and letting go. The awakening of genuine love, compassion, and the wisdom of the heart is the ultimate promise and purpose of this path. Fear is a major obstacle to fulfilling this promise – fear of the ego caught in its death throes, as it feels them to be; fear of the essential emptiness of existence; and the fear of those around us who witness our plight but cannot understand the significance of it, see only misery, failure, and waste, and fear that dark place in themselves which it reminds them of.

Breaking through is the journey of freeing the heart and spirit from the chains and illusions we have bound them in; this is the change that both the individual and humanity as a whole are needing to make in this time of global upheaval. It is the process of becoming more of whom we truly are, free from the concepts, judgements, and conditionings that weigh us down. Once we have made the commitment in our hearts to this path, we will be called to face whatever the path demands of us; there is no going back.

To free ourselves from our chains we must find the courage to face the darkness within, and then to bare our raw and tender broken hearts to the world. As we drop into our own heart of hearts, through the layers of hurt and fear that have surrounded it, we become opened, touched, moved by the hearts of others. Their love and their woundedness touches us, and we feel with them, cry with them. In this is the seed of compassion, which means to 'suffer with'. To suffer alone and unseen, unheard is a terrible burden on our hearts. With compassion, we are no longer alone in our suffering, for we are deeply felt and witnessed by another. This heart meeting brings healing, and it is the fulfilment of facing the fear and pain we encounter in the dark night of the soul.

On this journey we must also learn compassion for ourselves, for the 'little one' within us who is too afraid to make those great leaps of transformation all at once. The fearing mind jumps in to protect the wounded inner child from what she is not yet ready to encounter, but we cannot just say 'don't fear, little one, take the leap', for the wounded child will resist and rebel if her experience is denied in this way. We must embrace our fear, or the battle of the ego to maintain its unrightful rule and keep things just as they are will escalate fiercely and sabotage any attempts to grow free. Denying the fear does not make it go away, but will more likely escalate it into uncontrollable anxiety.

We must include the wounded child on this journey, not only because if we try to rush on without her, she will forever hold us back with her anguished feelings of abandonment; but also because her presence within us is essential to the work of inner transformation, for she connects us to the authentic feelings of our heart and to our creative spirit. Healing the wounded child is essential to our spiritual work, to the building of both the foundations and the golden roof. Without this, our heart cannot be freed of the fear that binds it, and true empathy and compassion cannot develop.

Father dear, you loved me

Mother dear, you gave me life, this life
and a tattered cloak
of grey home
spun cloth
to wrap me in
loosely
like last year's cocoon shell
hanging dryly from a sun-less ledge,
around itself,
empty now.

Father dear, you loved me
so I trusted
as your sweet-dream wishes cradled me
into my pillows
peacefully to sleep.
I looked to you for everything.
Your strong hand soothed the wild dark nights
joined the broken things of life
and made me safe. I looked to you
for tenderness.
You loved me so I thought.

Father why then did you tear
my cloak of rags
in your unmarked rage and passion?
Why then did you beat me
like a dog, a helpless child?
Your arm of strength against my trembling body
against my sex
        my innocence.

I hurt I feared I raged
but my rage was swept away in torrents
- driftwood in the flood
that catches on a rock
and breaks.

A child, I feared your violent lash
against my naked young and
tender flesh.
A woman now, I fear the men who hurl their glances, stones
or foul words
at my womanhood
and silently I hate the violence in their passion.
You made of me a victim, father dear,
to men's abuse.
I cry the victim's tears
and lick the wounds beneath my tattered cloak
as children hide their bitter secrets
in the night
between the covers
crying softly
all alone.

For love, for love
I wear my cloak of love and tatters
ripped through and torn again by winds that blow.
Rain comes in and cold dark nights come in
and fear comes in again.
I dare not walk the streets
half naked in my rags and shame, still trembling
from a memory lost down through the darkened days.
I patch the tears with poems
snatched from my mind and woven close,
but many winds cross through my life
and rend the stitches open,
stab their cold
into the wounds that never heal.

I love you Mother for the life you gave me
and this strange cloak of rags.
I'd like to find another tougher one, a smarter one
but only this one seems to fit.

I love you Father
though I cannot understand
your way of loving me
so fiercely.

3 The Wounded Child

When powerful experiences of a transpersonal or spiritual nature emerge into consciousness, we may be plunged into a crisis of many dimensions. As we begin to open more fully, and are called to surrender to our spiritual values and purpose, our orientation towards life and our own place within it may be deeply shaken. A realignment of our physical and psychological reality with a new experience of spirit is underway, but the old alignment needs to break before the new can be fully experienced and integrated. The breaking of the old, as we seek a new relationship to spirit, causes much of the pain and confusion we feel at such times.

A similar process happens, though usually at a less disturbing and perhaps more tangible level, in bodywork for example. When a realignment is first experienced in the body, there is often an initial feeling of disorientation before the new sensations are fully integrated. Perceptual responses have shifted and the new alignment may feel not only unfamiliar and strange, but unstable and even wrong to us; we are still relating to it from the old perceptual framework out of which we are used to evaluating our experience of ourselves and the world around us. Even gravity, the earth, may feel less familiar and certain during the period of adjustment and integration, as our sensory channels receive new information and old patterns of perception are disrupted.

The disturbance we feel when spirit is realigning may feel like loss of home and ground within, at the deepest level of being. Until we can integrate the new experiences and perceptions, we feel lost, unheld, like homeless wanderers in the universe. This integration may take very many years, if the experience has touched to a deep level. The spacious experience of spirit can, if we are not ready to receive it, throw us into the chaos of the unfathomable void. As long as we are still being influenced or controlled by old ways of perceiving, we cannot feel the holding quality of spirit which is both our home and the ground of our essential being. It is so close to us that we cannot see or feel it, and if the fearing mind holds too tightly to the old orientation it cannot trust and surrender to what is actually present.

Such crises involve facing issues of the purpose and meaning of our own life and death, confronting the existential suffering of the human condition and the inherently empty nature of reality; but they may also evoke the forgotten experiences of childhood trauma, and regression to earlier states of consciousness may occur. When dealing with these crises, all levels of experience must be acknowledged. Mainstream psychology has tended to exclude the presence of soul and spirit in its approach to mental health and illness. It frequently pathologises what is in fact an opportunity, even a necessity, to bring spirituality and sacredness into a person's life, by seeing the crisis only as regressive and indicative of the ego's failure to cope with reality.

On the other hand, transpersonal psychology may tend towards the other extreme, not giving enough attention to the needs of the wounded child, or the necessity of building a stable enough ego in order to contain and integrate transpersonal experiences safely. I experienced my own therapist responding with impatience when he felt I was taking 'too much time' to reach states of 'higher' consciousness, not accepting that the psyche has its own timing and needs to take as much time as it takes. If the childhood trauma that has been evoked is not adequately addressed, no genuine growth or transformation can occur at other levels. Both attitudes are one-dimensional approaches to a multi-dimensional crisis, and can equally lead to real pathology if the true nature of the crisis is not recognised and dealt with appropriately.

What we inevitably find is that our ability to accept and integrate the callings of our soul, or the touch of spirit as it begins to awaken in us, is conditioned by experiences in early childhood and infancy. This of course means the relationship, first of all, to parents, or those fulfilling the parental role. The unresolved issues of parental complexes are reconstellated and may be felt as severe obstacles to the resolution of the crisis. However, they *are* the crisis. Growth does not happen by eliminating the obstacles of parental complexes; rather what we need for our growth lies within them, and our task is to mine them until we find the seed that may bring healing for the particular sickness of soul and spirit from which we suffer.

We come into this life with a disposition towards experiencing things in a particular way, a certain tendency which is personal to each of us – our karma, if you like. This tendency is not dependent on our parents or the environment, but rather will condition the way we experience and respond to them. The complexes therefore evolve out of the meeting of the child's disposition with its parental environment. Jung writes:

'...[T]he individual disposition is already a factor in childhood; it is innate, and not acquired in the course of life. The parental complex is therefore nothing but the first manifestation of a clash between reality and the individual's constitutional inability to meet the requirements it demands of him. The first form of the complex cannot be other than a parental complex, because the parents are the first reality with which the child comes into conflict.'[1]

Of course, the child must respond to the reality of her particular parents, but she will respond in her own unique way. There can be value in understanding what our parents did or did not do for us, if it gives us insight into our own nature and patterns of behaviour, and where our own qualities and limitations lie. Through understanding the responses and the sometimes failures of others towards us, we can see our own nature more clearly and learn what it is we need for our growth – the lesson this life has to teach us. Our parents are the first to offer us this lesson.

When we come to face and accept the wounds of our childhood, we may discover the seed of redemption of that wounding. The wounded child within carries our deepest hurts and violations, but she also carries the pure essence and power of being which brought us into the world at birth, the power that can open hearts. Within her woundedness and brokenness, the child carries our integrity, our truth, and the intactness of our being – the authentic child long-hidden from the threat of further violation. It is in embracing the wounded child within us, in including her hurt, despair, fear, and rage, that we can open to the love that is her deepest nature; in accepting and loving the child within, we find the path to loving and feeling compassion for ourselves, and beyond this to developing genuine love and compassion for others.

When the tragedies of life open us to our deepest pain and grief, it is into the well of all our past suffering and loss that we are plunged. The flood gates to the tide of hurt, fear, and deepest longing, for ages buried in unconsciousness, are opened wide. We are opened to the authentic feelings of our heart, but we are also opened to the experience of boundarylessness. In reconnecting to the raw, pre-verbal experiences of the infant and young child, we are also confronted again with the essential nature of existence, before the ego created boundaries and separation, and the mind conceived definitions, limitations, and distance from pure direct experience. The more open and permeable state of consciousness of the child is closer than the adult's to the awareness of intrinsic emptiness, which exists before and beyond ego.

The way that we experienced the nature of voidness, the lack of boundaries, and states of disintegration as an infant and child will be reflected in our ability to cope with such experiences later in life. And in this personal confrontation with our depths, again without boundaries intact, our awareness pours into the collective archetypal layers of psyche, into the existential suffering of mankind, the pain and suffering of life itself. The infant and child, in her acute sensitivity and vulnerability, feels all of this, the rawness of the experience of life. How the child relates to this raw experience depends on the interface between her own nature and the quality of parenting she receives. As we re-experience these states during times of profound crisis, we are again given opportunities to learn the most important lessons of our lives.

Mother and Child – The Bond

The embryonic experience of self begins to develop *inutero*, through the sensations of the body at a basic cellular level. The unborn child first learns about herself and the world through the movement, touch, warmth, sound, and rhythm of her mother's body and her own; and through the emotional life with which her mother's body is imbued. Experiences of intrauterine life can be recalled in special circumstances, as has been documented by Stanislav Grof in his pioneering work with perinatal experiences in therapy.[2] Alessandra Piontelli also presents fascinating evidence of the development of the personality and the possibility of an emergent sense of self *inutero*.[3]

It is generally understood that the foetus experiences psychosomatic unity, and that emotional experience is only gradually differentiated out of the sensory-based experiences of the body. The distinction between the psyche-soma of the foetus and that of the mother is also not yet clearly defined; the walls of the womb are both its whole universe and a part of itself, and they are also part of the mother. The unborn child has no clear boundary separating and defining her experience as distinct from her mother's. She lives in a state of pre-conscious unity with all that is her world, the maternal matrix. In this psychically undefended state, the very cells of the body must be impressed with nuances of the physical, emotional, and psychic life of the mother, and all that she is consciously and unconsciously subject to. These memories are held deep within the tissues of the body, at the cellular level of being; the body knows and remembers from where we have come, and through what experiences we passed before ever the mind began to develop and differentiate this from that.

Early life in the womb concerns the incarnating or grounding of being in physical matter, and on the earth; this is the first level of holding and bonding which we experience, and upon it depends our ability to trust, surrender, love, and be loved. Without a feeling of trust and security at this fundamental level, we are unable to fully inhabit our bodies or access and express our instinctual life; we can be neither fully present nor spontaneously ourselves. Love of self, which is the basis of all love, is grounded in the early experiences of body and soul feeling held and cherished by the mother, both in the womb and after birth. 'Genuine love,' writes Marion Woodman, 'permeates every cell of the body.'[4] Incarnating on earth and bonding with mother-as-ground relates to the root chakra; it is an the essential foundation for spiritual growth. This level of experience concerns issues of basic survival, and is the root of our connection to instinctual feeling, power, and sexuality. Woodman writes on this issue, as related to feminine psychology:

> '...[T]he grounding of the life force in the lowest chakra has to
> be secure, open to the energies of the earth, before the radiance
> of the spirit can take up residence...'[5]

When holding at this fundamental level fails, the mother is unable to pass on to her daughter a sense of confidence in herself, her body, and her nature as a female being. She will fail to endow her child with a sense of trust in her body, herself, or life itself, which leaves the daughter without the essential ground within:

'A mother who cannot welcome her baby girl into the world leaves her daughter groundless. Similarly, the mother's mother and grandmother were probably without the deep roots that connect a woman's body to earth. Whatever the cause, her own instinctual life is unavailable to her and, disempowered as a woman, she runs her household as she runs herself – with shoulds, oughts and have tos that add up to power. Life is not fed from the waters of love, but from will power that demands perfection, *frozen* perfection...*[6]*

'Disconnected from the instinctual level of her femininity, she is disconnected from the passion of her soul in her own matter. In other words, she is disconnected from the life force in the lowest chakra, *muladhara*, and since that chakra is related to the crown chakra, she is unable to endure the potential energy of spiritual light. In archetypal language, she is disconnected from the Earth Mother and at the same time disconnected from the virile masculinity that would be her natural bridegroom.'[7]

Bonding of the mother and child begins within the womb, and some experts tell us that it is already well established within three days of birth. It is out of a positive experience of bonding that our sense of well-being and security in the world can flourish. In the womb, an underlying sense of trust or mistrust of life develops, depending on the quality and depth of the early experience of holding. In her unboundaried state, the growing child's experience will be subject to and influenced by every joy, sadness, fear, love, pain, and anger of her mother, and may be particularly susceptible to all that is unconscious in the mother's psyche. In this way, the child has already met with the emotional environment into which she will be born, and those people who are closest to the mother, through her responses to them. The child will have experience of the presence or absence of the father, and the level of unconscious collective experience that the parents are connected to and share in. It is an awesome prospect, and one that connects each one of us deeply with the soul of humanity.

When healthy bonding between mother and child has occurred before birth, the child is more likely to experience the environment into which she is born as a secure place, and out of this a loving and trusting relationship with it can be more readily nurtured. The child can experience her fundamental 'yes' to life as a growing sense of well-being born out of self love. But the child who has felt her womb-universe to be hostile, unsafe, or frightening cannot emerge with such a well-founded sense of security and trust. The mother's feelings towards herself, her child, and life in general can adversely affect the child if the mother herself has been subject to continued negative emotions or unresolved trauma, or if she has not experienced nurturing affirmation of her own feminine being and the ground within her. The infant will not experience her wholehearted 'yes' to life, but will come into the world with feelings of ambivalence towards it. Lack of the feminine ground within creates an attitude of fear and anxiety towards life.

The new-born infant at first experiences herself as vaguely at-one with the mother, the sense of separate self not yet clearly differentiated. In this relatively diffuse state of consciousness, she is extremely open and sensitive to the emotional undercurrents in her environment. Her early experience of herself and the world, upon which many subsequent feelings, attitudes, and beliefs will develop, will be filtered through and profoundly influenced by the mother's own feelings and attitudes towards life, herself, and her child. Whether the womb-environment was filled with love, joy, and confidence, or fear, anxiety, and repressed anger, these will become part of the child's, and later the adult's, experience of its interface with the world; life will be perceived through the veil of these feelings and attitudes. Only gradually does the child's sense of separate self and ego boundary form, as she interacts in a variety of ways with the world. At least in modern westernised cultures, the development of ego function and the defining of individuality gives some psychological distance and protection from the emotional and psychic energies of others, as the child learns to separate 'what is me' from 'what is not-me'.

In place of the walls of the mother's womb, an embracing energetic aura, a skin or boundary of the subtle body has developed to contain and protect the child psychically. It might be experienced as a psychic womb which surrounds, contains, and protects us, and the quality of this energetic boundary both reflects and influences the quality of the individual's psychological boundary. It seems to me that the intactness of this boundary or 'skin' may depend, at least in part, on the quality of intrauterine and early life experiences, particularly experiences of holding, and is necessary to an integrated and contained sense of self. When it is weak, damaged, or extremely permeable we experience a high degree of sensitivity to unconscious influences, and a lack of clear separation between inner and outer. On the other hand, it could well be that the condition of the subtle body and its 'skin' is as much a part of the disposition with which we enter life as our physical and psychological tendencies; it may be that the degree of strength, permeability, and intactness of this boundary affects the child's experience of the womb and early infancy. This possibility opens up interesting questions as to the meaningful potential and the liabilities of such sensitivity, which I will return to later.

There may be both joy and suffering in the child's separation from her mother, for she begins to experience the existential pain of separation from that which she loves and depends on, the reality of her aloneness. The child may suffer in this process even as she joys and prides in her growing sense of power and independence. But a foundation of healthy bonding provides the security of a 'facilitating environment' (Winnicott) within which the child may learn to embrace her individuality and autonomy, without fear of loss of that continuity of being-ness which is the experience of self.

From her experiences of living with Stone Age Indians in the South American jungle, Jean Liedloff developed an understanding of basic expectations with which every human child enters the world. Just as our lungs *expect* to receive breath, our stomach food, and the cells of the body the oxygen and nutrients which will sustain our life processes, so too is the infant born with an *expectation* that certain conditions will be provided at specific stages of development. These expectations have evolved within us over millions of years, and their fulfilment has ensured the survival of our species. An infant has an inbuilt expectation that it will be carried in-arms more or less constantly for the first few months of life, never being left to suffer and cry alone, but always in the midst of life, held securely within the reassuring warmth and movement of another's body.

The infants of the Yequana tribe, whom Liedloff studied, were fulfilled in this basic expectation, and grew up to be independent, competent, happy, and innately social children and adults. When each stage of development is met with the appropriate kind and degree of holding, support, and encouragement, but no more than is necessary, the child grows into an adult who experiences a sense of well-being rarely encountered in our modern world; her sense of self is securely embodied, grounded, and held within a stable social fabric.[8]

If the child has not been adequately held by her environment at each stage of development, she may not be able to internalise from her experience a secure foundation of selfhood; she will then be bound ever to seek to be held by others and to draw her sense of self from her relationship to them. In this, she is not truly free to make her tentative steps into the larger world. The steps will be made, for they inevitably must, but they will be made with anxiety, fear, and holding back. The fear is greater when we have not learnt to trust, when we are not sure we will be held, not sure the familiar world will still be there to meet us on our return from our adventures. In fearing those she loves will not be there to hold her, will abandon her in her moment of need, the child fears the loss, the annihilation of her own self, for to the child the parents are the first carriers of the image of the self.

The child will also feel abandoned if the parents have projected onto her the image of their own inner child:

'The overwhelming sense of abandonment which terrorizes so many people is rooted not in the parents' abandonment of the child, but in the abandonment of the child's soul. By projecting their own image of their child, they obliterate the actual child who then goes underground, abandoned not only by the parents, but by the child itself.'[9]

The infant's development from a state of complete dependency to relative independence requires the establishing of an integrated and stable ego. Winnicott states that this healthy ego-integration develops out of many moments of restful un-integration, where:

'...[I]n the quiet moments let us say that there is no line but just lots of things they separate out, sky seen through trees, something to do with mother's eyes all going in and out, wandering around. Some lack of need for any integration.... Something to do with being calm, restful, relaxed and feeling one with people and things when no excitement is around.'[10]

The ability to rest in a state of un-integrated experience requires the presence of another being who does not make demands on the infant, but whose stable and loving presence in the environment can hold her through the moments of discontinuity of her sense of being-ness. The infant is enabled to experience safely herself as alone, in a state of restful un-integration, when adequately held in such a way. Winnicott described this experience as underlying the adult capacity to relax, to be alone, and to enjoy solitude. When these moments are felt to be safe, the child will be able to internalise the loving presence of the mother, and gradually be enabled to spend longer and longer periods of time without her actual physical presence in the environment.

> 'This sophisticated capacity to be alone can only come about when the mother's actual alive presence at the beginning makes a return to the state of un-integration possible. Hence the paradox that the capacity to be alone is "the experience of being alone while someone else is present".'[11]

When the environment repeatedly does not hold the infant through such moments of un-integration, or fails to protect her from trauma that she has not yet developed the ability to defend herself against, or integrate into her realm of experience, then the infant's sense of continuity of being is lost. And loss of being means annihilation. The defensive patterns of the false self begin to be organised to protect the authentic self from the experience of annihilation, from the traumas of what Winnicott termed the 'primitive agonies' or 'unthinkable anxieties'. This is the essence of latent psychosis:

> 'Clinical fear of breakdown is the fear of a breakdown that has already been experienced. It is the fear of the original agony which caused the defence organization which the patient displays as an illness syndrome.'[12]

Somewhere in our experience we hold the memory of early losses of being-ness, the trauma of unheld disintegration states, and fear their return. As we live in a culture which does not fully meet the needs and expectations of the infant to be securely held and accompanied through this most vulnerable stage of life, we may all carry these early fears within us; but if the holding of our environment has been adequate, enough ego-integration will be established to contain them and enable us to live a fairly normal life. Many children who have not experienced adequate parental holding seek for it in experiences with nature, and may feel more closely bonded to the earth and nature than to other people. They will often seek solitude in times of deep need, and may undergo their most powerful healing and spiritual experiences through contact with nature.

Loss and trauma, and the crises of great change in later childhood, adolescence, and into adulthood, may open us once more to the frightening visions and experiences of early disintegration states. The tragedies and failures of life bring such openings; so can the use of hallucinogenic drugs, or the opening that occurs in depth therapy or intensive meditation practice, for example. The wounded child lives on within us, and may be evoked in times of crisis or deep inner exploration, when the defensive structures of the ego are expanded, weakened, or shattered.

In his classic novel *Lord of the Flies*, William Golding describes such a breakdown of the individual personalities of a group of young boys, and of the society they attempted to create for themselves. Stranded on an uninhabited island with no guidance and protection from the adult world, their initial euphoria at being free of adult rules and authority soon turns into fear, violence, and the eruption of dark, primeval forces that they cannot contain. Their still forming and fragile egos begin to crumble into the chaos of nightmare, as the loss of protective holding becomes manifest; and their deepest fears and nightmares begin to turn into savage reality, as the boundaries between them and the terrors of the unknown, or between their conscious egos and the archetypal depths of the unconscious, begin to disintegrate. This adventure story points to the potential danger and tragedy of the child unheld against the frightening power of realities beyond its understanding or control. For it is a reality that is being witnessed in these states – the reality that lies before and beyond the ordering process of the ego-mind, which seeks to make the great small, the terrifying safe, and the unknown clear and defined, in order to survive.

The loss of that which we trust to hold us in our vulnerability will inevitably feel like a death, an annihilation of self, to the ego which cannot contain its fear of that which is beyond. To the young infant every disappearance of her mother from view feels like death of the mother, and with it the fear of her own death is evoked. Death is felt to be the most extreme and final loss, for when a loved one dies then all hope may be lost; and we find it hard to live without hope. When the aching void that is left by their absence cannot be filled with hopes of joyful reunions or reconciliations, there is only the void.

In mourning – whether we mourn the loss of a loved one, or the betrayal of something or someone we innocently trusted – we may, if the grief opens us to our depths, descend within to the vulnerability, the terrible fear and neediness of the infant. Melanie Klein has described the experience of mourning as similar to what she calls the 'depressive position' of the infant:

> 'The object which is being mourned is the mother's breast and all that the breast and milk have come to stand for in the infant's mind: namely, love, goodness, security. All these are felt by the baby to be lost.'[13]

In adulthood, loss of whatever or whoever it is that represents for us love, goodness, and security can reawaken feelings and states of awareness experienced as an infant when, through abandonment or lack of holding, we were exposed to the terrors of the abyss beyond.

The way in which we experience and cope with loss, trauma, and crises of deep change or spiritual emergence in later life will inevitably be coloured by our early experiences of bonding with the mother-matrix, and of holding, or the lack of it, through those moments of un-integration. Our earliest and most direct experience of wounding is from the mother, from the absence of a wholly positive and affirming, embodied feminine principle, or violation by the negative feminine. As patterns repeat themselves, we may find ourselves re-experiencing the same issues around holding as we first did as a tiny infant and young child.

The hunger of our soul for loving, protective contact and holding from another is enormous at such times. The loving contact of another human being who can both witness us in this dark and hidden place, and keep us connected to, or grounded in reality is essential to the healing process. Without personal relationship the transpersonal experience cannot be grounded and integrated.

The person going through such a crisis does not need to be treated or cured, but to be held, witnessed, loved, and cared for until she is able to feel held again by the love that lives within her.

Breaking the Spiral

We have within us the predisposition to grow through particular stages of physical, psychological, intellectual, and spiritual development. Ken Wilber offers a description of the various levels of consciousness which we have the potentiality to evolve through.[14] His model integrates knowledge from various western psychological theories and psychotherapeutic perspectives with experience drawn from eastern spiritual traditions, and offers a useful formulation of the states of consciousness through which we may evolve during our lifetime.

Within this continuum of growth, we meet with and learn to organise experiences which we are able to integrate at that level of development. If life proceeds with relative normality, and we are given the appropriate and loving support that will nurture our integration of difficult and painful experiences, then a healthy development of the psyche can unfold.

We are unwarned and unprepared when trauma or violation to our sense of being occurs, which we have not yet developed sufficient ego-integration to contain and assimilate. This can, of course, occur at any stage. The process of development is not linear, but can better be described as a spirallic unfolding that incorporates both the height-depth dimension of evolution and the transpersonal, and the breadth dimension of integration and the personal. As we spiral round our cycles of development, there occur crises of changing levels of consciousness and states of being, which need to be integrated into everyday life through the horizontal dimension of experience in the world of materiality and relationship. The awakening and deepening of consciousness is thus grounded in the everyday reality of living.

Powerful and disturbing experiences that we cannot readily assimilate may break the thread of the spiral and propel us upwards or downwards to levels of awareness that are beyond our capacity to integrate. As the thread of the spiral breaks, a path is cut, through which we rise and plummet to the heights and depths of consciousness, into the farthest reaches of the realms of psyche, without the slow circling process of integration to contain and make safe our flights. Hence we encounter the burning power of our light and the engulfing of our darkest depths simultaneously. The connection between the root and crown chakras is made, perhaps prematurely forged with a suddenness and violence that can be extremely dangerous. The dangers of prematurely awakening the Kundalini, the *serpent* energy lying dormant in the root chakra, and the *kriyas* or disturbances which this can cause, have been spoken about for centuries in the traditions of eastern yoga. This may happen in a crisis of spiritual emergence, and when it does, every level of being is powerfully affected as a result.

There unfolds a crisis of many dimensions: a crisis of the soul, the spirit, the body, and of the wounded child. And through it all, the mundane everyday life that we no longer feel a part of looms as a futile and meaningless spectre, as we question very existence itself. Such a crisis is complex, and the handling of it requires a sensitivity to the many layers of experience involved. As traumatic experiences are relived, the wounded child needs to be safely held and reassured with acceptance, emotional and physical contact, and most of all, the warmth of human love. The soul is held by understanding of the meaning and purpose of the pain and wounding within the greater context of the individual's, and often the collective's, life. And the spirit must reach for the universal source which it dwells within, and is a part of, eternally held and nourished by.

It is easy to mistake the levels of holding needed through such crises, for the symptoms of a purely regressive disturbance (if there truly is such a thing) may look remarkably similar to those of an existential crisis or spiritual awakening, but it is important that the levels are recognised. Without the holding of human contact and love that will contain the woundedness of the child, we cannot reach for the heights of meaning and the purpose of our lives. And if every crisis is reduced to childhood experience and pathology, there can be no resolution of existential and spiritual issues, for the context of holding is too narrow and limited to contain the dimensions of soul and spirit.

Whilst psychology acknowledges the issues and problems caused by the absence of the father,[15] the mother is frequently viewed in psychological thought as over-present, 'smothering', or 'devouring'. But there is an even more fundamental issue in our culture concerning the absent mother – the mother who is unable to be present with the quality of unconditional love, holding, and affirmation of her unique being that the child needs, because she has never experienced this herself. The absent mother leaves a deep wounding to the core self; it can be felt as a weakness or a tear in the fabric of the child's protective boundary, the 'skin' or psychic 'womb', which may make the child particularly sensitive to unconscious forces within her own psyche, and to the archetypal powers of the collective unconscious.

The absence of the mother, and the particular sensitivity which this may engender, is a cultural issue which will be explored further in the following chapters.

Father and Daughter – The Bind

Although the mother is primary in the child's experience, the quality of this experience will be greatly affected by the presence or absence of the father, and by the mother's relationship to the one closest to her in her motherhood. The mother's ability to care for her child in a way that honours and fulfils the child's sense of being will depend to a large extent on the degree of security, love, and acceptance she receives from her own environment. In particular, it will depend on the support and protection she receives from the father, or the one taking that role, at a time when she is most vulnerable; traditionally the father's role is to provide the protective boundary within which the sacred mother-child relationship can be nurtured. And as the child grows she will of course be forming her own relationship with the father-figure. The quality of mothering a woman is able to give will also be influenced, perhaps subtly but nevertheless significantly, by the attitudes of the culture in general towards her, as a woman, and the role of motherhood itself.

We have all been born into a patriarchal culture, but one that is no longer fulfilling the true and positive function of a patriarchy. It has, for many centuries now, denied and repressed the feminine and its values, and hence has become imbalanced and distorted out of its positive role as provider of protection, the structure of an ordered and coherent society, and leadership born out of wisdom. In part, the patriarchy has declined into a rigid and controlling authority which often treats the weak and vulnerable, including women and children, with oppression, exploitation, and abuse; or it has degenerated into weak and ineffectual systems that serve primarily the self-interest of those in power.

It is hard for a daughter born into a negative patriarchy to feel herself valued as a girl-child and woman. Through the conscious or unconscious attitudes of those closest to her, and the culture at large, she may be made to feel early in life that being female she is necessarily inferior, weaker, less important than her brothers, and that she does not automatically have a valued and respected place in society. This may develop into an underlying feeling of guilt or shame for being who she is, which means that she feels driven to prove herself, her right to exist, at every turn, within and for the patriarchal culture. If she has sensed her mother's own insecurity in her womanhood, that her feminine nature has been undervalued and unfulfilled, the daughter will not be able to find her own sense of rightness of *being as woman* through the models her mother provides. The daughter who is not connected to her feminine ground may reject her mother and look instead to the father, who upholds the place of patriarchal values and authority in the home, for the validation, respect, and love of her feminine being which she craves. We are born to be father's daughters, daughters of the patriarch.

Linda Schierse Leonard describes some of the ways women have learnt to deal with unsatisfactory relationships to the father in a patriarchal society.[16] We may learn to adapt through taking on the various personae of the 'amazon warrior' or the 'eternal girl' for example, in order to maintain an illusory position of power or a protected place in society. There are a great variety of adaptations, all of which a woman may experience within herself at different times, but essentially all are reactions to a dominating or ineffectual father principle. All are ways of defending a violated sense of feminine being. Sometimes the violation is overt, as in sexual or physical abuse, abandonment, and neglect; sometimes it is an unconscious perception of what is not acknowledged or expressed directly by the parents, but acutely felt by the sensitive child. Having to struggle to survive as women in a patriarchal society also engenders competition, envy, and betrayal in relationships between women, which may begin in our earliest relationships with our mothers and sisters. In their book *Between Women*, Luise Eichenbaum and Susie Orbach sympathetically explore the issue of competition between women in a patriarchal society.

We are caught in a bind. Somehow we must either rebel against or succumb to the attitudes and demands of those we seek love and protection from in order to ensure our survival, and to maintain an illusion of safety and inner integrity. We attempt in these ways to compensate for an often unconscious and deep-felt sense of our unworthiness as women. But in doing this we inevitably betray our authentic nature, the deep and creative power of the conscious feminine, as has the culture which first devalued it. The deep wounds of these early self-betrayals are held within the body, and limit our expression of our womanhood. This felt inadequacy further ties us in the bind, for we will continually look to others, usually men, to provide the ground, the protection, and fulfilment we lack within ourselves. Men, says the culture, are the ones who hold this for us, and with no other ground to stand on, we again succumb or rebel. Either way, we are reacting to a power that is not our own, and one that holds the threat of exile and isolation over us if we don't play the game. However, it is exactly exile and isolation which many women today are actually choosing, as they seek to re-empower themselves. As Chani Smith writes:

> '...[O]ur exile is not an external one, imposed on us by the almighty, as we often think. It is we who choose to go into exile in order to find the Shekhinah.

> 'And when we find her and redeem her, we have found our soul.'[17]

There are times when we, as women, must actively seek isolation and exile, in order to hear our innermost truth.

The distortions and compromises which young girls and women have learnt to make, in order to adapt to patriarchal values, are compounded by the natural attraction between the sexes. The traditional view of psychoanalysis proposes that children desire sexual relations with the parent of the opposite sex. However, growing evidence of the trauma caused by incestuous relations clearly points to the highly questionable nature of this theory. Studies of some indigenous cultures which have a natural and healthy attitude towards sexuality have shown that the Oedipal complex does not exist at all amongst their peoples; it should therefore be viewed not as a biologically given, but as a culturally conditioned phenomenon.

Yet it seems not uncommon for a parent in our culture to feel sexual attraction towards a child of the opposite sex. Whilst sensuality is an important element in the child-parent relationship, the naturalness of a sexual attraction must be questioned; more likely such an attraction signifies that something is amiss or lacking in the parent's own sexuality and sexual relations. At a certain stage of development, such an attraction would have a particularly powerful influence on the child's growth. If the father is not clear about his own sexual feelings towards his daughter, or is repressing unresolved emotional content in relation to his sexuality, unmanageable or unconscious sexual feelings coloured by possessiveness, jealousy, violence, guilt, fear, shame, and rejection may arise between the parent and child during this delicate period. A bond of sexual attraction is tied between parent and child, containing all the associated emotional issues that are unconscious or unresolved in the parent, which swell like undercurrents through the flow of this bond.

The child's boundaries develop with strong emotional attachments to both parents. These attachments, which we might experience as psychological 'umbilical cords', often relate to the energy centres or chakras associated with specific psychological content. Through them, the child is particularly sensitive to the feeling life of the parent, by which her own emotional makeup will be strongly influenced. A flow and interchange of positive emotion will enable the child to develop a healthy relationship to her own inner feeling life, and to internalise a healthy sense of self, but the child will of course also be subject to the negative and unconscious feelings of the parent.

As described earlier, the root chakra is associated with early bonding with the maternal matrix, and issues of incarnating, survival, trust, and the instinctual, feeling life of the body. The next stage of development is associated with the sacral chakra; pleasure, sensuality, sexuality, relationship, emotional feelings, and physical creativity will lead us out of the dark womb world of the root chakra, into a world where our learning and relating is guided by pleasure and sensual play. Relationship with the father as well as the mother may take on primary significance at this stage,[18] and he becomes particularly important for the girl-child in the development of her sexuality, as well as her relationship to the world. However, if she is not securely grounded in her root chakra, the mother and father principles may become confused within her; without a secure basis of trust in her own feminine ground, the awakening of sexual feeling and relatedness may be experienced with uncertainty, anxiety, or fear. This is the child whose vulnerability and sensitive openness is likely to 'invite' unwanted sexual advances and abuse because she does not have a clear and boundaried sense of self. Later, as a woman, she may be one who finds it difficult to say no to a man's wishes, or who feels compelled to reject men as a defence against her vulnerability.

If the primary bond with the mother, and hence with her own inner ground, at the root level is not secure and self-affirming, then the sensual-sexual bond with the father may serve as a substitute for it. As a child and a woman she learns to find her essential ground and the affirmation of her selfhood through relationship with the father-lover, because she has not been able to experience it within her own feminine being. In this, she essentially gives herself away to the man, and should he abandon her, she again loses her ground and her core sense of self.

The woman who seeks help with this dilemma from a male therapist has a right to expect that he will recognise and help her to free herself from the vicious cycle, and not become personally entangled in the destructive pattern himself. However, the experience of many women in therapy suggests that all too often male therapists do not in fact have adequate understanding, self-awareness, detachment, or skill to avoid this trap, and are as much the victims of negative patriarchal values and conditioning as are the women who come to them for help. They are as much in need of healing of their wounded feminine nature as are their women clients.

The daughter who forms such a bond with the father will be bound, as a woman, to keep seeking relationship with father-lover figures who can fulfil the attachment, and through it give her a sense of her own identity and worth. Or alternatively she may seek self-validation by competing with men; this may be another manifestation of the same compulsion. Most often we look to other people who in some way resemble the parent, or are motivated by the same unconscious tendencies as the parent, and onto whom we can project the emotional tie. When these emotional cords are cut with the ending of a relationship, the experience is of a hole opened within our psychic boundaries at the place where the attachment was made and then broken; we are not whole without relationship to the person who has become an essential part of us.

This will happen every time we form a close attachment to someone, as long as we are unable to internalise a sense of inner ground and experience our own being-ness. As long as we succeed in finding replacement figures, we may not have to experience too acutely the hole that is left in the psychic boundary, but it is impossible to maintain this illusion of connectedness forever. At each separation in life, we are opened to feel again the pain of these wounds in our protective boundary, as the cords of attachment are ripped apart. Each time they bleed a little more, and until we are able to stop looking outside for the person to whom we may tie ourselves, we will run forever in futile search for solace from this wounding. For a woman, wounded in her relationship to the mother and father in such a way, to live her life authentically and creatively she must find the feminine creative ground and spirit within herself, and cultivate through her own actions and life an internalised positive masculine which will neither abuse nor betray her, but will support, protect, and wisely guide her.

Only by recreating a more positive relationship to the mother and father principle within, can she successfully, and with confidence, deal with the issues of personal power, individuality, assertiveness, and her place in society which are the issues associated with the solar plexus centre, and the next stages of development in adolescence and young adulthood. The development of a healthy ego, which results in a successful expression of personal power and individuality, can only take place when there is a healthy enough relationship with the mother and father within. Without this, self-expression and steps towards independence will always be hampered by the needs of the inner child in relationship to the negative or absent parents; and personal power will be expressed, not freely, but manipulatively, in attempts to meet those unmet needs of the child. In this way, confusion of the solar plexus chakra with issues related to the root and sacral chakras takes place – the needs of the wounded child for acceptance, holding, and love, or the expression of sexuality, creativity, and feeling can become a battleground of power, control, competitiveness, hostility, abandonment, and victimisation.

As suggested earlier, the parents represent the child's first experience of God. If there is wounding, neglect, and abandonment, or a sense of violation associated with the parent-child relationship, at some deep level of the psyche a wounding of the personal relationship with spirit will also be experienced. God-the-Mother has been devalued and ignored, rejected, and her positive presence may be absent from the child's experience. God-the-Father has usurped all the power and suffers from the distortions of a too-rigid and unfeeling, sometimes brutal rule. The child is bequeathed the enormous task of redeeming this wound within, and uniting once again that which has been torn apart – her own heart and the integrity of her being. And in that, the healing, wholing of the child within, lies the hope of healing for humanity's great wound, uniting again God-the-Mother and God-the-Father, the feminine and masculine principles in a mutually enlivening and creative relationship. Beyond the healing of the wounded child is the rebirth of the divine child within, the seed of spirit, that part of us which remains unharmed and unchanged by even the worst ravages of life. Within the wounded heart earth and heaven meet, and here the child of light is born.

A Cultural Context for the Wounding

In an 'ideal' process of development the individual would, in his or her middle or later years, (though earlier in some instances) make the transition from the solar plexus and its ego-oriented concerns to the heart centre. When this transition is successfully made, an individual's life and actions become motivated by concern for the welfare of others; the benefit of the greater whole takes precedence over the meeting of one's personal needs. If such a development is genuine it does not result in martyr-like self-sacrifice and do-gooding, but is a natural, uncontrived outpouring and expression of the individual's heart values and wishes. These become a more centrally motivating force than the power-centred values and needs of the ego. Not all, in fact possibly very few individuals make this transition fully in the course of their lives, but it is the potential which all spiritual traditions aim to guide their followers towards.

I would like to take the description of the chakras, which I have been using here as a model for personal development, and apply it to the development of the culture as a whole. In *Return of the Goddess* Whitmont describes the evolution of culture through the Magical, Mythical, and Mental phases of development. The Magical phase represents the earliest origins of human society:

> 'By *magical* is implied the preverbal, unitary symbiotic identity level of existence or consciousness prior to the arising of mythical imagery or rational thought.'[19]

This stage relates to the root chakra and its associations with earth, mother, pre-conscious life in the womb, the feminine ground, instinctual life of the body, and unity of experience.

The second phase, the Mythical, is also matriarchal; the Great Goddess is at the centre of religious practice and its myths and symbols, but polarity has now emerged into consciousness, expressed in the form of her consort who will:

> '...[C]omplement and serve her in the roles of child, lover, partner, playmate, and sacrificial victim. Their cycles of birth, death and rebirth embody the endless tides of physical life.

'The total figure depicts the androgynous wholeness of natural existence: growth and decay, life and death, are both opposites and yet contained, even embraced, by a continuum. The male experience is one of discontinuity, contrast, and opposition. This is subordinate to the feminine continuity just as the ephemeral is to the eternal. The Great Goddess represents being and becoming. The Feminine is not concerned with achieving or ideating. It is not heroic, self-willed and bent upon battling against opposition. Rather it exists in the here and now and the endless flow. It values the vegetal dimension of growth-decay, the continuity and conservation of natural orders. It expresses the will of nature and of instinctual forces rather than the self-will of a particular person. The feminine form of consciousness is global, field, and process oriented. It is functional rather than abstract and conceptual. It is devoid as yet of the strict dichotomy of inner-outer or body-mind.'[20]

Society based on such consciousness viewed everything as sacred; nature was an expression of the divine, and communities practised a morality based on an instinctive feeling for the immediate welfare of the collective. This consciousness is expressed in myth and fairy tale; it is pre-rational and feeling based, and relates to nature and the sacral centre of the body.

With the onset of the patriarchal or Mental age, abstract, conceptual thinking and reason replace the magical and mythical perception of reality, and the masculine principle takes ascendancy over the Goddess. Nature is to be controlled by reason and repression of the instinctual and feeling life of the body. Consciousness has become dualistic and materialistic; the sacred now lives in God-given and abstract laws and judgements by which society is ruled. The individual must serve the society and obey its laws by virtue of duty and obedience rather than a felt-sense of what is most beneficial for the community as a whole.

The patriarchal or Mental age marks the development of ego-consciousness and hence is concerned with control, assertion of personal will and power, and the fulfilling of one's individual place in society:

'*Ego* is a Roman word. Divide and rule was the motto of ancient Rome, the first fully ego-conscious society. It is also the motto of the ego. The orientation of the ego, of space-thing consciousness, is toward aggressive competitiveness, the use of manipulative power, and wilful rule. Ego strength is measured by the capacity to assert one's will over nature, forcing it to serve ego's striving for permanence, comfort, and avoidance of pain, and by the capacity to control one's urges, needs and desires. Existence is perceived as limited to the world of space; hence it is irrevocably terminated by death and decay of the space-visible body.'[21]

I am sure there is no need to convince the reader that this description fits our present age quite well. Developmentally we are, as a culture, dominated by the concerns of the ego, operating primarily from the solar plexus centre. The orientation of our modern culture is primarily mental, but the fruits of our intelligence are generally put to the service of the ego; it is the ego that rules. The fact that so many people no longer consider this consciousness to be positive and beneficial is a sign that the age is coming to an end; we have developed as far as we can or need to in this direction and change is now inevitable. This is not to say that the kind of consciousness developed during this age has not been useful, beneficial, even necessary for an earlier time. Undoubtedly it has served us in many ways, even though it has ultimately led us to a dangerous edge. Clearly matriarchal consciousness at one point in history became oppressive and abusive; the patriarchal myths of monster or dragon-slaying show us that human consciousness needed to free itself from the claustrophobic power of the Great Mother, that her bounteousness had ingrown and become poisonous, devouring, and destructive to emerging individual consciousness. This consciousness too, at one time, became distorted and outlived its usefulness in the way it was then operating.

Part of our problem now is that too many individuals are still benefiting too much from the patriarchal state of existence to allow willingly the changes that are beginning to force themselves upon us. It is of course the people with power – usually economic – those who are most successfully benefiting from this kind of existence, who would like to maintain it; the more vulnerable, sensitive, and oppressed are naturally the ones to call first for change.

The challenge of our time, if we are to continue to grow and evolve and not decline further into some form of sophisticated barbarism, must be the transition from the ego-centred consciousness and values of the solar plexus to a consciousness that is centred in the heart, whose values are founded on sharing, caring, honest communication, generosity, and love for others. As we are confronted with this challenge, what we experience is a re-emergence of the earlier, pre-patriarchal forms of consciousness which may have been forgotten, suppressed, or deemed overcome during the Mental epoch, but which are in fact the very foundations of our present forms of consciousness. The Magical and Mythical aspects of consciousness have to be re-embraced and included as we take the step into our next phase of growth, or the step cannot be made. This means the return of the Goddess and the values of the feminine – awareness of the earth, of our bodies and souls, of right relationship to each other, to nature, and to the greater whole of which we are a part.

This does not mean a wholesale going back to old matriarchal ways, but an inclusion of the qualities of every phase we have been through, both matriarchal and patriarchal, in a new consciousness. This implies a potential marriage of the creative aspects of each, and what we have learnt from them. As the feminine principle re-emerges into our psychological awareness, the new direction need not involve a regression to the feared dark, abysmal, chaotic, and unconscious feminine, but could be an integration of both masculine and feminine values and principles in a movement which embraces the *conscious* feminine. The conscious woman, conscious body, and conscious earth are the sacred ground to which the positive masculine spirit can be wed; when this happens with awareness, then genuine creativity can flourish.

It is the same with the individual's development. As awareness begins to emerge, we are confronted with all that is unresolved in our past, with any weaknesses in our psychological foundations which would make us unready to embrace fully the new. Bringing these feelings and consciousness into awareness again, we are able to include those lost parts of ourselves and trust them as necessary supports for our growth, rather than obstacles. In the language of chakra development, as consciousness unfolds, each centre in turn is cleansed of all the obstructions that have blocked its free and full flow: as this is happening we experience the burning off of all the dross of our past hurts, fears, and wrong actions so that the natural qualities of each centre may shine out clearly.

Given the control and repression by the patriarchy of feminine feeling values and natural wisdom, of nature, the body and its instincts, it is not surprising that we have all been wounded to some degree in the development of our root and sacral centres. That the woundedness of the child at these levels is a cultural phenomenon cannot be denied, but it is only as the patriarchal age draws to its close that we are becoming aware of this woundedness to its full extent. The wound has always been there but we are only now becoming conscious of it, and finding the means to articulate what it is we feel. With the demise of God and the God-given order of society, the wound that tells of the absent Mother, the lack of ground within, gapes open wide.

The individual woman who becomes aware of this woundedness to her feminine being is given an opportunity to look at what is missing, not only for herself, but for humanity as a whole at this point in history. Through the painful work of uncovering her hidden wounds, she may help to bring back into the cultural consciousness an awareness of the values and qualities that have been lost, repressed, and denied. It is not at all surprising that in the midst of the crisis of consciousness that we are facing there is now emerging an enormous interest in all things relating to the health of the body, ranging from healthy diets and exercise routines, to massage, bodywork and body-oriented therapies, alternative natural medicine, dance, martial arts, yoga and so on. All of these activities can, if practised with awareness rather than goal-oriented competitiveness, be part of the process of reclaiming the body as our natural home, and reawakening sensation and the feeling life it holds; that is, they can be an important part of the move towards reclaiming the Goddess and the feminine ground within. Concern about the environment and the ecology of our planet is another vital expression of this movement.

Many people involved in the work of healing, therapy, and consciousness development are now encouraging us to see that our wounds and difficulties can be opportunities for learning and growth. They can be seen as signals warning of some distortion, deficiency, or excess that is creating imbalance and disharmony in the body, mind, and spirit of the individual. Through paying attention to the messages, we can often make changes that will bring us back into a better balance and state of health. But there is yet another turn of the spiral which we can make from here.

At this moment, we may actually need our wounds, not just to warn us of some imbalance, but simply that we need them. We may need the woundedness of the child because we need her sensitivity; without the sensitivity and openness of the wounded child we may be unable to respond to the needs of the soul, the forces of life and spirit, the necessity for change. We may need the insubstantiality and permeability of our wounded feminine nature to allow in new consciousness and the transpersonal dimensions of experience. We may need the loss of our sense of ground because we need to lose our ground in order to find a deeper and more meaningful foundation for our life; we need to lose self in order to find freedom. All the great religions and philosophies of the world speak of emptying out, of non-doing, non-achieving, of losing all to gain 'the kingdom of heaven'. And we need to consciously feel the pain of our human suffering in order that we can see and understand the suffering of others; without the ability to feel and understand suffering we cannot develop the qualities of love and compassion that make us fully human. Perhaps we need to be wounded because it is only through the openness and sensitivity which the wound engenders that we can both perceive the dangers that humanity and our planet are now facing, and also be aware of and receptive to the healing, regenerating, and evolutionary powers that are there amidst the danger.

There is such a growing awareness today of abuse to children, to women, and to the earth, and it is the awareness of this wounding which is the catalyst for change, which is in fact changing the consciousness, attitudes and, very slowly, the behaviour of humanity as a whole. The wounds of the child and of the feminine are alerting us to the dangers of misdirected power, control, repression, oppression, and greed; we need to become aware of and consciously feel our own wounds, in order to be able to take real responsibility for our power, and stop the abuse.

It is also through these cracks in our defences, the chasms that our wounds open up, that our inner light can shine through. I used to work with people, adults and children, with severe disabilities – autistic children and people so badly damaged that most kinds of normal social activity and interaction were impossible. Yet with these most wounded of people there could sometimes be made a quality of contact that was extraordinary in its depth, immediacy, and love. Their spirit shone through, with none of the usual social barriers most of us have created to veil our brightness. I would be reminded of my nephew's birth. At such moments, these children and adults gave me far more than I could ever hope to give to them. I experienced them like powerful lights shining out in a world that has become bedded down and constricted by oppressive social conventions and rules; their naked spirits are gifts to the world.

So it may be that, instead of fighting endlessly against our suffering and sickness, trying to remove or overcome it in the dominating and controlling fashion of an ego-oriented approach, with ever more sophisticated methods of medicine and therapy, we need to learn to accept and love even this part of our experience, and recognise that our wounds truly are the gateways into deeper levels of being and awareness. If the masculine drives us to seek perfection, the feminine is concerned with wholeness and completion, which involves embracing the failures as well as the successes of life, the sickness as well as the health.

Today we are witnessing a deadly race between the advances of medical research and ever more virulent and uncontrollable diseases, sicknesses of both body and mind. Perhaps it is time we stopped to take an honest look at our collective attitudes towards illness and suffering, for there seems to be no prospect of ever winning in this escalating race. It is time to ask why it is that, even faster than we discover new cures for old illnesses, new diseases emerge which thwart even our most sophisticated methods of control. Might we not need to ask if sickness itself has something within it which we need to bear witness to, something even more than the means to remove it. Just as we can never create true peace through violent means, so too we cannot achieve real health and wholeness through attacking, destroying, or attempting to cast out the wounds and sickness. We will be whole when we can include and accept the wounds, and the people who suffer from them most, and when we can include them we may be surprised by what they reveal to us. I don't mean that we should not do all we can to help those who are wounded or sick, nor try our best to relieve their suffering, but there is much more to a healthy life than simply prolonging its length. Sometimes healing means embracing the suffering, accepting its gifts, and learning from it; sometimes healing means conscious dying.

Love, my heart, be with me

Death burns down through
the candle flame
falls in spirals
like a broken limb turning inwards.
Still red pool that holds the wavering flame below.

My heart, flame in my heart.

Wandering homeless
this is my own
my home my own wilderness
within.
No door to open
love to greet
hope
gone like smoke ringing to the heavens
and the earth.
To lie there in dying
grief wrenched out and thrown
to foreign lands.

Home of my heart.

Where love is lost
I travel long through wild nights
again — alone
snatched from comfort.

This was to be my time this
my world
of lost worlds created this
my lover and my life.

Love of my heart, I die
for you.

Love, my heart, be with me.

4 Body and Soul

*A*lternative and orthodox medicine today are again recognising the truth that ancient healing practices have adhered to for centuries – that the psychological and spiritual state of a person profoundly affects their physical health, and that the condition of the physical body influences the state of mind in both subtle and specific ways. Psyche and soma cannot be separated if significant healing is to take place, for they interact in complex and subtle ways as an undivided whole. In ancient traditions world-wide, from primitive shamanic religions to the early roots of modern western culture in ancient Greece, healing practices addressed the body and mind, or soul, as an inseparable unity. C A Meier writes:

> 'In the first place, the sources constantly emphasize that Asclepius cares for *soma kai psyche*, both body and mind – "body and soul" is the corresponding Christian term; and second, bodily sickness and psychic defect were for the ancient world an inseparable unity... .

> 'Thus in antiquity the "symptom" is an expression of the *sympatheia*, the *consensus* or *coniunctio naturae*, the point of correspondence between the outer and the inner.'[1]

We have looked at how psyche and soma seem to be experienced in early infancy as a unity; the physical body is alive with sensation, feeling, and consciousness, and mind is embodied through neuro-physiological processes and bodily activity. As the sense of self develops, it is through the body that the infant first begins to experience herself as a separate and unique individual, as she touches and is touched by the world, moves and is moved. The surface of the physical body is the primary boundary separating 'I' from 'other', and contains all that is experienced as self; the body contains, embodies, and is an expression of the subtleties of mind, or soul. As James Schultz writes:

'Piaget has shown that the child thinks with and through bodily activity. Infantile sensory-motor cognition gradually develops into concrete thinking which only later emerges as adult language and logic.'[2]

As mental and social development proceeds, the ego boundary also develops, providing a mentally based containment for experience. Whilst still being inherently connected to, and affected by, the feeling life of the deep psyche, the physical body and ego-mind provide a sense of containment for these feelings. They define the experience of a separate self and a social persona by which we are known and can meet the world.

This differentiation is a natural and necessary developmental process for the young child, but fragmentation occurs when we not only differentiate but unnaturally separate the different aspects of ourselves. Separation and fragmentation have been encouraged in modern western culture by religious beliefs that view the body as inferior and inherently sinful, and by the dualism of the mechanistic paradigm which has dominated scientific thinking for the last three to four centuries.[3] Today there is renewed awareness of the intrinsic relatedness of psyche and soma, and of the need to consider this relationship in all areas of growth and healing. Yet the process of discriminating between different levels and dimensions of experience is still useful in helping us to understand the conflicts, imbalances, and sickness that afflict us, and the paths that lead towards healing.

James Hillman makes a distinction between *ego-soul* and *psyche-soul*, and these terms are useful indicators of two levels of experience which I wish to discuss further.[4] Ego relates to the personal sense of self and all by which I define and identify myself as 'I'; in this context it includes the physical body, the functions of the conscious mind, and all that pertain to these, such as the possessions, roles, relationships, place and status in society by which we formulate our identity. Psyche, in this context, is that subtler, invisible realm of experience that includes the deep and unconscious workings of the mind, the apparently autonomous psychological forces which manifest as archetypal patterns of feeling and behaviour.

These two aspects of our being are continuously interacting and influencing one another to create the constant changes and swings of mood, feeling, and attitude with which we are assailed throughout our daily lives. Each seems to be guided by an independent force, tendency, or motivation that is what we might refer to as its soul. There are times when the will of ego-soul and that of psyche-soul feel in harmony and aligned with each other in a common direction and purpose, but more often we experience some conflict between these two levels of our being. What our personal ego would wish and need for its own comfort and well-being is not always compatible with the needs of the deeper and transpersonal forces that are working themselves out through our personal lives. According to our different philosophical and religious perspectives, we might call these deeper forces karma, fate, the will of God, personal destiny, or purpose. They contain the patterns that underlie our conscious lives, and that need to be brought into awareness if ego-soul and psyche-soul are to be aligned in a common purpose.

When our immediate personal needs and will are in conflict with the greater direction and purpose of our lives, then we experience two clearly different processes going on within us, as if being pulled in two opposing directions. The depth crisis which we are exploring here is essentially an initiation into death, the underworld, and when we can follow and survive the calling of this pull from the deeper levels of our being, then psyche-soul is deepened and enriched. However, the ego is broken down in the process and we can suffer immeasurably in this. It is as if the ego-soul that would lead us into experience and success in the outer material world, into life itself, is defeated by the will that would lead us into deepening inner experience, surrender, and ultimately death. This inevitably brings great suffering at the level of the body, for the will towards life and the will towards death both directly affect and are expressed through the body in some way; the battle between these two forces is waged through the body itself, one force pulling us towards life and the other towards death.

We frequently experience the movement of psyche-soul during an initiatory process through psychosomatic or physical symptoms, often a serious or life-threatening illness, and sometimes through accident. 'Transformation,' says Hillman, 'to be genuine and thorough, always affects the body.... Initiation rites are ordeals of the flesh.'[5] The initiatory journey of descent demands that we let go, at least temporarily, of the *doing* of the ego level of our existence and immerse ourselves in *being*. We experience *being* at the level of psyche-soul when ego function breaks down, and aspects of our deeper nature are revealed to us. We must be touched and immersed deeply in our own being-nature to bring these qualities back into expression in the upper world.

Because of the inseparable nature of psyche and soma, and the subtle but profound and pervasive influences they have upon each other, the question as to whether an illness has a physical or psychological origin will always elude general agreement. There is not one simple answer for all situations. In the homoeopathic view some diseases may originate within, from a mental, psychological, or spiritual disturbance, and work their way to manifestation in symptoms on the physical level. Other illnesses we contract from external agents, such as viral or bacterial infections; these can, if they remain in the body, affect deeper and subtler levels of the mind, eventually contributing to the development of symptoms of mental illness and spiritual crisis. In the ancient tradition of Tibetan medicine a third category of disease is identified; some illnesses are viewed as karmic, and for these medicine has no cure. Karmic illness cannot be cured by normal medical or therapeutic intervention, and only a spiritual approach may help us to understand and work through its root causes.

Today, because modern medicine is able to alleviate symptoms and often artificially prolong life, people do not so readily die from such 'incurable' diseases, whether they be of karmic or other origin. What we are seeing instead is an increase in the presence of chronic illness that seems to be, at its root, stubbornly irresponsive to any kind of medical or therapeutic treatment, orthodox or alternative.

Whether an illness appears to have a physical or psychological origin, there is no doubt that disturbances and imbalances at any level will directly affect all others. Research has revealed a great and growing amount of evidence concerning the effects that emotions, mental attitudes, anxiety, and stress have on the body's immune system, biochemical balance, and nervous system, effects which in time lead to a host of debilitating and sometimes fatal conditions. So many people today are plagued by a variety of seemingly unrelated physical symptoms, or a general state of ill-health, low-grade chronic infection, lowered immune system functioning, or 'non-specific' illnesses and syndromes, which can often be found to be associated with states of prolonged and unresolved emotional stress, anxiety, grief and so on. Conversely, we are also rediscovering the many ways that physical states of ill health (and of course good health too) profoundly affect the emotional and mental state of the individual. Hence vicious, and also benign, cycles of interaction are set up between the body, mind, and feelings, between psyche and soma, whether we view the original cause as essentially organic, psychological, or both.

An emotional state or mental attitude might trigger neurochemical changes that adversely affect the functioning and homeostasis of the whole body; these bodily changes further reinforce the psychological condition, which triggers a further escalation of the physical symptoms, and so on. Layer upon layer of conditions and symptoms can be accumulated throughout our lives, behind which the original causes may become lost from view and inaccessible to any of our own interventions, and most medical ones too. It is often impossible even to begin to extricate ourselves from such self-defeating cycles without expert outside help.

This is why, when dealing with a psycho-spiritual crisis, we are also going to be confronted with some form of physical disturbance or illness. Sometimes a person is plunged into the 'dark night of the soul' as a result of a serious or long-drawn-out illness of the body, or an accident which leaves them disabled or forces unwanted life changes upon them. In other instances the crisis may seem to be of a psycho-spiritual nature but the extremity of mental and emotional distress experienced may produce harmful changes in the body and its immune function.

Ordeals of the Flesh

Cancer is an example of an 'ordeal of the flesh' that may precipitate the sufferer upon a journey within, to the depths of their soul. As well as the physical pain and discomfort which must be endured, the sufferer may find herself overwhelmed at times by depression, fear, anger, grief, or stress as she struggles to overcome or come to terms with the disease. Such feelings may have contributed to the onset of the illness in the first place, and so the vicious cycle may escalate further. However, I have met people who have come through such ordeals with a renewed love of life, a sense of purpose and of service to others, and an ability to live in the present which is truly inspiring. They are the ones who have embarked upon and completed the journey of initiatory illness with courage and a commitment to true healing.

Another illness which must be mentioned here, because of the psychosomatic nature of both symptoms and origins, and also the mysteriousness and ambiguity which surrounds the disease, is ME (myalgic encephalomyelitis) or chronic fatigue syndrome. There is still dispute amongst professionals about the medical reality of this disease, despite its recognition by the World Health Organisation and a growing number of doctors and health practitioners. A wide variety of symptoms and possible causes, both physiological, psychological, and environmental, are associated with ME. Its elusive and manifold nature has made it particularly difficult to diagnose, but it is now becoming increasingly clear that the disease follows recognisable biological pathways, usually involving viral infection, immune system dysfunction, cellular pathology, and neurological damage.

Extreme chronic exhaustion and painful muscles, lowered resistance to infections, allergies, inability to concentrate, memory loss, depression, and anxiety are some of the most common experiences of the ME sufferer. These symptoms have caused many to consider it a psychiatric illness, 'all-in-the-mind'; but those who have seriously studied the disease now recognise identifiable physiological changes in people with the disease. However, ME does generally affect people whose immune system response has become imbalanced due to extreme emotional or mental stress, and it produces symptoms of body, mind, and spirit. It clearly is a disease that points to the interrelationship of these levels of being.

In the experience of many ME sufferers whom I have talked to, there has been, at the onset of the disease, an ambivalent attitude towards life, towards being fully present and incarnate in this world. It is as if there were an indecisiveness between the forces of ego-soul and psyche-soul, the will toward life and the will toward death, which causes a fundamental and existential conflict within the body itself. Bereavement, childhood abuse, and other deep trauma, which can create dissociation and a not fully embodied state, seem often to be at the root of contracting an illness like ME. When both forces are pulling strongly a stasis may ensue in which we cannot move at all – we can neither recover nor fully surrender to the death which psyche-soul is drawing us towards. We may not recover until we *do* surrender.

For many sufferers ME is an initiation into the underworld experience, and in this it is also a disease of our times, as are other epidemic illnesses such as cancer, heart disease, and AIDS. By this I mean that the symptoms of the disease are drawing our attention to issues that we need to address collectively, or offering a potential that we as a culture need to open to. When we suffer from such an illness, and are involved in the depth processes of the archetypal and collective psyche, we are also suffering the world's sickness; our symptoms are also the world's symptoms and they tell us what the world needs. Seeming to have equally physical and psychological, external and internal causes, and symptoms that manifest on all levels of being, ME speaks to that inextricably connected unity of the bodymind. And it inevitably leads us into the deepening of psyche-soul in an ordeal that challenges the ego-soul to surrender to the deeper impulses. It is this act of surrender that is one of the challenges, and also one of the greatest difficulties for an ego-oriented culture such as ours, which such chronic and incurable diseases pose.

Healing does not always mean a cure and freedom from the symptoms. Sometimes there is a deeper meaning that we must access – and even then the symptoms may not leave us. We may, collectively we may, need to keep accessing this meaning. When there is no healing at the physical and psychological levels, we are impelled to go beyond and search deeper for meaning and healing within a cultural and spiritual context.

When we are ill, particularly if the symptoms of the illness are hard to diagnose, we usually feel relieved when our condition can be identified and named. It is much easier to deal with a known disease, even if it has no known cure, than it is to live with a host of non-specific, chronic, and seemingly unrelated symptoms of body and mind. Most sufferers feel this way. If we cannot identify our condition, society tends not to acknowledge or believe in our suffering, and we don't know how best to treat it, so we often feel it is preferable to know and name. However, even as we accept the labels, we need also to remember the symptoms themselves, and the potential meaning that they may hold. It is too easy, as with mental illness, to allow the labelling to mask or take away the real experience and the potential for growth that it carries. Exploring the symptoms themselves can lead to valuable and meaningful experiences, for the symptoms bring awareness to what is, to what we lack, and to what we most need. Suffering brings us to our senses – back to the senses of our body; from misery and anguish, through to the heart of the pain, we come back to our senses, to what is present, essential, and necessary. The body holds locked within it not only memories of past pain and trauma; it also carries wisdom and knowledge.

Instead of battling against our symptoms of ill-health, trying to get rid of, alleviate, deny, control, or overcome them, which are some of the attitudes we most commonly take towards whatever is painful, uncomfortable, or diseased, we could try instead to get to know them, just exactly as they are. By bringing awareness into the heart of what we are actually experiencing, with full acceptance and openness, we may find there is something of immense value to us, and maybe even to the collective, which is attempting to make itself felt in and through that symptom.

Arnold Mindell, in his theory of the dreambody,[6] proposes that there is an underlying life process which is expressed through various channels, including involuntary movements of the body, physical symptoms, dreams, visual and auditory signals, relationship problems, and world issues. He developed methods to help access the meaning and healing potential contained within disturbances and symptoms of ill-health, both physical, psychological, and collective; the approach has similarities to ancient practices such as shamanism and the healing rites of ancient Greece. There is a very simple, in a way obvious, but quite radical attitude that underlies this approach; if something is happening then, for some as yet unknown reason, it actually needs to happen, just as it is. A symptom is an incompleted process, and to complete the process we need to *allow* the symptom fully, let it fully enter awareness and amplify it, so that we can feel what is actually trying to take place within and through it. Practical methods have been developed to facilitate the unfolding of a process until meaning, resolution, and sometimes healing are found.

The approach taken in Mindell's process-oriented psychology may at first appear similar to other alternative approaches to therapy and healing, but it is based on an attitude which is subtly different from the attitudes underlying many of these. There is a tendency within some current therapeutic approaches, despite conscious intentions, and perhaps as a reflection of the society which engendered them, to make us feel that our symptoms of illness are inherently bad, signs that we have erred somewhere, failed or done something wrong. This attitude, which may be overt or covert, can lead to the feeling that we ourselves are somehow at fault, guilty. Such underlying attitudes cannot lead to a truly positive approach towards health; because guilt is one of the major causes of neurosis in our scapegoating society, they are more likely subtly to reinforce the vicious cycles that perpetuate the problem. Feelings of guilt and of ambivalence towards life, towards fully incarnating here on the earth and in this body, can be closely related. They may also be connected to chronic symptoms, as bodily expressions of a deep-seated conflict between the will to live and the will to die. Existential guilt is a fundamental experience for most people in our society.

In a more creative and generous approach, our physical symptoms, like our psychological wounds, become the gateways into experiences and altered states of consciousness which we, individually and collectively, are desperately in need of regaining access to. The pains that ravage and wrench apart the body and mind may be the cracks in consciousness that open to let in awareness of our lost soul, our forsaken spirit, and our deeper purpose. Soul can return as the old structures are broken down by sickness and pain.

In the case of ME – which is most notably an illness of chronic and extreme exhaustion which, more than anything else, makes the sufferer stop – there is something about slowing down, letting go, surrendering, giving in to the pull of gravity to reclaim our connectedness with the earth, which this disease seems to be telling us. We need to do it. Perhaps it is showing us that, individually and collectively, we need to stop in our blindly ego-oriented, ever faster, and materialistic tracks, and learn to let go and surrender to the processes of psyche-soul and spirit. The natural way of progress is cyclical or spirallic, not linear; life also needs death, movement needs stillness, creativity needs destruction and decay. Until we learn, collectively, about the way of surrender, many individuals may continue to suffer this disease, and endure the psychological fall, the burning, and the dying that the journey entails, for all of us.

Embodiment: the Bodymind Container

A few years after my friend's death I had left my academic studies to follow a career in dance. This decision came as a spontaneous impulse, without any conscious reflection about the direction of my life. In retrospect I understand that it came from an inner knowledge that at this time it was through my body that I needed to seek healing. Since his death, my world had been filled with darkness and a longing for my own death; I had, in a sense, already left my body. I needed to return home, to the earth, to bring my consciousness back into my body if I was truly to live again.

I have witnessed similar issues of deep-rooted dissociation from the body in other students of dance and bodywork with whom I have worked. This often relates to early childhood experiences of trauma or neglect, physical or sexual abuse, or bereavement, which can engender difficulties in embodying, or incarnating fully. Dissociation may stem from an ambivalence towards life, and also from fear of touching the repressed feelings and unconscious pain which the body holds, and which may be reawakened when awareness is brought back into the body. Yet that is what needs to be done if we are to live authentically and feelingly. Our lost soul must be found and returned to its earthly home. Soul loss, in the shamanic tradition, is considered a primary cause of illness, and the shaman's healing task is to travel to the worlds beyond to recover the wandering soul.

My own work as a dancer soon led me into the field of bodywork and movement therapy, into studies that addressed the subtleties of mind and body integration. I was seeking, though at first unconsciously, to heal the rift within myself. I trained with some of the best teachers in the field, disciplines from both ancient traditions and the pioneering work of those in the forefront of modern research and practice. Through this I learnt many effective techniques and processes of integration, and grew to feel at home again in my body. My bodymind was becoming a strong container, and through dance I also discovered a way to both experience and express my feeling life that was creative and satisfying. I became a teacher myself, and a movement therapist. My progress might have continued uninterrupted, for my work was going well, but something would not let me rest there. I would say it was the mysterious force of psyche-soul which was demanding acknowledgement; I had worked hard to create a strong container, but now other dimensions of experience were knocking on the door of my awareness.

It was at this point that I began counselling and psychotherapy training, recognising that I needed skills to further explore and integrate the deepening levels of experience that bodywork was opening up for my clients. Unfortunately, I chose a therapy that did not have an integrated methodology for working with somatic and movement processes. Its strong emphasis on the use of guided imagery and verbal dialogue, and an overly conceptual orientation, began to pull apart my body and mind again, until the container was weakened and unable to hold the deep psychological processes that were under way.

With the experience of ego-death, we are thrown back upon ourselves in a way that we may never encounter under normal circumstances. As the bodymind container disintegrates, psychological boundaries dissolve and personal resources, which we may have worked long to cultivate, are no longer available to us. As I was plunged into the crisis of undoing, I felt acutely disconnected from my body, and unable to utilise anything I had learnt through all my years of practice and studies in movement, bodywork, or psychotherapy. Yet at the same time I understood with great clarity what was happening in my body and what it needed.

This might have been humiliating to my ego had I not been faced with the deeper and more impelling issue of life and death, of struggling to maintain a tenuous connection between body and soul. In fact I felt deeply humbled to recognise powers, however destructive they at first seemed, in the face of which my learning and knowledge was so utterly inadequate. It gave me a more deeply felt perspective on both my hard-earned knowledge and experience, and the place of physical existence within the larger context of soul and spirit, and the cycles of life, death, and rebirth – a personally felt understanding that all form must be sacrificed in death.

The experience opened me to a deeper understanding of the bodymind connection, and appreciation of both the immense value and the limitations of body therapies in psycho-spiritual growth and healing. It was as if I had to start again right at the beginning, go through the whole process of learning and embodying which my earlier life experience and studies took me through, but this time with more conscious awareness of the psychological and spiritual dimensions of the experience, and their relationship to body needs and body process.

Life often feels like this. We labour to create a satisfactory life for ourselves, only to have the whole edifice collapse around us. Then we have no choice but to begin again, if we are not to withdraw into a defeated attitude of failure. Our culture sees this as an entirely negative process, against what we call progress, and so it is if we see our lives only in terms of building fortune, status, and security for ourselves, a linear path of development. But if we place our life in a context of soul and spirit, then we learn that everything must be offered up to some greater purpose. Such trials and disasters test to the utmost limits our faith and strength of purpose.

To quote Hillman again:

'Without a dying to the world of the old order, there is no place for renewal, because…it is illusory to hope that growth is but an additive process requiring neither sacrifice nor death. The soul favours the death experience to usher in change.'[7]

What is experienced as death to the ego, which has worked so hard to establish its tentative hold, is new life at the level of psyche-soul; this involves a new perspective and orientation towards life. Such calamities may be the impulses that stir us to seek for greater meaning in our lives. Much of the suffering involved in this process is the mourning for the death of some part of ourselves, an old life and identification that may have formerly served us well. The house we have so painstakingly built up comes crumbling down, but new life can always grow out of the void that has been left. To honour the experience of both the suffering *ego-soul* and the process of renewal of *psyche-soul* requires us to embrace the paradoxical coexistence of courage and fear, of trust and betrayal, and of hope with despair and anguish.

Boundaries and Unboundaried States

The issues which confront us in such crises will be reflected in the symptoms the body manifests. We may find out what is needed for our healing and renewal by paying attention to the body's signals. Ancient cultures understood this wisdom of the body, but it is only recently, with an urgent need for change and for renewed awareness of our lost connection to earth and ground within, that people are once again turning to the body itself as a source of guidance in the healing process. Discussing modern shamanism, Lewis E Mehl writes:

'Healing involves returning the clients to the path of their own lives. When we walk too far afield from our own true nature, illness arises as an alarm that we must get back onto our own path of destiny. Healing produces that return. The body is wonderfully wise. It reacts immediately when we stray from our path. It is modern culture that has taught us to ignore our body. Shamanic treatment requires listening to the unique wisdom of each individual body, not blindly following rules made by the mind. For the body is a part of the earth. The body is the earthly home for our soul. It knows more about life on earth than the mind. When in doubt, we ask the body.'[8]

The experience of the body as earth and home is essential to psychological well-being. When we lose this experience of containment, we risk losing our inner integrity, our sense of self and of wholeness; or, stated the other way round, when we are losing an old sense of identity and going through an experience of dissolution, we may also feel unheld and uncontained, out of relationship with earth and body. Boundaries dissolve. The body not only manifests symptoms; it also manifests boundaries. The quality of our relationship to our body reflects the quality of psychological boundaries and integration.

When psychologically fragmented and vulnerable, we might use muscular tension in an attempt to create boundaries and a sense of substance. It is a far from ideal way of creating a feeling of safety, but until some measure of psychological integration is restored, physical armouring may be needed to give quite literally a sense of being held, and held together. It provides a fragile containment for whatever degree of integration remains, and may also provide a feeling of being alive.

What we are attempting to do with the muscular tension is to create a safe place, a cocoon, within which the transformation process can take place undisturbed. It is not an effective way of doing this, but may be the only available substitute for a truly protective and safe external environment. A safe, cocoon-like environment is essential for the containment of the process of dissolution, in order for the transformatory and healing processes to occur. The body will attempt to create this safe container from within, when it is not available from any other source. Therapy which attempts to break down protective muscular tensions prematurely can create psychological fragmentation.

The creation of the cocoon, the alchemical vessel of transformation as protective holding environment, can be one of the most difficult and crucial issues of the healing crisis for us today. If it cannot be created, or if it breaks during the period of dissolution, the process is uncontained and may overwhelm the fragile ego. In the depths of the process, the initiate may be unable to sustain the boundaries by herself, so it is here that the understanding and support of the therapist, healer, friend, family, or community is essential. Without appropriate support, the healing process may turn into pathology, and the potential for transformation be aborted. Supportive containment might at times take the form of assistance with practical needs; it may mean being willing to listen and witness; it may involve holding, physically and emotionally, through the most difficult times; or it may entail simply being present. Most importantly it is expressed through an attitude of understanding, care, acceptance, and genuine respect towards the person herself, the process she is in, and its potential value.

We do not need to be treated during such crises; we need to be touched, held, protected, witnessed, cared for in order that the process can be contained and completed. Only when a certain degree of reintegration has occurred might it become possible to find or create for ourselves the safe and containing environment which will facilitate the completion of the process. Because our culture does not have an understanding of and a context for such processes, the creation of a safe place is usually fraught with difficulty and trauma. For many, hospital may be the only alternative, but it is usually not an appropriate place. Only within the external boundaries of a safe environment can the essential issue of personal boundaries, their formation, dissolution, and evolution, be addressed. Psychological boundaries are about awareness, and a change in boundaries through expanded awareness is a central theme of the crisis.

There are membranes, tissues, and fluids of the body which specifically embody boundary issues. The natural boundaries of the body, such as the skin and cellular membranes, serve as organs of communication and transformation. There seems to be an integral connection between the functioning of the cellular membranes, and the psychological and energetic boundaries of the individual. The strength, permeability, rigidity, or weakness of the cellular membranes, their ability to communicate, absorb, contain, protect, and release, expresses the condition of the psychological boundaries, and also the protective 'skin' of the subtle energy body. Conversely, the condition of psychological boundaries reflects the quality of cellular containment. Richard Moss discusses how boundaries that are extremely permeable may be expressed in schizophrenic conditions, whilst more rigid and less permeable boundaries may result in illnesses such as cancer.[9] These conditions are reflected in the quality of both cellular and psychological containment.

Expression of deep emotion moves the whole body. With the breakdown of psychological boundaries, the floodgates to buried feelings are opened, and we may experience the breakdown of the boundaries of the very cells themselves, as if ravaged by the flood in motion around them. It is not so hard to imagine this happening if we look at the destruction of solid structures caused by nature in the wake of a torrential flood. The cells are the relatively solid, yet nevertheless fragile, structures of the body, together making up its tissues, and their boundaries are delicate, membranous skins. They must be affected by a too-violent eruption of emotion. Research also shows that emotional stress produces chemical changes that can cause the delicate cellular membranes to malfunction or disintegrate. Deep emotions, when extreme and uncontained, can damage physical and psychological boundaries alike, setting in motion processes which can lead to organic disease, as well as psychological disturbance.

The ability to protect ourselves against disease is a function of the immune system, and this body system provides another physical expression of boundaries and defence. The condition of the immune system also reflects the state of psychological boundaries. Caroline Myss relates the immune system to the root chakra, the place of embeddedness in the maternal matrix, and ground of our embodied existence.[10]

Weakened immune function is a major global health problem today, and is at the root of the epidemic of chronic illness discussed earlier. At a physical level the failure of our immune systems has in no small way been created by overuse of artificial means, medicines and drugs which suppress, weaken, and damage the body's natural immunity; and by toxic pollutants in our environment. At the same time, we are suffering collectively from difficulties in maintaining clear psychological boundaries, and from the resulting failure to protect ourselves in effective and humane ways. Military defence is a major concern for every government, and the more we create sophisticated means of defending ourselves at a distance, the less we seem able to communicate and protect ourselves in an effectively natural and humane fashion.

We might take this reflection further to compare the individual's experience with that of the planet as a whole. The boundary of the earth's atmosphere, its outer 'skin', is also in trouble. With the threat to the ozone layer, the earth is being made vulnerable to harmful radiation from the sun. As this process is allowed to continue unchecked, we are clearly inviting a level of destruction that we may be unable to control or alleviate. What the individual in crisis is experiencing is also a reflection of a process that is going on at a global and planetary level. This is one important reason why it is essential that we take seriously the experience of the individual, and learn from this of the dangers, the potential, and what is needed in such a crisis.

At a personal level, protective psychological boundaries need to be maintained to the extent that we are unable to endure the burning light and the expansiveness of spirit; as our endurance grows, the boundaries too can change, grow, become more permeable, perhaps eventually dissolve in the final stages of Enlightenment. Maybe it is the same with planet earth and the many forms of life that she nurtures. She needs protection; if her protective layer is damaged she may be burnt up, or at least cease to be able to sustain the life forms that are nurtured by her now.

But perhaps the present ecological crisis we are creating also carries a potential for evolution of the earth-soul, an opening to new awareness and life for the earth herself. In this age of the return of the feminine, is earth-awareness and earth-knowledge not also reawakening, perhaps to some new way of being?[11] How can we know what the present crisis means for the earth herself? Yet there is one thing that we can be fairly sure of – that the damage humankind is causing will destroy the conditions that ensure our own survival long before the earth herself will be destroyed. A remarkable process of rebalancing and healing takes place between the earth, her oceans, plant and animal life, and atmosphere. So far, this system of self-regulation has been able to counter the effects of pollution and destruction of natural resources, but it may not be able to continue to do so under increasingly threatening conditions. Yet the earth herself will certainly outlive human foolishness and greed, regaining ecological equilibrium once our excesses and abuses end.

For the individual, and maybe also for the earth, weak, permeable, or damaged boundaries can more readily let in both healing as well as harmful influences. Perhaps when the protective boundaries are too rigid and unresponsive to allow in new consciousness, they may first need to weaken in order to become more flexible, permeable, or expanded, and hence more able to include new perspectives and attitudes. However, even though the crisis may hold potential for positive change and expanded awareness, we need to take very good practical care of the vulnerable condition of both the earth and ourselves, each individual person, going through this process of growth and transformation. Damage to or breaks in protective boundaries, which may occur as signs that we need to be more flexible and receptive in our outlook, can also be lethal. Without proper care, the openings become too great and harmful, and the potential cannot unfold.

Cellular integrity and health is related to, and nurtured by, the experience of being held, beginning in the womb and developing through infancy.[12] When cellular and psychological boundaries are in need of strengthening, or indeed also of softening and opening, we need to be held, deeply and trustfully held, grounded, earthed again, like an infant in a nurturing womb-environment. The very cells of the body need to be held, supported, encouraged to relate to the earth in a responsive way – to surrender to the pull of gravity rather than strain and fight against it – and so return to a healthy, balanced state. In this nurturing space the body at the deepest cellular level feels itself acknowledged, loved, contained, reassured, and its own healing process can begin to unfold. This is the path of embodying, of grounding awareness in the body, awakening cellular and earth-consciousness.

The loving presence of the therapist or healer can make any approach to healing truly effective; but in times when we are in the throes of ego-death, when we have descended into the depths of psyche and the body and mind are suffering and fragmented, then what we may most need is to be physically held, contained by the touch of loving human contact. If the therapist or healer knows how to make deep and mindful contact, then as the boundary of the skin is touched, so too is the membrane of every cell, and through this deep contact, awareness can gently return to the body. Little more may need to be done. If the contact can support at this deep level then cellular, and with it psychological, integrity may be restored. It is a healing of being together at the most basic of levels, where we may begin to recreate the foundations of our home, our embodied being, in a more supported and expanded way.

Body Process and the Search for Meaning

We know that the denial and repression of emotional feeling causes our wounds to live on within us unrecognised, and it is frequently the body that becomes the victim of this process. As we bring awareness to our bodily experience, we begin to remember and re-experience the original woundings and pain, but we also begin to access wisdom. Archetypally, the suffering of the body can be a manifestation of the negative aspect of the denied, repressed feminine; through her destructive assault upon our bodies the Dark Goddess demands that we listen to and honour her. We listen to her when we pay attention to the symptoms of our own sickness, and through them her forgotten and wordless knowledge may be felt again. I hope that one day we will no longer wait until we are sick before we are prepared to listen to this inner knowledge; it is available to us in health too.

> 'Matriarchal wisdom knows – as all body therapies and holistic medicine know – that ancestral intelligence is communicated through the body: particularly the wisdom that for one reason or another is silent. The vicissitudes of the "occluded intelligence" are also carried in the body.'[13]

Patterns of emotional repression and physical disease are often passed down from one generation to the next. The choice bequeathed to us is to accept unconsciously the inheritance of our ancestors and continue our family line, denying ourselves awareness of our own feelings and reality; or to attempt the painful journey of bringing the denial to light and feeling the pain of our own wounds, and those of our family which we also carry. I believe that this can be an act of redemption not only for ourselves, but for our ancestors, for their silent and hidden suffering, and in some small way for the family of humanity too. To move forward we need to free ourselves from the pains and chains of the past so that we may live in the present, by our own inner truth.

This difficult path holds risk, and there is no guarantee of its success. Some do not get through; some die of their sickness or do not get beyond despair. Sometimes suicides occur, which may be attempts to kill the old false self and empty life, to become free of pain and be reborn into a fuller life. Suicide may occur out of a passionate love and longing for life which has been thwarted, rather than a hatred of it. It often appears to be an attempt to re-enact the rituals of initiation that we need to experience as we let old parts of ourselves die in order to cross important thresholds. Our society no longer provides or understands the enduring need of the soul for such rites of passage during processes of transformation, and so the need may be subverted into self-destructive acts.

Suicides rarely occur during the deepest stages of the dark night; feeling already dead, inhabitants of the underworld, death is not a way out of suffering. There is no will for even this ultimate act. But when a person is beginning to emerge from the long winter of the soul, and enough will and energy to act are mobilised again, then the risk of suicide is greatest. As we begin to emerge, but are not yet free of the darkness, we are intensely aware of the great gap between reality and potential. We have glimpsed something profound and sublime, but are confronted once again with the suffering and ordinariness of everyday life, and the distance between them may seem too painful to tolerate and too large to bridge. Until the depth experience has been fully integrated, and we are able to give expression to what we have experienced and learnt in the underworld journey, this can be a period of utmost desolation. We emerge like the new-born infant, our hearts open and raw, but may find we are not welcomed back, and there is no place for us in the world we have returned to. Initiation is not complete until we return with our gift to the world; many initiations today are thwarted because the return is unrecognised and the gift of knowledge of the underworld journey is not received and valued.

At some level, we make a choice to consciously feel our woundedness in order to redeem it. As women, we are choosing to redeem the wounds of the feminine by listening to the body, to our broken dreams, our own pain and that of our mothers and grandmothers before us, searching for the meaning within it all. Finding meaning in the suffering is to discover the underlying pattern, the myth, which contains our life experience in an order that is intuitively felt and recognised as somehow right. Myth gives a greater perspective from which we can view our personal life experience within the context of the life of soul and spirit. It contains all that feels unbearable, tragic, wrong, unnecessary, wasteful, and makes it endurable, right, and sacred again. Myth takes us beyond the small, beyond the personal, beyond the concerns of bodily and ego survival, progress, material comfort and security, to hold the experiences of our lives within the greater context of the unfolding process of Life itself.

The tragedy of my friend's death was the knife which cut through my family line, forced me eventually to seek beyond all that I had inherited, beyond the silent and unacknowledged suffering of my ancestors, towards heal-ing. I had to search for meaning in what was a cruel and meaningless event, and now, many years later and after much soul searching, I can acknowledge a level at which this wounding was a necessity for my own soul. It was an initial awakening out of the ignorance and denial I had both inherited and was recreating for myself, an opening to the potential healing of the deeper wounds of existence. Without such openings, we may remain forever blind to our deeper nature. It was a cruel and wasteful tragedy, yet it initiated a proc-ess that was necessary for my soul and for my understanding.

> 'There are deaths that are wrong, like that of the hero, of the helpful companion, of the soul's love image, of the Man on that cross, which are yet tragically right. They fit with a definite mythic pattern. Myths have a place for what is wrong and yet necessary.

> 'Myths govern our lives.'[14]

Right and wrong in this sense are not about value judgements. Something is right simply because it *is*. Rightness here is about recognising what is actual, real, existent, rather than imposing our own concepts and attitudes upon reality. This is not to deny the grief of bereavement or betrayal, nor the wrongness of abuse of any kind. It simply says that this is what is, and it exists as part of a pattern, a mythic or karmic pattern that underlies and creates our life experience. In discovering the myths that are reflected in our lives, we can come to a better understanding of ourselves. Without such awareness, the myths or karmic patterns unconsciously control us, and the archetypal dynamics may be played out in our human lives with tragic consequences. When these patterns are recognised, seen as the flow of our own mindstream, the power behind them is internalised rather than projected out into the events of the world. Discovering the mythic patterns of our lives can reinvest our experience with sacredness and bring us greater freedom from their unconscious tyranny.

Understanding at a mythological level is not meant to replace the personal work of healing our personal wounds. If we are too quick to try to find the myth which speaks to our situation, without properly working through the personal level of our suffering, we may end up by denying, 'jumping over', and again repressing our real feelings. The wounded child within can be re-victimised by such acts of denial and abandonment. This can happen in a therapeutic approach that places too much or sole emphasis on the mythological realm. We can also abuse ourselves if an internal hierarchy is operating which allows the search for meaning, a mythological or spiritual context, to dominate at the expense of the needs of the wounded child and the body for healing. Alice Miller gives an example of this:

> 'The patient of a Jungian analyst, for instance, can allow himself to confront the "savage goddess Kali" – that is socially acceptable, because Kali is abstract and not the concrete mother. Then painful memories, such as being dragged across the floor as a child by his drunken mother, unfortunately will not have to come to the surface, and he will consequently be unable to free himself from the repetition compulsion. When he later reenacts his repressed experiences with his own child, other archetypal explanations can be offered.'[15]

Personal feeling and relationship, the wounds and betrayals of the child, and the scars the body carries, must be felt, acknowledged, and healed. And yet there also come moments in therapeutic work where we do need to step out of the endless contents of our personal story and see it from another perspective, within a wider context. Sometimes, when the soil has been dug over again and again, we need to step back and let the sun shine upon it for the seeds to grow. A process can become stuck, cycling endlessly around the contents of personal history, if the dimension of meaning and a context of sacredness is not included. The skill lies in knowing when to dig the earth and when to step back and let the light of meaning shine upon it. If we do not recognise the myths that guide our life, the karmic tendencies and patterns that underlie our actions and experiences, we may carry our unbearable wounds forever. There may ultimately be no healing because there is no meaning, no purpose, and no acceptance of the 'suchness' of the experience.

The myth we are exploring here is the universally told story of initiation into death, the journey into the underworld, where the body is wounded and ego dies in order that the soul can be healed, the inner heart touched, and the creative source of life renewed. Suffering consciously the descent of the soul into its depths, self is embodied and grounded in deepened awareness; spirit and matter reunite and the fundamental split between them may be healed. The soul, in its journey of descent, serves as mediator in this marriage. The journey of descent is travelled by the wounded healer and the artist, and it is the path of initiation into the dark feminine, the banished aspect of the Great Goddess.

Part Two

Myth, Meaning and the Quest of the Feminine

The Burning

The crowd closes in. Stones fall
on exact parts of her body.
These wounds will be carried on into the future
worn as scars on the bodies of her daughters.
Marks of the lineage
of initiation into dark feeling.

Women know this, the stoning and the burning,
as secrets bedded in flesh, impressed into every cell.
With bodies bruised, still, from old wounds
we are set aflame each time injustice whips around our feet.
But smoke chokes the web of fine passageways
that would bring life to our beating hearts
and voice to our pain.
Remembering how it was for our grandmothers
we are weakened by fear of the burning.

At the very centre of the stoning crowd she stands tall,
tied to a pole, a pillar joining heaven and earth,
branch of the life-giving tree.
She cries out, her limbs jolted into dance, as flames rise.
She is burning.
Her dance is wildness.
A bird screeches from her throat.
Instead of succour she is sacrifice
but sacredness is cast out with the thud of stones
falling on her body.

Who heard the call of the wild bird
as it escaped in gasps from her burning throat?

'You may burn me but I will not die. Forever
I will return. So listen now.' Craw craws the bird.
'I know death. I have been often to her home
and she has grown me in wordless knowledge
she has shown me her face and it made me whole
she gives me fear and courage.
She is guide when all else fails, teacher
of unspoken wisdom.
Listen.
Listen to the silence. Hear her voice within it.
Listen to the cry which pierces through the night.
Hear the wisdom that it carries.'

Her last breath flees the burning.

The bird is freed, soars, spreads her wings.
Plumes of fire cascade rainbow-coloured from her graceful brow.
Now she circles round the earth
enfolds the sorrow pain fear hatred that consumed her.
Embraces earth in fiery plumes.

Be in awe now
for she will not die. Forever she returns.
She is power of life born
and reborn of dying.
She is beauty, rapture. She is spirit.
So be still now. Listen
and within the silence
hear her calling.

5 Woman's Story – Redemption of the Feminine

Myths tell the tales of the gods and goddesses, archetypal patterns that are played out through our individual and collective lives. When we study the myths of the world throughout time, we find underlying patterns that are universal to all humanity. Each culture throughout the ages had its own unique way of retelling the stories of creation, birth, life, death, and transformation, its own symbols and cosmology. In speaking to these great themes, myth is the way by which human beings, sensing their individual insignificance and vulnerability within the grand scheme of the universe, attempt to make containable and meaningful the harsh and often inexplicable experiences of life. Myth makes sacred, and returns us to the path of our soul. It also serves to maintain a degree of stability within society. The archetypal stories of the gods and goddesses can guide and orientate us in those places where we feel most lost. 'Mythology', writes Stephen Larsen, 'fulfills the function of a psychological womb that brings the developing psyche to maturity.'[1]

We might also speak of karma or destiny; when we are unconscious of the deeper forces which move us, we continually create cycles of action and reaction, patterns of cause and effect which must inevitably unfold and be played out, repeating themselves endlessly through many lifetimes. Unless awareness is brought to these mythic or karmic patterns, and their function and origins in the psyche understood, we will remain victim to them – playthings of the gods and goddesses, rather than willing co-creators acting as their conscious voice in the world. We cannot escape the mythic patterns of our own lives, and indeed of the collective life of our culture. But we can recognise them and work with them in a conscious and creative way.

'Now it appears that when the mythic imagination is cultivated it is the creative source realm of the highest and best in human endeavour, the inspiration of the finest flowerings of our culture. But when neglected, deprived of conscious cultivation, it is equally capable of becoming a choked and tangled garden of weeds. Instead of giving birth to the useful and the beautiful, the profound and the sublime, the same creative force can produce titans, monsters, and grotesques...'[2]

When we deny the gods and goddesses, being unconscious of, repressing, or castigating the psychological energies that they represent, their destructive aspects will create chaos and turmoil in both our inner and outer worlds. It is the god or goddess, the archetype that has been denied and relegated to unconsciousness, that will in fact control us. Only through conscious acceptance can it be integrated creatively within the personality, or the culture and society, as a whole.

The exclusive identification with one archetype has brought modern western society to a dangerous edge. In being impelled to worship one God and forsake all others throughout several millennia of Jewish and Christian religion, we have effectively denied all but one of a rich pantheon of gods and goddesses. They are messengers of the soul, mediators between the individual human being and the creative sources of life and universal spirit; each one represents specific aspects of psychological and transpersonal awareness. Monotheism has led us along a severe and narrow path that in particular has denied the Divine Feminine, the Goddess in her many aspects, and the consciousness and values associated with her. Though banished underground for so long she has nevertheless, as we have seen earlier, come to dominate the psyche of modern man through destructive materialism and greed. Mankind has feared and tried to control her, even as it sought to deny her in worship of the solitary male Godhead; being thus denied and dishonoured, her wisdom too has gone underground, unvalued, and she is able to make herself known and felt only through her dark, destructive side in conflict, war, disease and disasters both natural and man-made. The very dividing of consciousness and divinity into a polarised masculine and feminine, and the denial of one aspect, is fundamental to the dualism of our culture and the conflict of interests that dualism necessarily engenders.

The feminine weaves together the threads of *what is* into a rich and multi-layered tapestry; the masculine separates out and focuses in one direction, moving towards a goal *beyond*. Clearly, these are complementary tendencies that need to coexist creatively. So do the many other qualities represented by the various gods and goddesses of antiquity. We are impoverished when any one of them is excluded, and risk both the vengeance of the ones denied, and the distortion and inflation of the one solely upheld, as has happened in patriarchal Christianity.

The feminine is inclusive, embracing the whole even as it represents one aspect of the polarity. Early mythologies, and even the sources of most present day religious and philosophic systems, were rooted in gynolatric and matriarchal consciousness, and they generally reflect an appreciation of the feminine principle in their cosmologies. Before there was a God and Goddess, consorts and co-creators of life, there was the creative void, ocean, or pristine awareness, which engendered the polarities of masculine and feminine and all the forms which sprung from their creative union. Whilst being understood as beyond gender, this original source has an embracing, inclusive, eternally creating, nurturing, and reabsorbing nature which is often symbolically described as feminine in essence, and is depicted in many mythologies and early religions as the Great Goddess.

In Taoist philosophy, *Wu Chi* is the mother of the *T'ai Chi*, the feminine and masculine polarity, *Yin* and *Yang;* represented by the empty circle, *Wu Chi* is the primordial cosmic womb that engenders and embraces all that comes into existence.[3]

Although the religious institutions of Buddhism have been, inevitably, male-dominated in a patriarchal age, essential Buddhist philosophy gives equal value to both masculine and feminine principles.[4] Like the two sides of the hand, they are intrinsically connected and complementary parts of a whole, and without both, enlightenment cannot be realised. The feminine reflects inwards and is associated with wisdom; the masculine expresses outwards in skilful and compassionate action. Wisdom and compassion are likened to the two wings of a bird, without both of which the bird cannot fly. Buddhism also describes the primordial state of awareness, out of which all phenomena arise, as essentially feminine in nature, even whilst it exists both before and beyond the duality of opposites. In speaking of the feminine principle in Tibetan Buddhism, Tsultrim Allione writes:

'Any discussion of the feminine must begin with "The Great Mother or Consort".... She may be called "Yum Chenmo", "The Mother of the Buddhas", the "Womb of Tathagatas", or "Prajna Paramita". This is the primordial feminine which is the basic ground. It is described as feminine because it has the power to give birth.

'Trungpa Rinpoche explains the "Great Mother" in this way:

' "In phenomenal experience, whether pleasure or pain, birth or death, sanity or insanity, good or bad, it is necessary to have a basic ground. This basic ground is known in Buddhist literature as the mother principle. Prajnaparamita (the perfection of wisdom) is called the mother-consort of all the Buddhas .... As a principle of cosmic structure, the all-accommodating basic ground is neither male nor female. One might call it hermaphroditic, but due to its quality of fertility or potentiality, it is regarded as feminine."

'The "Great Mother" is different from the Christian God, because it does not intend to produce a world and set down laws. The whole thing is spontaneous rather than intentional. God separates himself to create the world, but the feminine just gives birth spontaneously.'[5]

In separating himself, the Christian God, as he is commonly understood, and man whom he is a reflection of, has cut off aspects of his own creative potentiality; he has also lost contact with the basic ground and grown inflated with a grandiose belief in his own powers. We in the modern western world need to return to the roots of our own culture and religion to see where it went astray, where it became divided within and against itself, and where the Goddess-principle was lost. God himself must be as much in need of the return of the Goddess as we are, for without contact with her creative ground his lonely kingdom in heaven may fall.

By claiming that there is only one God, that this God is a Father, and demanding that people worship only him, Christianity attempted to banish the Goddess in her many aspects completely. To a large degree it succeeded, although in Catholicism the Virgin Mary has been elevated to the status of Goddess within the hearts of the people. Mary has fulfilled for many Catholics the need for a female deity and mother-consort of the male God. As well as being the servant of God's divine will as mother of Jesus, Mary is also the Mother of God, and Holy Virgin. Her nature is ambiguous and mysterious, but essentially the epitome of goodness, purity, and holiness. For many Christians she represents the light aspect of the Goddess. But her dark sister, Eve, has been used to cast a slur upon womanhood itself, with the naming of women as the cause of all evil and temptation; in that, the dark aspect of the Goddess has been denied a rightful place in Christian worship. When the light and dark aspects of the deity are split off from each other, she is incapacitated and cannot fully serve in her creative, nurturing, healing, visionary, and protective functions. Writing on *The Divine Woman in Christianity* Roger Horrocks says:

'...[I]n relation to the Eve/Mary polarity, the Christian Church – and the society in which it existed – was unable to hold such a relativist view of light and dark. The figure of Eve has been used to castigate the inherent flaw in women: they are rebellious, sources, of evil, death, corruption. This has been one of the great problems for Christianity – that it has been unable to accept the necessary dark side of life, and of the divine, and has therefore *acted out* its own dark side, in religious wars, persecutions, acts of genocide, attitudes of patronizing contempt to other religions, all of which has been breathtakingly brutal and "unChristian". Christianity became a murderous force, precisely because it clung too fiercely to "the good".

'Thus the cult of Mary is the obverse of the suppression of the dark feminine. Mary is idealized and rendered ethereal; along with this goes a harsh refusal to accept women in themselves, a vengeful and murderous assault on women in the form of "witches", and an unpreparedness for the internal psychic assault of the Dark Goddess. This is a dangerously schizoid fantasy about the feminine. Mary is idealized in order to suppress the feminine shadow, and therefore ordinary women, confronted with Mary, can easily feel failures.' [6]

However, it was Protestantism that took the banishment of the Goddess to its limit. As Horrocks writes:

'But then in the Renaissance, something even more drastic happens to Mary: she is removed completely. In Northern Europe the religious Reformation sweeps away the "idolatry" of saints, chief among whom is Mary.

'The stained glass windows were smashed; the statues of Our Lady were toppled and destroyed; the numinous Word became the prosaic word. Religion became rational, non-symbolic, individualized – we might say "privatized". Its function as a binding of community values was weakened. God became fiercer, more judgmental, as the intercessionary powers of Mary were lost.'[7]

Whilst no doubt introducing some healthy changes into a corrupted Catholic Church, the Reformation left a heavy toll. Horrocks continues:

'But as part of the price paid for this development, the values of Mary were rejected in the northern part of Europe. Protestantism became a religion with a huge hole in it. The Goddess was completely removed. She became an unperson. The feminine aspect of the divine went completely underground.

'The consequences of this revolution are incalculable. On the positive side, there was enormous release of energy into masculine thought and activity, leading to scientific and geographical discovery, new philosophical currents, the development of political democracy, inventions, manufacturing. On the debit side, we find a growing sense of the alienation of the individual within the community; an increasing feeling of soul-lessness, rootlessness and violence, that has come to dominate our culture.

'What happens to the feminine? It cannot be made to disappear. It is driven underground, into the unconscious. There it becomes darker, more violent, vengeful. Surely it is not an accident that after the bright dawn of the Renaissance, and then the Age of Reason, we come to the twentieth century, one of the most irrational, destructive, genocidal eras in modern civilization? Is it fanciful to imagine the Goddesses of death and destruction stalking the planet, perched on the standards of Hitler, Pol Pot and Stalin? The Goddess unheard, unwitnessed, becomes a Fury.'[8]

When the feminine is driven underground it is not only women who are repressed and cannot grow to their fullest maturity, are not given the possibilities to develop their gifts or express their own particular feminine perspective and wisdom. The feminine within men can also not grow and mature, and men remain sons bound under the unconscious domination of their mothers, as much as women remain daughters of the patriarchy. In the patriarchal age, we have all been denied our full inheritance and freedom as adult human beings by a repressive and judgmental God-the-Father, and an exiled God-the-Mother grown violent, vengeful, and controlling.

The Goddess did not completely disappear from Christianity. Sophia, Goddess and wisdom-aspect of the divinity, was originally consort with God, but has no place in modern orthodox Christianity. She was in fact incorporated into the image of Jesus; her wisdom, compassion, and humanness – for the Goddess always has a closer connection with the earthly, human aspect of existence than her male consort, and often functioned as mediator between God and humankind – were assumed as the qualities of Jesus, as was her femininity. The figure of Jesus is potentially that of the divine androgyne, representing the marriage of masculine and feminine, a symbol of wholeness and integration. Sadly the androlatric view of orthodox Christianity could not consciously accept this possibility and instead manipulated the message of Jesus to further castigate the feminine in women. Only today, two centuries after the birth of Christianity, is the name of Sophia, wisdom, beginning to be spoken again.

It is a mark of the importance and necessity to the human psyche, which the Dark Goddess has always held, that orthodoxy has never been able to completely eradicate her presence, despite banishment, reformations, witch-hunting and other abuses that she has suffered. Throughout the world today there are still images of the Black Virgin, powerful icons which are worshipped with great devotion by ordinary Christians, despite the fact that the religion has no place for the Dark Goddess. And despite the terrors that have been inflicted upon her and her worshippers throughout the ages, she survives. Clearly, she holds a power that is greater than that of all the destruction that has been wrought against her.[9]

If we look at Judaism, the mother religion of Christianity, and in particular at early Judaism, the Goddess was originally present. As Asherah she was the consort or feminine aspect of God, though this early worship was eventually suppressed and denied by the male leaders of the Jewish tradition. As Hochmah, Wisdom, she was co-creator of the universe with God, and is also 'the preexistent cosmic order that is the source of the world and sustains it'.[10] As a way of maintaining the essence of wisdom but eradicating the feminine deity, Hochmah later became identified with the Torah and was thus subsumed under the patriarchal tradition. As the Shekhinah she was God's Bride, sometimes identified in this role as the people of Israel, comforting and protecting them in exile, exiled herself; although the name is feminine, some orthodox thinking ascribes the Shekhinah not to the feminine aspect or consort of God, but to the 'presence' of God, or the Face of God.

Lilith is the Goddess of Judaism that orthodoxy did not incorporate into the patriarchal version of the religion.[11] Lilith became the demon of destruction, the outcast, the dark and untameable side of the feminine that religion and society would not tolerate. Lilith is the original Dark Goddess of our modern western religion and culture, banished, reviled, yet nevertheless still present after centuries in exile. She is sister and predecessor to Eve. Lilith was consort to God and first wife of Adam. The husband-son-lover relationship that Adam had with Lilith is one recurring frequently in matriarchal mythology; it symbolises, in the death and rebirth of the Goddess's son-lover, surrender to the Great Round of Nature, the cycles of fertility, death, and rebirth, over which the Goddess presides. The Lilith-Adam-Eve story, however, follows a different course, and marks the turning away from matriarchal to patriarchal and androlatric consciousness.

As his wife, Adam expected Lilith to be submissive and subservient to his wishes, in the same way that he himself was subservient towards his God. One version of the story tells that he wanted her to assume the 'missionary position' when they made love, but she wanted to express her sexuality freely and in her own way. Being a strong and self-determining woman, a woman of self-respect and spirit, and as Goddess also consort to

God himself, Lilith refused to be subservient to Adam. Adam should have known that he could not use or overpower the Goddess; this would amount to a dangerous form of hubris. Lilith defied both Adam and God and called on the secret name of God that should not be uttered; knowing his secret name signifies that she was the holder of the knowledge of good and evil. As a result she disappeared, forced to flee into exile from the Garden of Eden, and was doomed to a life on the outside, scapegoated, feared, denounced, and cursed by man and God alike.

As the story goes, Adam complained to God about Lilith's insubordinate behaviour, and asked for God's help. He then fell asleep one night with Lilith at his side, but when he awoke in the morning Lilith had gone, and in her place lay the beautiful young Eve. God had indeed sorted out Adam's problem; Lilith had been banished, or perhaps chose of her own accord to flee an intolerable situation, and in her place was the sweet and compliant Eve. Many women today, particularly strong and independent women, or women in their middle or later years, will recognise this story being played out in their own lives. Adam was well pleased with his new wife. Until...until, of course, Lilith returns in the form of a serpent, ancient symbol of wisdom and healing, and tempts her sister to taste the fruit of the Tree of Knowledge. The rest of the story we are all well familiar with. So, first through Lilith and then through Eve, woman was twice castigated as sinful, the source of evil and suffering.

Lilith was exiled into darkness, the denied, repressed feminine spirit cast out from her home, a refugee. This is a state that women of the patriarchy know well, exiled from the home and ground within and without. It was believed that she became wrathful at being denied and dishonoured in this way, and sought revenge by causing disharmony in marital relationships and murdering infants at their birth. Thus the Goddess denied, instead of being worshipped as creator and protector of life, is transformed into the abuser of women and babies, the very ones for whom she should be a source of nurturance, inner strength, and support. The self-hatred and self-negation that poisons women's relationship to themselves, their children, and their partners finds expression in the images of Lilith – witch-mother, old hag, and demon of destruction. Her true wisdom is thus debased, as her function and place in the sacred order is distorted and denied.

Some women still wear talismans and make prayers and offerings to Lilith during pregnancy and labour, to ward off her evil. She was both feared and revered as the demon-goddess presiding over pregnancy and childbirth. With her death-in-life consciousness, she represents the function of woman as mediator of birth and death, officiator of the passage between the worlds, Goddess of the night and the dark:

> 'Patriarchy has turned her into queen of the demons, killer of children, particularly to be feared by mothers in childbirth. And that sums it up; instead of the creatrix she has been made the destroyer. The symbol of women's wisdom and power, she has become a source of evil to be feared most particularly by women. She represents to us our innermost herstory. In reclaiming Her, we women throw off and pour away for ever the poison about ourselves, our so-called inferiority, our evil inner selves, our guilt. On reclaiming Lilith we reclaim the breath of life that emerges as we give birth to our children, to our works of all kind; we reclaim our wisdom, our knowledge, our power, our autonomy.'[12]

These bold and courageous words of Asphodel Long feel to me like the breath of the Goddess herself as she returns, reborn into our consciousness; this is how her voice sounds when she is free to speak out clearly, without malice or revenge, but with passion and conviction.

Reclaiming Lilith, the repressed and banished Goddess within us, means including and redeeming, through our own conscious suffering, the dark aspect of the feminine, recovering the creative potential buried within our depths, and regaining a sense of awe and reverence in the face of the Goddess. It also means redeeming the madness that her exile has thrown us into. We are being called now to redeem the Dark Goddess and heal the splitting of the feminine, both within itself and from the masculine; we do this for ourselves, for humanity, and for the earth.

Sacred Body, Sacred Ground

All cultures that have worshipped a Goddess have held nature, the earth, and womanhood as sacred. These cultures have an understanding of the natural processes of life, death, and rebirth; they respect all forms of life, whilst also accepting the inevitability of sacrifice in death in order to create new life. They honour woman's death-in-life and life-in-death consciousness, and her place in the natural order of things as mediator of birth and death. Menstruation, childbearing, and the menopause are all held as sacred. Our culture does not worship a Goddess – at least not consciously and creatively – and womanhood is not truly held in honour and respect. Long treated as a second-rate human being, woman became little more than object to man's subjectivity. When man, and woman too, treats the sacred as it is embodied in women, nature, and in the earth, as an object of desire, conquest, greed, hatred, or fear, he or she undoubtedly incurs the wrath of the Goddess.

The archetypal forces of the deep psyche that are represented by the gods and goddesses cannot be controlled by the conscious ego. Those irrepressible and powerful forces might at any moment sweep away our conscious hold; it is they that endlessly shape and reshape our lives, whether we choose to consciously accept and co-operate with this or not. When we alienate ourselves from their creative powers, we are left spiritually empty and desolate, lost in the wasteland within. And today the inner wasteland is manifesting in the external world as well, as the sacred ground of the earth and of womanhood is desacralised, used, and abused. The Goddess's experience of exile in the wilderness has become a living inner reality for most modern men and women, and at the same time a living outer reality for the poorest, weakest, and most vulnerable individuals and communities amongst us.

In the lives of individual women the repression and betrayal of the Goddess within them, of the deepest, most essential, and creative feminine aspect of their being, begins early on in childhood. It begins with adaptations they are forced to make in order to secure the love, protection, and approval of the parents who are, to the child, the upholders of society's values. Women have been conditioned into martyring their womanhood for the sake of acceptance into, and compliance with the rules of patriarchal society, and in this the principle of the feminine is denied. A woman may remain forever a 'child-bride', first to her father, then to her husband, never maturing into full womanhood but remaining 'as if' a child in the possession of and under the protection of the father-husband. She may be a child-bride, psychologically, to the church, the state, the workplace, or whatever authority protects and controls her simultaneously.

Today many women, rejecting this model of passive and ineffectual femininity bestowed upon them by their mothers and grandmothers, have chosen instead the path of independent activity in the world. However, they often find themselves unconsciously seeking to become 'as if' men in heroic attempts to master the exigencies of a male-dominated society that may otherwise exile them for not acquiescing in the traditional female roles. In all of this the patriarchy tends to set women against women – against their own friends, mothers, sisters, daughters – through competitiveness, betrayal, and fear of the loss of their special and protected place in family or society.

Both Lilith and Eve, as they are depicted in the version of the story outlined above, are present in every woman. We may find ourselves moving between these two archetypes at different times; we can be the woman who refuses to conform, in an attempt to keep intact our self-respect and inner integrity as woman, and also the one who acquiesces in order to maintain the love and protection of the male, and hence also of society. Frequently one side will dominate a woman's personality, and the other may be relatively unconscious to her. Both patterns of behaviour are reactions to male authority, and not responses coming from our own true nature and feminine wisdom. Whether we react through rejection of, or compliance with, male authority and standards, we are still being controlled by them, not responding out of our own feminine authority and power.

We cannot simply blame the men in our lives and throughout history for doing this to us, though they do have their part to play. As women we have, individually and collectively, colluded in the betrayal of our authentic feminine being, however innocently or unconsciously. Because the influence of patriarchy has been so deep, widespread, and almost total throughout the world, we cannot avoid the conclusion that it must also have been necessary, at one point in our collective development, to move in this direction. We needed to separate and individuate from the Mother in order to free ourselves from an identification, a *participation mystique*, with the Great Goddess that must have become suffocating and stifling to further growth. The masculine spirit and intellect needed to emerge, and the hero had to 'slay the dragon', which had become oppressive, in order for this consciousness to evolve. But now this movement has also outlived its usefulness and turned in upon itself in a madness of unconsciously motivated and meaningless violence and destruction. It is time to redress the balance and move forwards again. It is time to heal the wound of the rejected Goddess so that she may once more participate with joy and delight, instead of fury and vengeance, in the great cosmic dance, the creative play of the universe.

To heal the feminine wound it is within ourselves that we, as women, must first look. We cannot heal the gaping void we feel within, the loss of our feminine ground, through our relationships to men. We must first free ourselves from the constricting roles we have been caught in, and make contact once more with the sacred ground within, the creative feminine spirit. Only by doing this can we begin to redefine and heal our relationship to men and the masculine within and without. And through it women may also serve, as I believe we are intended to, in the initiation of men into the mysteries of the Divine Feminine, and the healing of their own wounds through the journey of descent into the realm of the Dark Goddess.

This must have been a sacred function of women, understood by old religions that worshipped the Goddess and respected the roles of the priestess and the sacred prostitute. Through her connection to the earth and the cyclical processes of nature, through her monthly bleeding and the rupture of childbirth, woman is naturally more attuned to the dark, wounded side of life. She feels each month the possibility of new life, the wound of her torn womb, and the energy of that potential for life that may be transformed and released into other areas of creative activity. Woman is by nature a traveller to the underworld, and when she learns to go there consciously, she can bring back guidance, wisdom, and healing to others on this path.

At this point in history, women have the possibility, the will, the responsibility, and I believe now also the collective strength to initiate the way towards the redemption of the feminine, for the benefit of all life, not just our own. We are beginning now to do it, and we must remember as we suffer the dismemberment that the path entails, that we do it not only for ourselves, and are not alone in the ordeals we go through. In the concluding words of her poem 'For strong women', Marge Piercy says:

'...Strong is what we make
each other. Until we are all strong together,
a strong woman is a woman strongly afraid.'[13]

When each of us chooses, in our isolation and aloneness, to face our fear and go beyond it, we come eventually to find that we are not alone, but part of a community of spiritual warriors who feel as we do – women who want to create, care for, and celebrate life, not destroy it, but who also have the inner strength and wisdom to embrace death as well as life.

Many of the issues explored here are common to both men and women, but there are significant differences in the process we each go through, different myths which shed light on our own stories and give them meaning. The redemption of the feminine is a personal issue for every man as well as every woman in our Goddess-forsaken culture, but the path towards it may take a different course for each. We will be exploring the experience of woman in particular, and the myths that may speak to and guide the woman of today as she seeks to heal the wound of the feminine, which is both her own and her culture's wound.

Healing the feminine within ourselves is intimately connected with healing the relationship we have to our own bodies and the earth. Woman's spirituality, her sense of sacredness, is rooted in, and often accessed through her body and her experiences in nature. Abuse of the sacred ground of our own bodies, the earth, and other beings living on it has become a way of life in the modern world; healing means *re-membering* ourselves and relearning to tread gently on this sacred ground, to respect and care for, to nurture, appreciate, and celebrate it. Holistic bodywork, natural approaches to healing, living closer to nature, empathic and respectful parenting and relating, Goddess-worship, and the ecology movement are some expressions of this path, and are all essentially political as well as personal quests in our present-day crisis. They are also some of the different ways that women are beginning to express their new-found sense of self as they reconnect to their feminine ground.

I would like to go back at this point to the primary relationship of the child with her mother, and the issue of holding which was discussed earlier. As was suggested, the quality of holding an infant receives from her mother, or other primary caretaker, is not only a personal but also a cultural issue. Lack of adequate holding in the early years contributes to, if it does not directly result in, many of the forms of psychological distress and physical disease so widespread in our culture today. Whilst many so-called 'third world' and 'primitive' societies suffer from extreme physical hardships, we don't hear of such an epidemic of mental and stress-related illness occurring in their midst. The epidemic proportion of emotional suffering and mental illness is a phenomenon of modern western culture, and whilst we can trace many causes, most of them lead us back to the devaluing of feminine consciousness and values, of woman herself, and thus to the quality of holding she is able to give as a mother. In a culture that deeply values womanhood and motherhood, a mother can feel secure within herself, and this will inevitably affect her child positively. If she does not feel herself embraced by, and securely held within, the structures and values of her society, then her own unease will inevitably affect the quality of holding she can offer her child; the child will suffer as a result, in the ways discussed earlier.

By holding, I mean the ability to make a quality of contact with the child that includes every level of her being: that she feel warmly and securely held physically, and can enjoy the comfort of her mother's body; that she is held emotionally, accepted and loved unconditionally, knowing that no matter what she does or feels she will still be loved for who she is; that she feels cherished in a way that allows her to develop a deep sense of love and acceptance of herself and her own feminine body; that she is seen, understood, and respected as a unique and individual being with her own life and soul. When the mother can hold in her awareness the being-ness of her child at all levels, the child will feel deeply loved and held. This is first communicated to the infant essentially through the quality of physical and sensory contact; the mother who can truly hold her child is the woman who is at home in her own body. She is herself embodied, is attuned to her own rhythms and the subtle feelings and needs that flow through her, and so also to those that flow through her child. Such a woman lives in and perceives through her body, not only her mind; she perceives and communicates with her child through every cell of her body. Feminine wisdom and intuition is deeply connected to the body, to cellular awareness and intelligence.

The mother who is in touch with herself in this way is able to nurture in her child a healthy relationship to her own body and body wisdom; from this a healthy relationship to feelings and self can more readily develop. She sees from her heart – she sees her child for what she is and not for what she does. If the mother herself has not experienced this quality of holding as a child, the validation of her feminine being, and acceptance of her self for who she truly and uniquely is, she may not be able to convey such loving security to her own daughter – unless she has been able, through later positive life experiences, to learn it, through loving relationships, healing bodywork, or psychotherapy for example, or through deep suffering and surrender.

Not all modern women pass on this inheritance to their daughters, but it has become an increasingly widespread phenomenon of our western culture, and one that, like child abuse, will likely be passed down through generations until awareness of the need for healing is awakened. Joseph Chilton Pearce describes the results of research done by Marcelle Geber into birthing and child-rearing practices in Kenya and Uganda:

'She found the most precocious, brilliant, and advanced infants and children ever observed anywhere. These infants had smiled, continuously and rapturously, from, at least, their fourth day of life. Blood analyses showed that all the adrenal steroids connected with birth stress were totally absent by that fourth day after birth. Sensorimotor learning and general development were phenomenal, indeed miraculous. These Ugandan infants were months ahead of American and European children... .

'These infants were born in the home, generally delivered by the mother herself. The child was never separated from the mother, who massaged, caressed, sang to, and fondled her infant continually. The mother carried her unswaddled infant in a sling, next to her bare breasts, continually. She slept with her infant. The infant fed continuously, according to its own schedule. These infants were awake a surprising amount of time – alert, watchful, happy, calm. They virtually never cried. Their mothers were bonded to them and sensed their every need before that need had to be expressed by crying. The mother responded to the infant's every gesture and assisted the child in any and every move that was undertaken, so that every move initiated by the child ended in immediate success. At two days of age (forty-eight hours) these infants sat bolt upright, held only by the forearms, with a beautifully straight back and perfect head balance, their finely focused eyes staring intently, intelligently at their mothers. And they smiled and smiled.'[14]

This is a far cry from the experience of many western mothers and babies, particularly during the last several decades, as Pearce so poignantly describes. Women have been alienated from their natural childbearing instincts, subjected to the male authority of medical practice and hospital procedures. The power of woman in this, one of her most intimate functions, has been largely usurped by male ideology. Lilith has been controlled, disempowered, shackled to the hospital bed. The Goddess has been denied her place as mediator of birth and death by the sterilising procedures of western medical practice. No one would deny its value in special circumstances, but we must deeply question the attitudes behind such practice, and the results of denying women their natural childbirth rights. (It was apparently Louis XIV who first introduced the practice of making women lie on their backs to give birth, which inevitably creates a more passive attitude and a more difficult and painful birth for both mother and child, so that he could watch the whole procedure as his own children were born!)

Ideology about the care of the infant and child after birth has also been dominated by the beliefs and requirements of this same patriarchal authority. Women of this century, often lacking the opportunity to learn in a natural way about the care of their children from their mothers and grandmothers, through the breakdown of the extended family, and robbed of confidence in their own feminine authority through centuries of gradual but insidious erosion, have turned to male ideologies in their uncertainty. They have been told, for example, that it is good to let the infant cry until exhaustion brings on sleep; that they should not feed on demand or pamper to its every need, but should introduce discipline from the very earliest age. Anyone who has relived their experience of this kind of practice, perhaps through experiential therapy or crises which evoke preverbal memory, will understand the wrongness and cruelty of it. Pearce's description offers a persuasive argument for the natural alternative, the mother's own instinctive wisdom.

In ancient Tibet, I have been told, it was a custom after the birth of a child for the mother and baby to retreat together for the first month after birth. They would be cared for, but have minimal contact with the outside world, including other family members. This was seen as an important time for the mother and her child to spend together, without other responsibilities and obligations that might take her attention and energy away from the new infant. Time for the bonding process was given absolute priority. In the west the new mother often withdraws into post-natal depression; perhaps this is a sign of the need for a time of quiet retreat.

For the Tibetans, the love of a child for her mother is also an extremely important element of their Buddhist religion; the mother is always loved and treated with the greatest respect. The Tibetan people are well known for their warmth, humour, and an aura of happiness and enjoyment that radiates from them. Despite the terrible destruction of their homeland by the invading Chinese, their indomitable spirit and good nature still shines through. I cannot help but wonder if this is not in some part due to their understanding of the needs of the young child, and the honour with which the mother is regarded. Such a healthy mother-child relationship must also provide a good foundation for the spiritual practice of the Tibetan people; with a positive experience of early holding, the states of consciousness accessed through meditation practice may be more easily contained and integrated, and the dangers of disintegration less likely to occur.

The issue for us in the modern world goes deeper and deeper still. We live in a society that has lost connection with the earth. We walk not on the earth, but on concrete; when we travel at high speeds by car, train, and especially aeroplane, we lose our ground. Always travelling so fast, we do not give ourselves the time that is needed to connect to the earth, to surrender our weight to gravity, even as we walk. It takes time and a certain kind of attentiveness to maintain an internal relationship with the earth. We hold ourselves up, and we hold ourselves back, unconsciously knowing that we are rushing ahead too fast for our own good, and this creates patterns of tension and pain in the body.

There is a story of a native American who was offered a lift in their car by some white men passing by. He accepted, and travelled with them for some hours. On arriving at his destination, he simply sat down by the roadside. They asked why he was sitting there, as they had now arrived. He replied that now he would have to wait two days for his soul to catch up with him. In my work at the moment it is necessary for me to do a lot of travelling by air, and I know exactly what the old man meant!

In our everyday living, many of the tasks that should involve us intimately with the earth have become mechanised, and city life has taken us further and further away from nature and her cycles. Food comes from the supermarket, not the earth. We can easily become oblivious to the changes of the moon, and even forget to notice the rising and setting of the sun, or the beauty of the changing of the seasons. Life has become one long effort to control or outwit nature in so many different ways. In losing the earth, we also lose the natural connection to our body and its instincts, the sensitivity to its rhythms and processes. To the Ugandan woman, the degree of constant care and sensitivity to her infant's needs would be natural and easy, an instinctive response from her own nature to the nature of her child. This attentiveness would seem to most western women to be impossible, for our bodies and sensitivities are no longer so well attuned, our ground within forsaken. If not coming from our natural body wisdom and sensitivity, such continual attentiveness and care would feel like an endless chore and a burden.

The splitting-off of children, and hence also mothers, from the 'more important' business of adult life and work is a fundamental problem in modern society. As the workplace has become alienated from home life, women have to make uncomfortable choices between career and family, and as mothers, they must often choose between social isolation, or abandonment of their children to the care of others. Workplace and workers alike are no longer oriented towards the inclusion of children in the midst of life. It is not so for the woman in a society living close to the earth, who will be going about her daily tasks, probably in the company of other women, as she carries her 'unswaddled infant in a sling, next to her bare breasts'. This can only be done with comfort and dignity in a society that is accepting of the presence of the mother-and-child, and comfortable with the sight of the sacred body of motherhood.

Our society is not truly accepting of this, and still gives mothering a place inferior in importance to that of achievement in the working world. Many women have also bought into this attitude. Pearce, describing how a woman at home in her pregnancy may feel, writes:

'She knows that the creation of life is the greatest of human acts and that the successful nurturing of a new life is a consummate art, greater even than being a successful accountant or advertising executive.

'She conceives because she wants to create life, as her intent drives her. Her pregnancy is then first in her life and the source of her strength and calm. She knows the creative thrust of life supports her, that she is acting with the flow and has the strength of that flow.'[15]

I am certainly not suggesting that a woman *only* feels the 'creative thrust of life' supporting her in pregnancy and motherhood. Today women are finally able to express their creative, nurturing, and life-enhancing qualities in many different ways and areas of life, both in and outside of the home, and rightly so. We do not have to be mothers in order to experience and express ourselves fully as women; such a judgement is a patriarchal way of oppressing women, and it really is time that society, men and women and alike, accepted that motherhood is not the only path to feminine maturity and wholeness. However, for many women it is a very important one.

As Jean Shinoda Bolen describes, every woman can be influenced by a number of very different archetypes which will shape her life accordingly.[16] For example, Artemis, Goddess of the Hunt and of the Moon, and Athena, Warrior-Goddess and Goddess of Wisdom may be strong forces in a woman's psyche, and she will find fulfilment in an individual life path which does not necessarily include, or require, marriage and motherhood. Another woman may be strongly influenced by the power or Demeter, the Earth Mother, or Hera, the Wife. Each woman has a right to the freedom to choose her own individual path.

However, it is still a concern that modern women may be at risk of losing the positive, instinctual connection to the process of creating and nurturing new life, and the self-affirming and life-affirming experience that pregnancy and motherhood may give. Some women may choose not to have children as a negative reaction to the burden of motherhood, or out of fear that they may not be able to give to a child what they have not received themselves, rather than as a positive choice coming from genuine feeling and the wish to direct creative energies towards other forms of expression.

We can trace roots of this dilemma back to the patriarchal fear, repression, and devaluing of the feminine, of woman herself, and all that pertains specifically to womanhood. The tasks and crafts that have naturally and traditionally been her domain, her special gifts and qualities, her intuitive wisdom and intelligence, and the work of bearing and mothering children, have all been devalued in patriarchal society. In this, the child herself is also devalued, and is inevitably wounded in her sense of self-love and worth as a human being.

A significant argument has also been put forward by feminist writers and some psychologists: as women are generally the primary and sometimes sole caregivers of children, early experiences of frustration, helplessness, impotence, and fear become associated in each person's unconscious with the mother. Later on these deep feelings of fear and rage are projected onto women in general, resulting in aggressive and controlling behaviour in men; feelings of low self-esteem and self-hatred develop in many women whose own self-image is formed out of the internalised image of a negative mother. And so the vicious cycle is perpetuated. Although the women's movement has won for women many opportunities and improved social status, the change to truly honouring and valuing woman and *all* of the qualities she embodies is slow; women's liberation and equality will be only skin deep until deeply embedded attitudes within both men and women change, and the authentic feminine is truly accepted and valued.

We become daughters of the patriarch when we have not been validated in our essence as women by mothers who know that essential nature in themselves. Marion Woodman describes this, the emptiness of self that unmothered women come to feel, and the negative relationship to their own femininity and their female bodies, which results in an 'Addiction to Perfection'. We will never easily, nor without great cost to ourselves, be as good as men in doing things 'men's way', and in our efforts to overcome the feelings of inadequacy, we strive endlessly towards a masculine model of excellence and achievement. It is well known that women in business must work and excel far more than their male contemporaries in order to reach the same status or level of promotion and income.

We will continue to feel like failures, and exhaust ourselves in the process, until we learn what it is to really do things 'in our own way' and have the courage to stand by that knowledge. In denying our feminine selves, we deny our bodies, our creativity, and our intelligence. Woodman, researching the psychology of eating disorders in women, describes the way in which these deep-rooted conflicts are embodied in destructive patterns of addiction and denial of the feminine body. We internalise the abuse that has been heaped upon us as women through generations, and act it out in various forms of self-negation and abuse against our own bodies. Overeating, not eating, drinking or drug-taking, depressive illness, overwork, punishing exercise regimes, or denying our selves and our bodies pleasure and rest, are some of the ways we may continue the abuses against our own persons as women.

Many women today must juggle the demands of a career with family life, sometimes with success, sometimes with exhaustion or dissatisfaction. But the answer doesn't lie in juggling the 'what we do' of our lives, but in transforming the quality of engagement with life by connecting to the 'who we are'. From here, we can make choices out of our own deepest needs, desires, and values about what we really want to give to and receive from life. Without connection to our inner authority and creativity, we may suffer from a need to remain weak and dependent on patriarchal power, or to be unnaturally strong in the face of it, competing for power and position in the world on the terms and values of this authority, not our own.

The process of redeeming the feminine within us often means facing an immense depth of pain, for the wounding reaches back through generations, through centuries of patriarchal culture in almost every part of the world. As we begin to connect to our own wounded feminine, we feel the pain of the wounding of the earth herself, of children starving in a world where there is plenty for all, of the homeless and exiled, of battered wives and abused children, of women victimised, oppressed and raped, the pain of our own mothers and grandmothers, and of the sensitive, vulnerable hearts of men who have been taught to deny this part of themselves.

When we first begin to awaken to the abuse of the feminine by the patriarchy, we may identify closely with the environmental rape we see all around us. Identifying with the suffering of the earth and collective womanhood, we are prey to anxieties, phobias, paranoia, and depression. The pain and rage of the repressed feminine, the Dark Goddess is deep, and it must be heard. She challenges the patriarchy that fears her, fears the chaotic power of her dark realm, her wrathful and destructive forces, and will try to put her down or patronise her into silence. But it is also attachment to the masculinised ego of the woman who has accepted, succumbed to, rebelled against, or struggled to be part of a distorted patriarchal power, which is challenged and must die, in order that we may live in the world fully as women, valued and valuing ourselves. Children will continue to be wounded by the absence of the mother, and all of us will suffer the consequences of this, until the wound of the feminine is healed.

A friend of mine who lived for some time in Bali recounted the loving respect with which all children were treated there. Their spirit was never belittled, or their needs subordinated to the wishes of adults. They grew up happy and content, feeling themselves valued as human beings. A child that grows up feeling valued will learn to value others more easily and naturally; the sickness of the modern world is that we have lost the ability to value the life of others as much as our own. We need to relearn the respect that was a natural ability for those cultures in which motherhood and childhood were revered as expressions of the sacredness of life, and the well-being of the community as a whole was every individual's concern.

The Journey of Descent

During a course on women's creativity that I led, one woman commented that we are always 'trying' to be women, rather than just 'being' women. We exhaust our resources in this futile striving. As their explorations of their creativity led them to contact themselves more deeply, almost unanimously these women felt that, for them, creativity primarily meant *being* and *feeling* creative in the ordinary, everyday details of their lives – feeling the magic of the moment, rather than *doing* creative things and *achieving* great goals. Of course there is also a place for doing and achieving, but so often in our goal-oriented approach to life we miss the magic of the moment and the joy of the creative process itself. For expressions and models of the creative feminine, these women found themselves looking to images from other cultures, for our culture has lost its own symbols of woman in her wholeness and creative power. In the images they were drawn to, these women felt the presence of Woman in her Being-ness – earthy, sensual, confident in her beauty and sexuality, her own feminine power embodied. There is a deep need for us, as women today, to rediscover from within ourselves those long-lost images of the feminine which will give meaning to our deepest experience of ourselves as women, redefining and expressing this in terms of our own subjective values, rather than as masculine ideals.

Connecting to our deep feminine nature involves letting go, at least for a while, of all the 'doings' that we have adopted as reactive patterns, and relearning what it really means to 'be' as women. It requires a journey of descent, a sacrifice of the masculinised ego to the feminine ground of being. In a culture that views growth as a continual and linear, upward path of progress, there has been an emphasis on the type of male heroic journey that is an ascent, a journey into adventure and the heights of conquest, achievement, and transcendence of physical and human limitations. The hero seeks the realms of light and spirit, but the hero also dies young. A symbol for ambitious masculine consciousness, Icarus was one such hero who flew too close to the sun, was burnt and suffered a humiliating fall. The life of soul and spirit require us to make journeys of both ascent and descent, and today we are being called to redress a tendency of our culture to see growth and development of consciousness as only an upward and accumulative movement. We must also descend through the depths of the deep psyche to the realm of the Dark Goddess, the place of undoing, to the creative ground of the feminine within.

> 'Depth is as important as height: the descent is the way of releasing and manifesting the divine into the world of action.'[17]

It is a process of renewal and regeneration without which life becomes dry and sterile, meaningless and unsanctified – a process as natural as the turning of the tide – but as Maureen Murdock writes *in The Heroine's Journey*:

> 'Like most journeys, the path of the heroine is not easy; it has no well-defined guideposts nor recognizable tour guides. There is no map, no navigational chart, no chronological age when the journey begins. It follows no straight lines. It is a journey that seldom receives validation from the outside world; in fact the outer world often sabotages and interferes with it.'[18]

For these reasons it is essential that we as women learn to share our experiences and support each other in these passages. For too long now, the woman on this journey has been outcast or branded as 'crazy', 'witch', or 'madwoman'. Today we can begin to redeem our madness by reclaiming the creativity and spirit that has been buried beneath the stigma of the labels of insanity or witch.

There is darkness within the light, as Icarus' story shows us; so too is there light within the dark, but we must journey deep to meet it. We must journey through the void of existence to touch the feminine ground of being, before we can truly open to the light of the creative spirit within us. I had a dream some years ago, which seemed to describe and prophesy the journey of descent I was soon to embark upon. My spiritual teacher had given me a scroll on which was a copy of a meditation practice. As we unrolled it, it turned out to be an enormous thangka, a picture as large as the room. At the top was a beautiful verse, decorated and written in illuminated letters – it said something about 'light' and 'thy world' – I don't recall the exact phrase. Most of the painting was in dark subdued colours and it seemed to tell the story of the journey in pictures, winding down from the top to the bottom. Here and there were small illuminated sections that coincided with particular points in the story that the images were telling. At the very bottom, shining out amidst the dark colours, was a final image ablaze with light. I was struck by a profound sense of beauty and meaningfulness as I contemplated the numinous image.

The journey of descent is not just a way through to the light; it is a way in itself – the way of deepening, of endarkenment. There can be no wholeness unless both dimensions are embraced. Bika Reed states:

> 'Illumination, like the sun has its day and its night. In the human dimension, despair is night and like the night, has its function…the soul is…directing the man's intention to the light beyond duality, from which both day and night emanate. The night is thus incorporated into the Light, although rationally incomparable with the day. The sunset has its spiritual function, as does decline and despair in man.'[19]

In our actual lived experience, the descent is often felt to be a journey of hopeless decline and the deepest despair. It is a journey of conscious suffering, fear, and danger. In order that we might touch again the deeper strength and wisdom which lies within us, we must feel and penetrate the pain of all that we have endured, the grief of what has been lost, the anguish, fear, and shame that haunts us. We become for a time weakened, so raw and vulnerable, as we pare away the layers that hide our inner self, ineffective in our doings in the world. This journey is more about being than travelling, for in the infinite depths of this dark place to which the soul descends there is no sense of place or path, nowhere to move towards or through. There is only being there, enduring the fall, the pain, the terror of being no one nowhere. We fall into the empty chasm within our hearts, the void left by the absent mother and the Goddess in exile, like a black hole in space which seems to suck all into it. Time and space lose their ordinary meaning. There is nothing to touch, nothing to do, nowhere to travel, and yet there is also much travelling and much to be touched by in this dark place. Even if light is seen or its presence felt, we cannot move towards or touch or pass through or into it, for it has no place or path that leads to it. We can but wait in the dying, and in the death and the waiting we learn to simply be. The journey into the deep feminine is not about going, but about coming more deeply into where we are, becoming present to what truly is, not seeking for what is beyond.

Myths to Guide Us – The Path of Trials

When we embark on the underworld journey and find ourselves submerged in unfamiliar realms of the unconscious psyche, we are treading the paths worn by the gods and goddesses of antiquity, whose stories may help to guide and orientate us in those places where we feel most lost. Myth, as Larsen points out, has always served two distinct but intrinsically related purposes within human society:

> 'We have, then, two dimensions of mythology which must be distinguished: the culture-bound aspect, which has a primarily socializing function, which I shall define as *orientation*, and the psychological aspect that lends depth and richness to human existence, whatever its setting, which I shall call *guidance*.'[20]

The socialising function has a stabilising and unifying effect upon the community, as expressed in the cosmology, art and ritual, the moral standards, religious and social traditions of the culture. However, to serve this function, mythology must speak to the hearts and souls of the people in a way that is meaningful and inspiratory. When this ceases to be the case:

> 'Whenever religious traditions have grown stale and outworn, there has come a time of psychological unease: dissatisfaction, criticism, alienation...
>
> 'At such times the visionary quest must again become dominant over the traditional religious forms. Man needs a living mythology

that springs out of the present conditions of his living, his joys and sorrows, fears and expectations. Guidance, the psychological aspect of myth, must continually be renewed within the experiencing of everyman, as he uses myth to measure his experience and finds that experience in turn must be the measure of myth.'[21]

It is the psychological aspect of myth, and its function of guidance for the individual's inner journeying, that I wish to explore here. We are at such a time of psychological unease, and it is down into the inner deep psyche that we must voyage on our quest to be touched by our innermost spirit, and connect with the myth which will bring meaning and healing to the fragments of our lives.

The deeper we travel, the more multi-dimensional and chaotic is our experience, for the depths of psyche are not ordered and organised as is the world of ego-mind. As we gain access to the deeper layers of the psyche, we encounter an intricate web of threads, interconnected stories that together create the fabric of our lives. Traditionally weaving has been a woman's skill, and psychologically it is one of the processes associated with the feminine, and the Goddess. Hence as we journey to the ground of the feminine within, we weave and are woven into the web of our own life story. In using the ancient myths to guide us in our quest, we need to keep a flexible and open mind, one that can include the many layers of experience and meaning simultaneously, and can hold the apparent contradictions and paradoxes without attempting to order them in a too rigidly linear or conceptual fashion. This is feminine consciousness, the mind which can allow disparate things to exist in relationship and dance together, without grasping too quickly for definition and certainty. Out of this attitude of mind can arise creative insight and intuitive knowing. It is in this way that we may approach an understanding of the deeper levels of the psyche, and give birth to that understanding through the discovery of new myths, new rituals, new definitions, and new values that speak to our present circumstances.

There are many myths and stories that tell of the hero's journey, but not so many remaining today which offer guidance to the heroine on her quest. In many of the patriarchal myths, the feminine, in the form of the female characters of the stories, is invariably defined and portrayed in relationship to the hero as his mother, lover, daughter, sister, or friend, for example; she may play essential roles in his unfolding drama as the helper, comforter, muse, damsel-in-distress, seductress, or downfall of the male, but she is usually on the periphery of the main drama, and does not really have a life and identity of her own apart from her relationship to masculine subjectivity.

In *Return of the Goddess*, Whitmont proposes the Grail legend as the myth that will guide us in our transition into the new age. Whilst appreciating the psychological depth and relevance of this myth for our time, it has never quite fully touched my heart and soul, never brought forth that deep sigh of recognition. For me it cannot be more than half of the myth that will guide us into the new age; it offers a vision of the quest for wholeness and spiritual integration from the masculine perspective, from the standpoint of a male-oriented culture and masculine consciousness, but the feminine is still portrayed as other, as object and not subject, peripheral to the central actions performed by the male characters. It offers guidance to the hero in his quest for a much-needed new way of relating to life, to the feminine, and to the divine, but does not speak so directly to the experience of the heroine and the very particular quest she today finds herself confronted with – that of healing the wound of the feminine within herself, of reclaiming her own subjectivity and spirituality, and finding new ways to relate from there to the masculine.

In the myth, the hero, Gawain, comes to understand that what is needed of him is 'to give sovereignty to the Goddess', his inner feminine. I have heard men interpret this on the interpersonal level as man needing to give sovereignty to woman, but this is to misunderstand woman's deepest need today, and risk further patronising her. In this interpretation, he continues to see the flesh-and-blood woman as a projection of his own sacred feminine. What woman really needs is to reclaim her subjectivity, her self-entitlement, and hence her genuine existence; it is only when she does not have this that she may seem to require 'sovereignty'. Before there can be a true meeting and marriage of the masculine and feminine, and an equal participation in the world by both men and women, woman needs to rediscover, redefine, and express who she is in her wholeness. She must do this on her own terms and not in relation to the needs and ideologies of men conditioned by the patriarchy. She needs to find her own myths to guide her in this.

There probably were many more myths of the heroine's journey alive in the matriarchal age than there are today. We know that many myths were rewritten by the patriarchal fathers to reflect the then new consciousness and male-oriented world view. However, there are a few surviving stories of the descent of the Goddess still known to us today, which show us that the heroine's journey to the underworld was recognised and understood by ancient cultures. Although we may feel more personally connected to one particular version, they each offer variations on this universal theme which can be helpful as maps for different stages and aspects of our own unfolding journey. Different aspects and depths of our own psyche may resonate with the various expressions of the age-old theme of descent, depending on the particularities of our own character and life experiences, as well as the age and culture we live in. Yet the underlying universal themes are clearly as relevant for women today as they were several thousand years ago. Today women are again beginning to consciously recognise and own the inner psychological meaning that the myths hold for them, and are also beginning to refuse to allow their experience of the descent to be scorned, interfered with, sabotaged, drugged out of existence, or even outlawed, as it has been for many centuries now.

The myth of Kore-Persephone is one of the most well-known, and has become popular in the area of archetypal psychology as a model of the path towards maturity of the feminine psyche. In this Greek version of the descent myth, the heroine Persephone is portrayed as the archetype of youthful beauty, innocence, and virginal purity. In order that she may grow into her wholeness as a woman, she must die to her innocence and a narcissistic preoccupation with her own beauty. She is snatched from the loving protection of her devoted mother Demeter, Earth Goddess, by Hades, God of the Underworld, taken to his realm and raped. She must remain there as his bride. She learns the price of beauty.

Eventually she is permitted by Zeus to return to the earth each spring-time, bringing the beauty and freshness of new life back with her; as it fades with the coming of autumn and winter she must descend again to the underworld. Her initiation into death in the underworld has brought her to experience the dark side of nature and the wisdom of the cycles of creation, destruction, transformation, and rebirth. It has made her whole. She becomes Goddess of the Underworld and of the transformational processes of death and rebirth. Reborn again to the upper world each spring, she also holds the secret of eternal youth and beauty.

In his book on feminine psychology, *She*, Robert Johnson describes how a woman might experience such an initiation through marriage. Psychologically a man gains something through marriage, but to a woman it is a psychological death. She must lose in order to gain.[22] Traditionally in the death-marriage she sacrifices her maidenhood, her family, and her name, in order to enter into her full womanhood through the union. This need not necessarily be initiated by an outer marriage; the process may be an inner event, a marriage of the masculine and feminine sides of the woman's nature. The work of psychotherapy may itself provide the initiating and penetrating force that carries the virgin soul into the underworld of death, and 'violates' its innocence with experience of the darker side of life. Life itself presents us with many such assaults, crises which precipitate a journey of initiation into full and conscious womanhood.

The myth of Kore-Persephone differs from the story of Inanna-Ereshkigal (which will be explored in the next chapter) in the motivating force behind the descent. Inanna is the woman of worldly experience and position who chooses her own path with conscious awareness, whereas Persephone, the vulnerable one, is innocently seized and made victim of another's intentions. Both archetypes may be operating within us, each in its own sphere of psychic activity. Yet I feel that the myth of Kore-Persephone does not speak so directly to the central experience of many modern women. It presupposes an idyllic, innocent and carefree, psychologically virgin existence close to the bosom of a loving, nurturing, protecting earth mother; her initiation into womanhood involves a brutal separation from the positive mother. She is initiated by and into the masculine, but this can only happen because she is well grounded in her own feminine being through the positive relationship she enjoyed with her mother.

This has not been the experience of many women today; many have not felt so loved and cherished, and many have witnessed or experienced events early in life which have brutally shattered their innocence even as young children. It is difficult for the daughter of even the most loving parents today not to grow up with some knowledge, and often personal experience, of 'man's inhumanity to man' and the suffering side of life, which has darkened the light of her 'Garden of Eden' experience. This must be taken into account before assuming a young woman is psychologically virginal and innocent, or grounded within her feminine self by a positive experience of the mother archetype. The myth of Persephone, as it is known today, may relate to a very early initiation through childhood trauma or abuse, or to women's collective rape through generations. If a woman has not experienced a truly positive, nurturing, and protective relationship with her mother, the experience of her core psyche may be of a different pattern of initiation that involves the Goddess in her dark and destructive aspect.

The Kore-Persephone myth does not touch so directly upon the nature of the original wounding of a woman's relationship with the feminine ground and mother-archetype. When the Goddess has been absent in her experience, a woman's quest is not of being returned to something she has previously been torn away from, but of seeking and discovering that which she has not yet known. For modern women the Goddess is in exile and cannot search for us; we have to go to her, join her in the wilderness. For a woman of the modern world the journey *to* the exiled Goddess relates to a more fundamental level of experience than the story of the abduction and rape of Kore-Persephone, which comes from an essentially patriarchal perspective. We are raped when we have been denied our power, our self-entitlement, and the feminine ground within which we stand, and thus we cannot protect ourselves. We are initiated when we reclaim this ground as our own.

The Roman myth of Psyche and Eros offers a beautiful rendering of the heroine's descent by way of Psyche's search for her beloved Eros, the God of Love, and their eventual joyful reunion in heaven. This myth speaks to the 'awakening of the sleeping soul through love',[23] of the human being touched by the divine, and is another way of initiation into psychological and spiritual maturity for woman, and for the feminine principle in man. It also describes another aspect of the journey – the series of trials that are encountered on the way. Psyche is put through a series of tests that enable her to access specific qualities and powers through surrendering to something beyond her ordinary capabilities.

The path of trials represents a way of psycho-spiritual integration and strengthening, whereby she can become grounded in the deep feminine and thus develop a sustaining relationship to her inner masculine. The trials she undergoes and the suffering she endures serve to initiate and prepare her for the divine marriage with the god Eros. They also remind us that this path is fraught with difficulties of all kinds and requires hard work and perseverance. There is no sudden release or breakthrough, but many successive crises, ordeals, victories, and failures following one upon the other. At each trial Psyche descends deeper and can consciously integrate a little more of her own powers and insight.

Like Persephone, we see Psyche at the beginning of the story as a paragon of beauty and innocent purity. So perfect is she that no man dare court her, but she is admired, even worshipped far and wide as the new Goddess. This leaves Psyche terribly lonely, her parents, the king and queen, distraught, and Aphrodite, the old Goddess of femininity and love, jealous and outraged that her place was about to be usurped by another, and a human at that. She plots to have Psyche destroyed through a marriage to the vile monster Death, but her plan takes an unexpected turn when her son Eros, the god of love and emissary of her fateful wishes, himself falls in love with the beautiful maiden and carries her off to a heavenly paradise to be his own bride. She is content for a time to live in a state of blissful but unconscious rapture in this magical nowhere world, where she is not allowed to know the true identity of her lover.

> 'Psyche is even forbidden to see her lover; she must know him only in the dark. The reason for this no-place atmosphere is that in the search of our own psyche for the god, for the agent of transformation, the two poles of heaven and earth, the realms of essence and existence are too extreme for the requirements of this mysterious conjunction. They are either too subtle or too strong. Thus Eros, as the intermediary between worlds, must create the world-in-between, providing sacred time and space to do the work of love and transformation. He has created a chrysalis from which the butterfly may emerge.' [24]

This magical world is the world of the imaginal, the crucible of gestation and transformation that must be retreated to in preparation for the initiatory tasks ahead, but it cannot be known or expressed in the language of the everyday: hence Psyche's enforced unconsciousness at the beginning. But she is not to be allowed to remain unconscious forever; her path is to grow into maturity through facing, after all, the death that Aphrodite had planned for her. Made to question and doubt by her visiting sisters, she finally does the forbidden thing; in the night, when Eros sleeps beside her, she lights a lamp and looks upon his face. She sees that he is not the vile snake, the monster that her sisters had warned her of, but in fact the God of Love himself. She accidentally pricks herself on one of his arrows and falls in love with him, with love itself; but she has disobeyed and the result is that Eros flees, burnt by oil from the lamp she has accidentally spilt on him.

The dream has vanished, the glimpse of divine love gone. Eros the god is burnt by the oil, tortured by his love for a human being, and Psyche is awakened to suffering and the pain of loss. Despairing and suicidal, Psyche searches for Eros everywhere. She implores the gods to help her but none dare defy Aphrodite's will. Yet, through the experience of love and suffering, the path towards her maturity and wholeness as a woman is opened to her. The wounding is the door through which she will eventually become fully conscious and complete as woman, both human and divine.

Before this can happen, Psyche must pass through a series of impossible trials set for her by the vengeful Aphrodite. Aphrodite is the one who actually initiates Psyche, through setting the initiatory ordeals that she must undergo. At each task Psyche falls into despair and tries to kill herself, but each time, just as she is about to give up, assistance comes. First, an army of ants, symbolic of instinctive forces of the psyche, help her to sort a great pile of seeds. Then a reed in the water advises her on how to collect just a small amount of the golden fleece, and avoid engaging directly the powerful energy of the rams. In the third task, Zeus sends his eagle to collect a small amount of the Waters of Life in a crystal goblet, and so saves her from the dragons that guard the Waters. At each task Psyche, by giving up her conscious will, surrenders to a power beyond her known resources, and through this she is able to integrate these attributes into her personality. Her suicidal impulses can be seen as attempts to let die an old consciousness and way of being, in order that she is deepened to a new one.

Many real-life heroines, like Psyche, also mistake this symbolic movement towards a psychological death and act out the impulse to tragic ends. What the myth tells us is that in the moment of giving in, the help we need is there; what we need to do is to yield, to *give over to*, rather than *give up*, in order to be able to perceive and be receptive to the level from which help and guidance comes, to be able to see and hear the messages from the 'other world'.

Psyche's fourth and last task is the most difficult and fearful of all, and one that most people do not undertake. She must go to the underworld and get from Persephone a jar of her own beauty ointment. The journey to the underworld is a task of a different order; the ordeals undergone there should not be approached without preparation. Robert Johnson writes of this:

> 'A woman may not undertake the fourth task unless she has first gathered all the necessary strength from the first three. Almost always one needs a teacher or a guide, and unless one has the strength and courage, it is best not to undertake the fourth task. It is a terrible experience to be stranded partway through the underworld journey. Unless one has the coins, the barley bread, and, most important of all, the necessary information gathered from the tower, one should not begin this journey.'[25]

In reality, the path of trials does not always unfold in the order set out in the myth. Sometimes we may be hurled headlong, or have to go out of necessity on this forbidding journey, before the other tasks are complete and we are fully prepared. I believe that more and more people are being called to this task today, whether personally ready or not, because it is a task of our times. We often find ourselves struggling with several of the tasks at once; or after surviving a premature descent to the underworld, having to go back and complete other tasks as part of the integrating process. Without proper guidance, the journey is anguish-ridden and dangerous. However, the myth points us towards potentialities; Psyche, by now well prepared and spiritually strengthened through having successfully completed her previous ordeals, is ready for her last test. Again, she first attempts suicide, but this time she is stopped and given guidance and very precise instructions by the tower from which she would have thrown herself. Johnson describes the tower thus:

> 'First one finds a proper tower, a human construction. The tower is masculine, a construct, a convention, a set of rules, a tradition, a system. Christianity is such a tower of strength and one of the best ones for us Westerners. Excellent examples of such towers are the spiritual exercises of Ignatius of Loyola, the lives of the saints, the liturgical year, and Christian retreats. Besides our own culture, there are many systems of yoga, Sufi mysticism, Zen, and other Oriental towers.'[26]

The tower is essential to the safety and success of the underworld journey. Whilst Christianity may be the way for some, I don't feel that it is necessarily the best tower for all of us – conventional Christianity is fundamentally dualistic, and a dualistic belief system may not adequately contain the consciousness encountered in this depth of journey. The non-dualism of most eastern philosophies may offer to some a more appropriate holding structure for the depth encounter. As Stephen Larsen says:

> 'The sacred reality of one's childhood indoctrination is entwined with an archetype and not easily expelled. Intellectual decisions do not really affect it, at root; nor do scientific beliefs. What may be needed to transform it, revitalize it, is another, perhaps complementary, alternative mythic system.'[27]

If we do adopt another mythic and spiritual system, from eastern traditions for example, or a deeper understanding of our own western mystical traditions, we need a time of preparation. We must build our tower and integrate its strength within us in such a way as may provide genuine support and guidance throughout our depth encounters. As Larsen points out, intellectual decision is not sufficient to affect a deep-seated archetypal pattern. We need to engage and immerse our psyche in the new mythic system in order to establish a meaningful relationship with it, and allow our sacred reality to be transformed. The foundation practices of a spiritual tradition, whatever form they may take, constitute the creation of a relationship to the tower, which can serve as guidance and support throughout the depth journey. Without this we may become lost and overwhelmed by unconsciousness or psychosis. If the foundations of one's tower are undermined by another's influence or will during the descent to the underworld, it may collapse just at the time when its support is most critical.

It is important to enter the underworld in full consciousness, aware of the purpose and meaning of one's task. To fall unconscious at this point may lead to pathology. Psyche does well; she keeps focussed on her task and follows the instructions given to her, receives from Persephone the jar of beauty ointment, but at the very last moment, when she has succeeded in her task and is returning with the priceless prize, her human weakness overcomes her. She cannot resist opening the jar, but instead of finally witnessing the gift of eternal youth and beauty Psyche falls into a death-like sleep. After all she has endured and gained, the impulsiveness of her all-too-human vanity, desire, and curiosity defeats her at the very last step of her journey. Yet it is in this moment of her symbolic death, which looks like her final undoing, that Eros can finally rescue her. He takes her to Olympus where Psyche is made a Goddess, and the sacred marriage takes place. We can assume that Eros was somehow behind the help that Psyche received throughout her tasks, but he has to wait for the right moment before he can intervene directly. The moment is when, after preparing and strengthening herself through completing successfully all the tasks, Psyche falls into unconsciousness; her old self symbolically dies in this moment. In this void of consciousness the god can enter and the transformation take place. Jean Houston writes of this:

> 'If, in the middle of the dark descent into yourself, you return to old consciousness or neglect to follow the discipline of your personal tower, you will probably fall into one or another kind of deep, deep sleep. But this need not be pathology, but rather, as in the story, the entrance into a place of deep gestation, like Jonah in the belly of the whale. Here you undergo the fetal sleep that prepares you for life lived out of a fullness you never knew before. In this place and time of gestation you are tended by the deep Eros powers of nature, of goddedness, of patterns of evolutionary quickening. These powers can now help you, for they recognize you as having opened to your many latent capacities of psyche by virtue of being seeded with instinct. You have gained the golden strength, received the waters of life, become mindful, suffered deeply, and are now ready for transformation.'[28]

This may be the time when we learn a genuine attitude of prayer. It is a time when we learn to wait patiently through the suffering and, remaking our connection with Mother Earth, find deep solace in nature and slowly allow her to heal us. It is the crucial time of surrendering personal will and allowing a deeper level of being to emerge to consciousness and inform our lives. In the death-sleep we reconnect to our intuitive wisdom and the wordless knowledge of the Goddess; only through this can the sacred marriage with the God within be fulfilled.

The myth of Psyche and Eros tells of the path of awakening through divine love and longing for the Beloved. It describes the spiritual quest as the heroine's journey towards integration of the human and divine, and of the masculine and feminine aspects of her nature. In particular this story speaks to the relationship between personal and divine will, to the necessity of surrender through deepening of consciousness, by which we are touched by the divine.

The trials of Psyche also show us that there are stages on the path; once one task has been completed and a level of psychological integration achieved, we are confronted with the next in an uncompromising succession of ordeals. When we seem to have won through and are then plunged back into despair, it is not necessarily a sign of failure, this story reassures us; we simply have not completed all the tasks, and so we cycle through the ups and downs of despair and release, as we gradually integrate the strength to confront new levels. This aspect of Psyche's story can help us to accept those inevitable turns, and to find the courage to go on through some of the darkest moments.

I have found both of these myths helpful in shedding light on aspects of my personal journey, but it is in the myth of Inanna-Ereshkigal that I feel the deepest sense of recognition and validation of my own inner experience. This myth, when I first discovered it through Sylvia Brinton Perera's insightful book, *Descent to the Goddess*, touched me deeply. It spoke to the essential core of my experience as a woman, and I have found much healing through my explorations of its themes over the years. I know that many other women have been similarly and profoundly touched by this myth, which signifies that it is truly a story for our age. The interest and recognition that the myth of Inanna is now receiving, not just in the minds but in the hearts and souls of so many women today, points to the necessity in our time for this journey of descent to the Dark Goddess, and the deep need we have of guidance on our way. The story of Inanna-Ereshkigal is one of a way of initiation for women, essentially into the feminine and by the feminine, and it has its origins in matriarchal times. For me, it embraces a depth and maturity of feminine experience and consciousness that the myths born out of, or rewritten during, the patriarchal ages do not. In this, it can guide us in our quest to reconnect to the innate wisdom and power of the creative feminine spirit that may have lain buried now for more than five thousand years.

Rock Woman of the Ages

Woman's power – rock, stone, ages of the earth.
No sword that cuts, but stone
that shapes the sword
> *and yields the world.*
Rock woman of the ages, earth woman,
soil and red clay woman.
Stone that heals
stone that cuts and
stone that bleeds.
She is trodden on, buried into, ravished, raped
and left a desolate wasteland.
Yet she goes on and on
to hold the child that will be born
and hold the child again
> *in death.*

Woman's power – rock, stone, ages of the earth—
and all the pain and flowers that she holds.
With her stone-knife
life so delicate as fallen petals
hand
she cuts my heart.
To show me that it bleeds.
And there is life in there
and love. Her claw-like tender
healing hand is gouging poison
from my heart.
Wound of the ages, ancient wound
of woman, life, betrayal, love and death.

Wound of the heart
        deep as stone.
And somewhere in that depth
is stillness
aching like an ocean full
of tears
        of joy and sadness... .

6 Inanna-Ereshkigal – the Journey of Descent

The myth of Inanna, Sumerian Queen of Heaven and Earth, is the oldest recorded version of the descent of the Goddess, dating back five thousand years at least. The theme is one that appears in the mythology and fairy tales of all cultures; Persephone and Psyche, as we have already seen, were later heroines of the great descent, as are Snow White and Sleeping Beauty for example, all daughters of the patriarchy. The culture in which Inanna ruled as Goddess of the Upperworld was poised, like our own, on a threshold, a turning point in history and the evolution of consciousness. Rooted in the matriarchal age and consciousness, it was a time when the patriarchy was just beginning to claim dominance.

This myth is particularly interesting to us now, as it points towards an image of the Goddess as she may have been before the patriarchy distorted her to fit into its own cosmology and theology. It follows the Goddess into her exile in the underworld, revealing to us where she went and what happened to her there. The myth also shows the path towards embracing her again as subject rather than regarding her, as patriarchal culture has done to Lilith, as object and as other than ourselves; and it offers guidance for the way of her return. Inanna's path of initiation is through a kind of death-marriage with the Dark Goddess. The Goddess in her dark or wrathful aspect has continually re-emerged throughout history in such forms as Kali, Lilith, the Gorgon, Medusa, Baba Yaga, and in this ancient story she appears as Ereshkigal, dark sister of Inanna and Queen of Death and the Underworld.

The story of Inanna tells of woman's quest to reclaim the power and wisdom of the dark aspect of the feminine, to reunite the two sides of the Goddess, and hence of herself, in an image of feminine wholeness which is both human and divine. Inanna is of the light and the realms of heaven and a fruitful earth; she is a beautiful and commanding queen of the upperworld, much loved bestower of blessings, and as Goddess of Love she delights unashamedly in her own female sexuality. The poem of her courtship and holy marriage with the shepherd Dumuzi is a celebration of erotic love.[1] In another poem we learn how Enki, God of Wisdom, bestows upon his daughter Inanna the holy *me*, symbols of secular and sacred powers.[2] Enki himself has undergone the journey to the underworld, and he also gives to Inanna the power of descent to and return from that dark realm; through the blessings of Enki and his holy offerings to her, Inanna's fate has already been decreed.

However, despite being the much loved and worshipped queen of heaven and earth, the story suggests that Inanna has already become, to some degree, a daughter of the patriarchy, of the masculine deities who are beginning to take on the reign supreme. Inanna stands on the threshold; she represents the fate of the feminine poised between the values of the old matriarchal order and those of the newly emerging patriarchy. In human terms, she represents the young woman today who commands her own life with confidence, who expresses freely and takes pleasure in her sexuality, and has achieved a measure of respect and success through her activity in the world; she is successful as a woman in a male-oriented society. She is not, however, conscious of her dark shadow side, and therefore not fully rooted in the wisdom of the deep feminine.

Her dark sister Ereshkigal, whose name means 'Lady of the Great Place Below', was once a grain goddess of the 'Great Above'. As Ninlil, wife of the sky-god Enlil, she was repeatedly raped by her husband; the gods punished Enlil for this offence to the young Goddess by sending him to the underworld, to his death, but Ninlil followed him there out of her great love for him. She became Ereshkigal, Goddess of the Great Below.

'Thus she symbolizes the Great Round of nature, grain above and growing, and seed below and dying to sprout again. To matriarchal consciousness she represents the continuum in which different states are simply experienced as transformations of one energy. To the patriarchy death becomes a rape of life, a violence to be feared and controlled as much as possible with distance and moral order.'[3]

We might imagine that Ereshkigal was originally worshipped as Goddess of the Great Round, within a matriarchy that was accepting of the inevitable transformations of nature. However, by the time of this story she has become the exiled Dark Goddess, split off from her light upperworldly aspect, 'to be feared and controlled as much as possible with distance and moral order' by both men and women of the patriarchy. It is of great interest that Ereshkigal consciously chooses the path of descent to the underworld; she willingly sacrifices herself out of love for her husband. This is in marked contrast to the patriarchal daughters who are usually in one way or another abducted, exiled, or sent to the underworld against their conscious will. The story will return us again to this theme which is of some significance to us today.

Ereshkigal represents many things. She is the silent, unheard, unwitnessed suffering of women and of rejected feminine nature; she is the agony of birth and death, the pain and the creative potential of menstruation; she is the anguished and unbounded chaos of repressed feeling and instinct; she is the rage and fury of woman denied, dishonoured, disrespected; and she is also the ancient knowledge and wordless wisdom of the feminine which is held in and accessed through the body and through attunement to nature and her cycles. We experience Ereshkigal in the part of ourselves that feels the pain of loss and knows what it is to live in exile. The woman who is unconsciously identified with her Ereshkigal-self moans and complains, is bitter, resentful, self-righteous, and full of self-pity; she might be labelled, in the derogatory sense, as 'witch' or 'old hag', particularly if she expresses her bitterness and resentment too actively for the comfort of those around her. She complains because she sees only too clearly what is wrong with things, but until she can become fully conscious of the pain behind the complaint she cannot articulate clearly the injustice she sees, and embody the creative and transformative aspect of Ereshkigal's power and wisdom.

Ereshkigal's suffering is unconscious, underground; she is the deep and often forgotten pain that we carry hidden within us, even while we go about, like Inanna, enjoying life and achieving our successes in the world. The myth of Inanna-Ereshkigal is an initiation for both aspects of the Goddess; each must become conscious of herself and of her other half in order that she be made whole again.

Although Inanna is not yet grounded in her feminine depths and her dark side, she is nevertheless not of the innocent virgin type; nor is she psychologically so immature and unaware as some of her successors. Inanna has not forgotten her dark sister, or the necessity of paying homage to her; nor is she unaware that Ereshkigal suffers. Like Ereshkigal herself, Inanna chooses the path of the underworld journey, the path of suffering and death, in full consciousness and out of her own free will. Inanna is aware that she must descend to Ereshkigal's realm to pay reverence to her sister, for it is recognition and reverence that the Dark Goddess requires, in order to balance and complete her own one-sided nature. The poem of Inanna's descent tells us that she left her upperworldly abode above for:

> '...[T]he road
> From which no traveller returns....'
> 'Because ... of my older sister, Ereshkigal,
> Her husband, Gugalanna, the Bull of Heaven, has died.
> I have come to witness the funeral rites.' [4]

A special relationship which Inanna had previously enjoyed with Enlil the Air God, thought to be the upperworld aspect of Gugalanna, suggests that this was genuinely her motivation for the descent. Perera suggests that Gugalanna, the 'great bull of heaven', also represents the repressed shadow of the patriarchal gods, which is:

> '...[B]ull-like passion, raw desire and power, sadistic bull-dozing violence, demonic bullying. That stubborn, bullish, defensive shadow of the gods is a fact of the patriarchy and its heroic ideals, ideals which overwhelm the feminine and struggle to control and hold their own in life, charging ahead, uncaring where they destroy playful sensitivity and empathetic relatedness. Inanna's descent implies her confrontation with this archetypal patriarchal shadow.' [5]

Inanna must experience the repressed and shadow aspects of both masculine and feminine in her initiatory journey, in order that she become whole and complete.

Another motivation for her descent is hinted at in one of the poems [6] which suggests that Inanna had been dispossessed of her home and power by the patriarchy, by whom she was perceived as 'fickle and unreliable, and the certain cause of grief to her beloved consorts'.[7] It would seem that her power had been claimed by the patriarchal gods, in fear of her overt and untamed sexuality, and Inanna left homeless, wandering in exile. Feelings of homelessness and exile are commonly experienced by women who are cut off from the ground of their feminine being. So for these several purposes Inanna goes, like her sister before her, of her own free will to meet her death in the realm of Ereshkigal, Goddess of the Dark. She goes, not as Persephone who was seized against her will, dragged helpless to the realm of Hades and raped, but in full consciousness. Inanna is the woman of a certain amount of maturity and knowledge of herself, who has not yet been fully grounded, consciously embedded in the dark side of her nature, and takes her fate into her own hands by consciously submitting herself to the sacrifice of her upperworldly self in symbolic death.

Inanna must enter the underworld naked, bowed low in humble reverence of Ereshkigal's power and sovereignty in this realm. At each of the seven gates which she must pass through she is stripped of her queenly robes and the adornments that symbolise her holy powers. Even the queen of heaven and earth must enter the underworld thus. We are reminded that in death all are equal, and all must be equally humbled by death, stripped naked of our achievements and power in the upperworld, for they have no place in this realm. Inanna, like each of us, must enter stripped bare to reveal what she essentially is before the cold and ruthless eye of the Goddess of the Great Below.

When we make the great descent we must submit to this stripping away of everything we are identified with; everything that is not our absolute, essential, and naked self is torn from us. We are scraped raw as we make the descent, so that we may enter humbled, helpless, powerless. From Inanna's descent, we learn that this is just as it should be. At each of the seven gates one of Inanna's royal garments are removed — the gates symbolise stages or levels of descent and of consciousness, and are reminiscent of Psyche's ordeals on the 'path of trials'. The seven garments which are removed, and later returned, may also be associated with the seven chakras over which they lie on her body, suggests Perera.[8] She is stripped down from the crown to the root chakra, the place of embeddedness in inert matter. Each time a garment is removed, Inanna questions why, and her questioning is repeatedly replied to by Neti, the chief gatekeeper, with the words:

'Quiet, Inanna, the ways of the underworld are perfect.
They may not be questioned.'⁹

There is no recourse to the laws and logic, even the compassion, of the
upperworld here. The underworld has its own law and reason, that of the
Great Round of Nature – nature in all her ruthless cruelty and indiscriminate
destruction, in her service to the eternal process of death, transformation,
and rebirth. The Goddess of this world will destroy everything in the end
– nothing escapes. Even the Queen of Heaven must submit to the laws of
the underworld and the power of death – surrender, as we all must, in this
most dangerous of journeys where there is no assurance of return. Nature
in her destructive aspect, the Goddess Ereshkigal, demands the giving over
of the energy of life into death, that the waters of life may continue to flow
and all may be renewed.

Inanna's descent into the underworld brings the light of consciousness
to Ereshkigal's realm. Her unconscious suffering and pain are illumined by
Inanna's presence, and through it she is initiated into self-awareness. She
must now also initiate Inanna into suffering and death. Judgement is passed
against Inanna:

'Then Ereshkigal fastened on Inanna the eye of death.
She spoke against her the word of wrath.
She uttered against her the cry of guilt.

'She struck her.

'Inanna was turned in to a corpse,
A piece of rotting meat,
And was hung from a hook on the wall.' ¹⁰

Reduced to a piece of rotting meat, Inanna's corpse is hung from a hook
on the wall, impaled on Ereshkigal's peg. The peg is also the phallus that
penetrates Inanna. Her initiation is a death-marriage, but rather than
through the masculine it is through the dark feminine, her elder sister
Ereshkigal, that she is impregnated and initiated into the depth and maturity
of her feminine being. Both masculine and feminine aspects of the Goddess
are embodied in this act. Through Ereshkigal, Inanna is transfixed in flesh,

incarnated, initiated into the mysteries of life-in-death and death-in-life, and the grounding of feminine spirit in matter. For Inanna, a Goddess of the light and a daughter of the patriarchal gods, such a sacrifice is necessary to complete her one-sided nature, to heal the split in her being and consciousness through a return to the feminine ground of being.

In my understanding, it is the primordial feminine ground, the pregnant void that exists before and beyond the differentiation of masculine and feminine, that Inanna is initiated into through her death-sleep. This can happen because she has confronted the shadow of the masculine, represented by Gugalanna, and of the feminine in the form of Ereshkigal herself. Through accepting her suffering, dismemberment, and death, Inanna descends to a depth within herself where she meets with and can surrender to the primordial feminine ground. This ground of being is the experience of voidness, of eternity, the eternal present, which contains but is also beyond the duality of masculine and feminine.

To the woman undergoing it, this depth of descent can feel like total and utter annihilation, as she confronts both patriarchal and matriarchal shadow. On the human level, her experience of deepest violation to her core self has been brought into consciousness, and must now be lived through. She suffers through immeasurable pain, terror, and humiliation as she is stripped naked, fastened with the eye of death, and impaled, helpless and devoid of spirit or will in the land of death. The deepest levels of depression and despair accompany this journey, from which she feels there is no release. When injury to the core self has been revealed she is stripped bare of all the resources she once possessed and can do nothing to help herself.

Time spent in the underworld feels eternal, beyond the bounds of marked time. Normal boundaries of time and space have no meaning here; it is the realm of the transpersonal and of universal suffering. When we journey within there are many depths to be encountered, but Ereshkigal's realm is the deepest we may descend to with the possibility of a safe return; beyond it is full-blown psychosis or actual physical death. The fine line that discriminates initiation from psychosis on this journey is essentially one of consciousness and the meaning we are able to give to the experience; this is dependent on the many levels of holding, discussed earlier. If we cannot open in consciousness to our suffering, then we may fall asleep as we descend to the underworld and be unable to return, embedded in inertia and depressive illness. If we are unable to surrender at the right moment to the experience of voidness, experiencing how we are actually deeply held within the void, then we become trapped in battle with the archetypal shadow figures which arise within that dimension of the psyche. They take on a dangerous quality of reality, quite literally devouring us as our body becomes weak and emaciated, like Inanna's impaled corpse, through the ordeal.

Meaning can be made of the terrible sacrifice if we can symbolically offer up to Ereshkigal our suffering, the loss of all that we once were and held dear, as our old identity dies, for she is the Goddess to whom we must pay reverence at this time. The descent to the underworld is a sacred journey, endured for a sacred purpose. We may not consciously know the purpose, but we feel it in our blood and in our bones. Often it is a woman's body that heralds the descent, which signals that she is going down, must go down, for such ordeals are always of the flesh. Our body suffers like Inanna's, stripped naked and impaled on the cruel stake. We suffer from exhaustion, the tiredness of the ages, pain and sickness, fear and terror, and the heavy, slow inertia of consciousness sunk to its depths. All our energy has gone underground, and there is little left to attend to upper worldly matters during this time. We must rest, and rest, and allow the slow putrefying forces to work upon us, even without the assurance that new life will gestate eventually from the decay. Without this sense of making sacred our losses, of offering ourselves and our suffering to the Goddess for whom our old identity must be sacrificed, the experience may be felt as meaningless waste, and the pain unbearable and irredeemable.

Finding the myth of Inanna-Ereshkigal, first in Sylvia Brinton Perera's study, and later in the translation and commentary by Wolkstein and Kramer, was enormously healing for me, as I struggled with my own pain and despair. It was essential to name the journey and the Goddess into whose hands I had submitted myself. In Inanna-Ereshkigal's ordeal I found a reflection of my own experience, and the sense of being witnessed and acknowledged through this ancient myth helped to restore a sense of my own place in life, and the 'rightness' of what I was enduring. My own personal story also seemed to parallel the myth with an uncanny accuracy. This of course can happen when we are unaware of the mythic or karmic patterns that shape our lives; when unconsciously identified with the myth, the archetypal powers are played out in the real and everyday events and relationships of our lives.

When we embark upon this journey of descent, we enter the place of deepest depression, yet it is rare for suicides to occur when we fall to this depth. We are already dead, so death can be no escape – it cannot even be considered as a possibility. In the depths of the descent, there is neither the will nor the energy for even this act. This is an unimaginable place to one who has not experienced it, where even the final release of death is no option because that threshold is felt to have already been crossed. However, though suicide at the point of deepest encounter may be rare, there is a very real danger of enduring depression or psychosis if we remain stuck in the underworld, impaled on the death stake, and cannot find the way of return.

Inanna's Return

This was not to be Inanna's fate, for she was aware of the perils of her journey and had made provision for her rescue should she become stuck in the world below. Before descending, she instructed her trusted servant Ninshubur to seek help if she had not returned within three days, and this Ninshubur did. Sylvia Brinton Perera describes Ninshubur's function for woman:

> 'Psychologically, she seems to embody that small part of us that stays above ground while the soul descends, the still conscious and functioning aspect of the psyche which can witness the events below and above and feel concern for the fate of the soul. It is the part in therapy open to feeling and taking responsibility for action and understanding while most of the patient's energy is below in the unconscious, the part capable of sustaining the therapeutic alliance. It is analogous to the remarkable, strong, humble, functioning consciousness that can permit life to continue, can prevent a psychotic episode and total loss of soul, that can persist in its journey to find what is necessary. It is the spokeswoman of the Self, the one who has heard Inanna, who keeps track of the days, and who cries out of her deep feeling that the Goddess must be roused. Ninshubur, for me, is a model of woman's deepest, reflective-of-the-Self, priestess function, one which operates as simple executive of the Self's commands, often when the soul is most threatened.'[11]

Most women will recognise this essential function operating at critical times in their lives. What the myth tells us is that a woman must have developed a conscious relationship to this part of herself if she is to return safely from the underworld, and not fall into the oblivion of chronic depression, psychosis, or physical death. If she falls unprepared, without having developed the connection to Ninshubur, her internal witness, she loses consciousness in the fall. In this, she loses her connection to the upper world reality and the possibility of rescue from Ereshkigal's womb-tomb, should she become too deeply embedded there.

In the myth Ninshubur proves herself to be a trustworthy servant:

'When, after three days and three nights, Inanna had not returned,
Ninshubur set up a lament for her by the ruins.
She beat the drum for her in the assembly places.
She circled the houses of the gods.
She tore at her eyes; she tore at her mouth, she tore at her thighs.
She dressed herself in a single garment like a beggar.
Alone, she set out for Nippur and the temple of Enlil.'[12]

Out of her deep love for her queen, Ninshubur grieves for Inanna's fate, but she also takes compassionate action to help her. This is important; it means that we can mourn our losses but also feel compassion towards ourselves in our own suffering. Without developing compassion towards ourselves, deep feeling and compassion for others cannot grow. But first we must circle the houses of the gods, dressed like beggars, in search of the one who will help rescue the Goddess.

As instructed, Ninshubur appeals first to Inanna's fathers – Enlil the Sky-god, then the Moon-god Nanna – but both refuse to help. The patriarchal gods will have nothing to do with the Great Below, and believe that those who go there do not return; Inanna has brought this upon herself and they will not dare to meddle in the ways of Ereshkigal. Ninshubur finally appeals to Enki, 'lord of the earth' and God of Wisdom and of the Waters. Enki is troubled by his daughter's plight and it is he who initiates Inanna's return by sending two little servants, created out of the dirt from under his fingernails, down to the underworld. It was Enki, remember, who gave Inanna the *me*, the power of descent to and return from the underworld, and he provides the impulse for her release. Through his bestowing of the holy *me* upon Inanna, a sacred bond of initiation has already been established between them.

When consciousness descends into the deepest layers of the psyche our personal will becomes ineffective. Like Inanna, we are impaled by the Dark Goddess, inert, unable to act on our own behalf. If the ego disintegrates, the mind breaks and can no longer function to contain or integrate the deep emotions which are surfacing, and the structures and resources it has developed to organise the personality into a coherent unity are lost. Help needs to come from some level beyond the ordinary containment and organisation of ego-will; we are called to open to relationship with some power greater than our personal self. Unable to act, we are called to surrender to a will greater than our own personal will. It is through relationship to this 'other' that we may be released from our static, inert condition. This power is ultimately within, at a higher and deeper level of consciousness, but this needs first to be touched, awakened by someone or something outside of ourself; the transpersonal source which will rescue us must initially be represented through personal relationship, or integration of the depth encounter into life cannot occur.

The return is initiated through relationship with one who can see us in our depths, one who feels for our suffering and has the capacity to travel between the worlds. Unless there is such a relationship, we may not be able to find our way back. Inanna's return is dependent upon both her human companion Ninshubur and the god Enki. The person – or perhaps a personal image of the divine – who can relate to us in our dying is one who knows her own death, and can meet us there without fear, grounded in the knowledge of her own experience and suffering. Because of the transpersonal nature of the crisis, help needs to come from a spiritual source, often mediated through a spiritual teacher or guide, or an experience of Christ, Buddha, God, or Goddess; this source of spiritual support also relates to Psyche's 'tower'. Nowadays it is often the therapist who comes to take on the role of guide in such journeys, and sometimes a special friend or partner who understands the process and has integrated its lessons for him or herself. The one who is capable of initiating our return is the one in whom we have the deepest trust and faith, who touches our spiritual core in a way which makes this the most deeply personal of relationships.

We saw that it was from the Sky-god, the Great Father and grandfather of Inanna, and the Moon-god, Inanna's own father, that she had instructed

Ninshubur first to seek help. Neither of these were able or willing to give assistance. It is so often the case that we, as father's daughters, will seek help from sources that cannot or will not give it. As unmothered daughters, we may look to men when we are in need, seeking again and again the father who may have given, or seemed to promise, protection, validation, or release from suffering. This is what we have some experience of, or, in our lack of feminine ground within, forever long for to fill the inner void. We may be compelled to refuse or find it hard to accept nurturing or spiritual guidance from a feminine source, if that was not felt to be given as a child. And so it was, perhaps, that Inanna went first to the gods who had once given her love, protection, and recognition in some form. Already becoming a daughter of the newly evolving patriarchy before her descent, it would seem that in her moment of need she looked first to the patriarchal fathers as the powerful holders of authority. But as we see, the laws of the underworld are different from those of the world above, and so Inanna's first pleas for help fell upon unwilling and inappropriate ears. The ordered world of patriarchal values will inevitably fear and reject the chaos and seeming unlawfulness of the realm of the Dark Goddess.

It may be that it is necessary for Inanna to be abandoned at this vital moment by the patriarchal gods; without the loss of what once held and sustained her in the upperworld, she would not be called to search deeper and find a source of spirituality which can truly embrace the depths of her being in the underworld. This is the darkest time, when soul is lost, and we may wander forever homeless in the dark night if help does not come. It is the time when we feel cut off from the source of spiritual nourishment and guidance within us. During this time, a woman is forced to cut the ties to the false gods and dependencies that do not serve her greater path in life, if she is ever to be freed from the underworld. Like Inanna, we must lose our soul in order to find it.

It is Enki, God of Wisdom who rules the seas and rivers and lives in the deep watery abysses, who sets into motion Inanna's return. Perera describes Enki as:

> '...[T]he generative, creative, playful, empathetic male. Like Mercurius he includes the opposites and has no abstract boundedness to the principle of law. Although Enki is said to have created the 'me', those ordering principles of the upper

world and civilization, his order is creative, not static and preservative. He is the culture bringer, not the preserver of the status quo. His wisdom is that of improvisation and empathy. And having a bisexual breadth...he can penetrate into any necessity – even into the underworld... . Enki's wisdom flows with, breaks up; it releases the inertia and rigidity of the underworld. His waters...restore the wasteland, symbolic of the never-ending flow of life's energies.'[13]

In my own journey of descent I looked first to the man who was my therapist for the relationship that would initiate my return, believing in my confusion that as he was the one who had guided me into those depths, he was the only one who could understand where I was and help me through the process I was in. But I was mistaken and, like Inanna, calling upon the wrong 'gods', those of the patriarch and the law of the upperworld, for at that time he was unable and, by his own confession later on, unwilling to see me where I was and help me through. I felt deeply betrayed, as might Inanna when the sky and moon gods refused to give her help, but I see now the inappropriateness of appealing to this source. The myth has helped me to understand the rightness of this failure; the patriarchy of today has not yet included the values of the dark feminine and the underworld, and will inevitably retreat from them in ignorance, fear, or defensiveness, for they seem to counter and destroy all that the upperworld upholds as good and right. And it takes much time and great patience to be witness to someone through the underworld journey; patient waiting and holding, with no positive end or results in sight, is not a characteristic of the masculine.

Initially, it was my spiritual teacher who was able to see and respond to me in the depths of the descent. He was the one, like the god Enki, who had embraced the totality of himself and could respond to any situation with wisdom, empathy, spontaneity, and playfulness. His responses to my situation served, like the flow of Enki's waters, to begin the loosening of the static hold of Ereshkigal's realm. Like Enki, he improvised with whatever was at hand, and through this play could initiate the release from the death-like state. Enki uses the dirt from under his fingernails to create the little servants who will secure Inanna's release; nothing is not useful in his creative approach, everything both ordinary and sacred to his far-seeing eye. Later on a healer, a man with Enki-like qualities and 'little servants' in the form of homoeopathic remedies, also helped in facilitating my return.

A woman who has integrated her masculine and feminine, her light and dark aspects, may of course also fulfil the function of Enki, but I think it is of interest that the god who helps Inanna is in fact male. He is not a typically patriarchal god, and therefore his role in this myth is not as a representative of the patriarchy; he has gone beyond dualities through his own initiation into the underworld, and represents a new form of masculine consciousness which also embraces feminine values and principles. It is here that I feel this myth dovetails with the myth of the Holy Grail; Enki represents the male who has embraced the Dark Goddess and knows the mysteries of the feminine through the sacred marriage. In the Grail Legend, the hero is made whole through his initiation into the dark feminine, and in this he simultaneously helps to heal the wounded feminine.

Inanna has been initiated by Ereshkigal; what she is unable to do is return to the upperworld. Returning to the upperworld will mean confronting the patriarchy from a new standpoint of feminine empowerment. She is deeply changed by her ordeal, but the change, in order to be integrated, must also be realised – made real – through expression of who she now is in the upperworld. Hers is the task of redeeming the feminine from old patriarchal attitudes and values that judge woman as inferior, weak, passive, fickle, irrational, and reasserting genuine feminine qualities and power out of her own feminine ground. Without this, the change remains only an inner experience of the imaginal world; she is caught in the liminal twilight zone of consciousness. Enki's connection with her return suggests that Inanna also needs to embody the wisdom of Enki and the creative, empathetic masculine in order to meet this challenge. There is a depth of her being which, in order to be healed, now needs to be touched by the energy of the positive masculine.

Inanna's quest is also for the integration of masculine and feminine energies, both interpersonally and intrapersonally. To bring back into the world the expression of her wholeness as woman, and to confront patriarchal law from there, Inanna needs both the penetrating power of the dark feminine to deepen her, and the life-giving waters of Enki to restore her. She must now internalise and integrate the qualities of Enki which are revealed to her as life-renewing powers; through this she can complete herself as a being not only of light and dark, but of feminine and masculine qualities as well. The story of Inanna's return shows us that the woman on this journey must connect to the inner positive masculine, the god within, in order to release her and bring back into the world the feminine power that has its source in the depths of her being.

The intervention of the male god Enki can also be understood to function at an energetic level. In terms of the subtle energies of the body, the root chakra is the place where we are embedded in flesh, enwombed before birth, and entombed in the darkness of descent as Inanna was, staked on Ereshkigal's hook, submerged in matter. It is the energy of the second, the sacral chakra, which is needed to release us from such a condition. In the submerged state, libido is withdrawn from outer relationship; death and the deep stirrings of the soul on its solitary journey have drawn desire inwards and down. To return, the energy of desire needs to be reawakened – desire of the body, desire of the heart, desire of the soul for life. The waters of Enki serve to break up the static condition and revive the flow of Inanna's life energies. The creative tension between the opposites stimulates the re-emergence into life. Thus, at some stage in the process of descent and return, the reviving of sexual feeling through relationship with the masculine may play a part in turning the flow of libido back towards life.

This is a point at which great caution must be taken, however; if a teacher, therapist, or other helper becomes sexually involved with the woman at this point, her healing process may be aborted. A man helping a woman through such a crisis must not rob her in this way of the god-like energies that her healing journey has evoked, for they belong essentially to her own healing process and not within their personal relationship. If the journey back is successful, however, and she is able to free herself from destructive patterns of relationship to the masculine, then the woman will experience a deepening of her sexuality, feel it rooted more strongly in her feminine ground and power, more closely connected to the feelings of her heart and to the earth.

To return to the story, Enki's two little servants slip unnoticed through the cracks in the gates of the underworld, and come to Ereshkigal. They find her:

'...[M]oaning
With the cries of a woman about to give birth.
No linen is spread over her body.

Her breasts are uncovered.
Her hair swirls about her head like leeks.'[14]

As Enki had predicted, the Goddess of the underworld suffers in abject misery and pain. As suggested earlier, the descent of Inanna into her dark unconscious realm has brought consciousness to the suffering of Ereshkigal, awakened her to the pains of her own death and birthing. The wise little servants of Enki empathise deeply with her misery, reflecting back her anguished groans; she is moved by this, and grateful. We see that Ereshkigal is not vengeful or rejecting of the patriarchal order above when respect is paid to her, when her suffering is acknowledged and met with empathy. Her wrath only becomes manifest when she is not accepted and honoured. And isn't that so for all who suffer; empathetic witnessing can dissolve so much of the pain, resentment, and anger that we hold. As a token of her gratitude, Ereshkigal responds with generosity and gives them Inanna's corpse. They sprinkle on it the food and water of life, and Inanna is revived. But the law of the Great Round must still hold, and Inanna is told that if she returns another must be sacrificed in her place:

'No one ascends from the underworld unmarked.
If Inanna wishes to return from the underworld,
She must provide someone in her place.'[15]

With these ominous words the face of our future is drawn. Inanna is only halfway through her journey, and she now faces the daunting task of integrating her new awareness and power as she returns to life. No woman who returns from this journey is left unmarked. Her face and her body bear the lines and scars of suffering, and she is deeply changed by her ordeal – not always in ways that she had hoped or expected. From this deepened sense of herself, she must learn to relate anew to the world to which she returns; and she must find an appropriate sacrifice. Sometimes this part of the initiation can be as hard to endure as the underworld ordeal; she must learn how to face alone the challenges and responsibility that her reclaimed power entails.

As Inanna returns from the underworld, the *galla*, demons of the underworld, cling to her side. They will capture the one who is to take her place in the underworld, and they will be persuaded or bribed from their task by nothing. The *galla* don't eat or drink; they accept neither gifts nor offerings. They embody the indiscriminate destruction of Ereshkigal, the Goddess in her dark and devouring aspect, not knowing good from evil.

When a woman returns from the underworld journey, when she has witnessed the pain and indiscriminate fury of her dark sister, and suffered her own dismemberment and death, she does not return with all-loving sweetness and radiant light. Around her cling Ereshkigal's demons, emissaries of the dark; we see them in the deepened furrows on her brow, the tension she holds in her body, her darkened eyes, and cheeks scored by tears. These are the marks she bears as she returns; this is the woman who must search for a sacrifice, and she will not be released by the clinging demons until she finds one.

Just as a woman may get lost in the underworld, she may also get stuck at this point of her journey. If she does not complete her task by offering the sacrifice to Ereshkigal she will live in a state of limbo, tied to the underworld, unfree to move fully back into her life, and will be consumed by the demons of rage and bitterness turned against herself or others. A few people may recognise and respect her for what she has been through, but most will try at all costs to avoid her. She is not comfortable to be with for anyone who has not made this journey him or herself.

We saw this energy expressed most forcibly in the anger and militancy of the early women's movement; strong women, finally able to express their outrage at what women have collectively suffered through the ages, sought with vengeance the 'sacrificial blood' of the chauvinistic male ego and the patriarchy. We have needed to go through this expression of anger in order to learn to embody our collective power as women, and each individual woman on her own journey also needs to experience her power in a similar way; but we should be wary of the danger of not getting beyond this point, for we are still wandering in the wilderness with the *galla* at our heels, still not free. At such a point, our healing journey is not yet complete. The personal and the sacred dimensions of the return of the deep feminine both need to be integrated.

If the fall has been deep, then the return may be long and difficult, and may bring further depression and despair. We may seem to fail at first, and have to descend again and again, only gradually learning to make our descents with consciousness, assimilating and embodying our new knowledge and power piece by piece. We must remember that the loss has been great and the pain deep. It is not to be redeemed all at once, but step by step, death by death, and by many of us as we repeatedly make our descents with ever-deepening consciousness.

For a woman on the journey this is also a time when it may be tempting to forget what has been learnt in the underworld and try to regress back to the consciousness of the father's daughter. There are many tests during this period, and in particular we are called to find a new way of relating to the masculine, both within and without, but now from the ground of feminine being rather than the precarious position of the patriarchal daughter. It is easy to fall back again into old ways of relating as we first emerge, still vulnerable with our new skins not yet fully formed, not quite sure of who we are in this newness, and how we will relate from here. We may return feeling like the butterfly who hasn't yet realised she is no longer a caterpillar, dazed from the long months cocooned in darkness, and unused to our own brightness. We try to crawl again, as we once did, instead of fly, knowing that it doesn't feel quite right.

After an encounter with the mythic or transpersonal depths of being, the healing journey then necessitates a shift back to the personal, to the psychological work of integrating the experience in the dimensions of intrapsychic and interpersonal relationship. Whereas the myth of Psyche advises that this psychological work be done before the journey to the underworld is undertaken, Inanna's story suggests that a process of personal integration must follow the experience of encounter with the transpersonal, and that the journey between the upperworld and the underworld is cyclical and continuous. Whether it is wise or unwise, the reality is that many people today *are* experiencing the depth encounter without adequate psychological preparation, and perhaps the myth of Inanna can offer useful guidance in such cases.

For women this myth presents a way of reclaiming our womanhood in its wholeness, first through healing the deep wound of the feminine, and then through relationship to the masculine from the place of grounded feminine authority and truth, rather than the subordinate place of a daughter of the patriarch. Sometimes connecting to our truth leads us in directions contrary to where we had hoped or intended to be. Return from the abyss experience may lead us away from, rather than into relationship. Whatever emerges, it serves to balance what was missing or one-sided before. If we have been caught in negative and destructive patterns of relationship then we need to find, through encounter with our depths, the insight and strength that will enable us to let go of these roles and relationships. We need to learn to discriminate what in our relationships is genuinely loving, healthy, and creative, and what is manipulative, destructive, and abusive. Hence before we can create relationships that fulfil our need for real depth, intimacy, and authenticity, we may need to let go of the search for relationship and find true independence.

What a woman must learn through this period is to stand her own ground, to be able to stand alone in her own authentic truth — what Marion Woodman calls 'empowered aloneness'.[16] She must learn to be first and foremost a woman unto herself, to cease giving herself and the treasures she has gained through her hard work and suffering away to others, and in particular to men, if that has been her tendency. She has to stop bleeding away the creative power of her 'dark moon', to use the life-giving and healing energy she accesses in her depths, first to renew her own spirit and nurture her own creativity. This is an important part of the task of the father's daughter, who has learnt to succeed by pleasing or adapting to others, as she returns from her descent into the underworld. It means she has to learn to be tough when necessary, with herself as well as others, to embody Ereshkigal's ruthless power that sees through to the heart of things and lets nothing escape her scrutinising eye. She has to learn to see what is, and to act on what she sees. Like Ereshkigal, she can nurture into form, give birth, and destroy in death. But unless she can integrate Ereshkigal's forbidding wisdom and the knowledge she has gained through her ordeals she cannot develop true compassion, but may lapse into sentimentality or martyrdom. Meanwhile, the consciousness that has been gained, if not integrated into her life, will turn into a fury that consumes her. As Marie-Louise von Franz writes:

'Unrealized consciousness becomes a burning fire'.[17]

And so Inanna returns to the upperworld to search for the one who will be sacrificed to Ereshkigal in her place. First she is met by Ninshubur, then her two sons. All express their great love and devotion to Inanna, throwing themselves in the dust at her feet, so Inanna tells the *galla* not to take them. Because they recognise their Queen and Goddess, and humble themselves in her holy presence, they will not be sacrificed. They represent the ability of the personality to bow down before the sacred.

Inanna then comes to Dumuzi, the one who was her husband-lover and on whom she had bestowed the holy kingship. She finds him sitting on his throne, dressed in his royal garments. As she approaches, he does not move; he does not bow down to Inanna or acknowledge the sovereignty of the Goddess. During her absence, he has usurped her place, and because of this he is the one she chooses to be sacrificed to the underworld. Dumuzi, proud king who refuses to revere the Goddess, now represents the one-sided and inflated patriarchy. For this he must be forced to confront his own shadow and taken to his death. This is Inanna's purpose – to restore reverence for the Goddess – and she has now integrated the powers of the Dark Goddess that will enable her to fulfil this task. Now, just as Ereshkigal formerly did to her:

> 'Inanna fastened on Dumuzi the eye of death.
> She spoke against him the word of wrath.
> She uttered against him the cry of guilt;
> "Take him! Take Dumuzi away!" ' [18]

In the oldest kingdoms that we have knowledge of, it was a custom for the king to be sacrificially killed when he had served his reign, or when there was trouble in the kingdom. This custom symbolically reflects the annual death and rebirth of the lover-son-consort of the Goddess, a theme we see recurring in most matriarchal mythologies. The sacrifice represents the transformational processes of life, and ensures the continued fertility of the community and the earth. It also ensured that the king did not become inflated by confusing his own person with the power and authority of his role, which was held to be a sacred one. (In modern democracies, the periodic election of new leaders seeks to serve the same function.)

> 'The King was to serve as sacrifice to the transpersonal powers;
> to renew relationship with them .... The king, symbolic offering
> of the kingdom, must be sacrificed so that rebirth and a new
> beginning might take place for the community at large.' [19]

There is an element of this old theme in the story of Dumuzi, consort of the Goddess. However, he has become inflated in his role and has rigidified into an upholder of the patriarchy. In refusing to acknowledge

Inanna, he dissociates himself from his inner feminine, feeling nature, and the flow of life. This must inevitably reconstellate the wrath of the Goddess. Because of his pride and inflation, he must be sent to the underworld in Inanna's place. But Dumuzi is not a willing sacrifice; he does not understand the necessity and inevitability of his death and struggles all the way against it. He does not go willingly, as Inanna did, but tries by every means to escape the clutches of the demons. He is terrified; he runs, he hides, and he seeks help from the gods, his friend, and his sister, as the *galla* relentlessly pursue him.

Dumuzi represents the one-sided, inflated, patriarchal gods, and the values they represent, which must be confronted by the woman returning from her initiatory ordeal into the deep feminine. They must be confronted both within and without. At an intrapersonal level he represents her masculinised ego, and the distorted and repressive aspects of the patriarchy which she has internalised and lived by. All this must now be sacrificed, transformed. As Inanna, her light, upperworldly feminine aspect has been transformed through her encounter with her dark side; now, as Dumuzi, her masculine side must also be deepened, initiated, reconnected with its own dark aspect. Through this, a woman's relationship with the outer masculine can also transform. She might serve in some way to initiate others into the mysteries of the dark feminine, as Inanna serves to initiate Dumuzi. Woman becomes again spokesperson for the values of the feminine expressed in human life, priestess of the Goddess on earth.

Inanna represents the intuitive, feminine, receptive, inclusive consciousness which can accept necessity and the inevitability of suffering. When she is called, she goes willingly and purposefully into the depths of the underworld. She can accept the trials endured in order to come to her inner threshold where both the light and dark sides of life and of the psyche are embraced. Inanna's story at first felt incomplete to me, for although during my own crisis I could feel this deep level of acceptance and an intuitive understanding of the rightness and necessity of the journey, there was also a turbulent resistance to the process going on; something within me was opposing my recognition of the meaning and purpose of the descent, and threatened to overthrow completely the attitude of acceptance and surrender.

It was in later finding the poem of Dumuzi's capture, that I began to understand the conflict that had been going on within me. Dumuzi represents the proud male, and the masculinised ego of woman, who resists in terror his capture and fall. The poem shows him fleeing into hiding, calling on all those who might help him to evade, through slippery tricks, or kindness, the claws of the ruthless *galla*. Dumuzi is the part of us that resists the inevitable pain of dismemberment and creates all kinds of neurotic suffering to hide from it; he is the ego that cannot accept its death, and out of its non-acceptance and inability to face the dark feminine, generates pathological disturbances in the psyche. Dumuzi struggles all the way against the wisdom of Inanna-Ereshkigal and the inevitability of his fate within the cycles of transformation over which the Goddess presides. He does not understand the ways of the realm below, the unconscious, and cannot, like Inanna, foresee the need to make provision for his own release. Dumuzi is the part of us that is completely helpless and uncomprehending in this situation, out of its depth. He is the broken ego, shattered vessel that cannot hold or tolerate the woundings and the fear. Both attitudes may be present simultaneously, creating an agonising split between Inanna's acceptance and Dumuzi's fear and resistance, if we don't understand the different levels that are operating, and the relationship between them.

When, during a process of deep transformation such as the myth of Inanna describes, we are simultaneously retraumatised in a way that cannot be contained and integrated, then we also suffer this splitting of experience. In this instance, Dumuzi represents the traumatised self whose structure has disintegrated in the face of overwhelming emotions; from this place we are incapacitated and cannot safely and creatively engage with the depth of process that has been initiated. The evocation of trauma must be dealt with as such, or the violated self will continue to suffer, and we cannot fully engage with and complete the underworld journey. Thus we may experience the emergence of an Inanna-like intuition and acceptance of the process of dissolution, simultaneously with the eruption of the pain, fear, and helplessness of our traumatised core self.

Geshtinanna, the Unifying Principle of Love

Finally, the unwilling Dumuzi is seized by the *galla*. They strike him, destroy his possessions and, as Inanna suffered before him, his royal garments, holy crown, and sceptre are taken from him. Naked, he is dragged to the underworld. And Dumuzi may have been lost there forever, but for his sister, Geshtinanna, who now comes to his rescue. She is grief-stricken at her beloved brother's death and offers to sacrifice herself in his place. Seeing Geshtinanna's grief and great love, Inanna is deeply moved and agrees to let brother and sister share Dumuzi's fate, spending half of the year each in the underworld.

Geshtinanna's offer is not the martyrdom of a woman who cannot stand her own ground and gives herself away out of false motives; she offers herself out of her deep love and compassion for her brother in his suffering. Geshtinanna is a woman of wisdom, a seer and prophetess. Dumuzi describes her thus:

> '...Geshtinanna, my little sister,
> My tablet-knowing scribe,
> My singer who knows many songs,
> My sister who knows the meaning of words,
> My wise woman who knows the meaning of dreams.'[20]

We see in Geshtinanna a further transformation of Inanna, and of the feminine. Through embracing her dark feminine side in the underworld journey, incorporating her light and dark masculine aspects through her connection with Gugalanna and Enki, and the realisation of this in relationship through her marriage and later confrontation with Dumuzi, the Goddess has now integrated the many sides of her nature. The light and dark, the masculine and feminine are now joined within her in the sacred mandala of the Self. From here, the Goddess as Geshtinanna can act with genuine compassion and wisdom out of the strength of her own grounded feminine being, and her knowledge of suffering and the dark world below. Knowing the underworld, and how to go and return from there, she does not need to fear it. She embodies the light and dark aspects of the Goddess, and the masculine and feminine energies as symbolised by the brother and sister.

Like Ereshkigal and Inanna, Geshtinanna goes willingly and consciously to the underworld. But where Ereshkigal was exiled there and spilt off from her light aspect, Inanna's descent heals the splitting of the Goddess into light and dark aspects. Finally, the feminine is made whole and fully redeemed through the action of Geshtinanna. Through Geshtinanna's love, a deeper level of consciousness and integration has been reached. The consciousness that is attained honours and respects both worlds, and enables the continued process of passage between the worlds that serves both life and death, spirit and matter, consciousness and soul, within the Great Round of the transformation of Life itself.

The vengeful and demonic aspect of Inanna's search for the one to be sacrificed in her place is first transformed through appropriate expression of her power in relation to Dumuzi, symbol of inflated and rigidified power; only then can she be further transformed as she witnesses Geshtinanna's love and finds in her own heart compassion for Dumuzi. Inanna can now serve in a positive role as initiator of Dumuzi into the feminine mysteries. Like Inanna, women may serve to initiate aspects of men's growth and evolution, but unless the transpersonal and sacred dimension of the descent has been integrated, elements of aggression or revenge, rather than compassion, may be present in the motivation; this can only lead to further conflict and defensiveness on both sides. Inanna understands the necessity and inevitability of Dumuzi's descent from a transpersonal perspective, and so in the very act of sacrificing him, compassion is awakened in her.

If a woman is able to complete this journey, she may find expression of her new consciousness in many different ways. In her family and other relationships, her presence may help others deepen to their authentic feelings and creativity, serving as initiatress into the feminine mysteries; she may express her new awareness simply in the quality of her life, in the way she creates her home, in actively working to heal the earth, or in bringing awareness of and aid to those who are suffering; she may discover gifts that lead her into work in the creative or healing arts, for example, or find that in her encounter with her depths she has been opened to psychic abilities which can be of help to others on their own inner journeys. But she can only do all of this in a way that is true to her own nature if Dumuzi, her inner masculine, has also been initiated and transformed.

> 'Inanna tells Dumuzi:
> "You will go to the underworld
> Half the year.
> Your sister, since she has asked,
> Will go the other half."
> Inanna placed Dumuzi in the hands of the eternal.'[21]

Thus Dumuzi, through his death, is also healed, made whole. He is initiated into the mysteries of the feminine and the cycles of creativity, death, and rebirth. In this way he becomes as Enki, able to encompass both his masculine and feminine nature, and the wisdom, creativity, empathy, and playfulness of the god who can travel between the worlds. He receives the blessing of immortality; his proud ego dies and he is spiritually reborn into the eternal, the transpersonal.

If Dumuzi's fate had not been softened by his sister's self-sacrifice, then Dumuzi would have been lost, exiled as Ereshkigal has been, in the underworld. If a woman's masculine is split off in this way, she is again in deep trouble. Masculine consciousness is necessary to order, structure, and understand certain experiences; it delineates, orientates, and puts each thing in its appropriate place in the universe. If we are plunged into the depth dimension of consciousness and lose touch with our capacity for rational thought and psychological organisation, then we are as much at risk of psychosis as we are if the Ninshubur function is absent. If Dumuzi had not been allowed to periodically return, the masculine would have been split off and consciousness would descend into the realm of the imaginal without access to upperworld orientation. Reconstituting herself, reintegrating her ego, and reorganising her life is part of a woman's healing process which can and must occur when Dumuzi is allowed to return to the upperworld. The myth teaches that the masculine principle of woman must also be periodically reconnected with and immersed in the feminine ground, but in order to return deepened, renewed, redefined, and ever humbled.

What we learn through Geshtinanna's transforming action is that we are called, through love of our fellow beings, to make the journey of descent consciously, not just once, but again and again. We can participate willingly and consciously in the cyclical processes of the Great Round, continually reflecting on our two faces, ever reminded that we must give all away in order to be received into the 'hands of the eternal'. It is not an end to be achieved once and for all, but a process with which we must engage continuously. Each time we descend and return we access a little more of our heights and depths; a little more wisdom is born out of our experience. Each time we must give up ego and all we have gained in the upperworld to be deepened and renewed in our depths. It is always painful, but as we learn to travel between the worlds with consciousness and understanding, we may go with less fear; as we gain acceptance of the suffering, we are able to redeem and bring back to the world more of our gifts that may have been long buried.

The way of the Goddess is about process and transformation, and even the fruits of our difficult journeys to her must be sacrificed once more in the Great Round, as we continually let die our small concerns for the sake of something greater. Our old ways are so deeply engrained that it may take many cycles of descent to slowly erode their traces and realise a new way of being in the world. But our spirit is like the gold that is repeatedly melted down and beaten, emerging each time purer and finer; it does not lose its essential nature, but is refined through the repeated transformations. At each descent, we access the power to go deeper, and so come a little closer to the essence of whom we essentially are.

It is interesting to compare the outcome of this myth with the fate of Psyche in the later patriarchal version of the descent. Psyche, after her trials and journey to the underworld, receives a place with the gods in heaven and gives birth to a daughter called 'Pleasure of Joy'. Her journey reaches completion with the divine marriage in a heavenly paradise. This reflects the aspirations of a patriarchal orientation towards spirituality – the soul finds its final fulfilment in a return to a transcendent heavenly sphere. The Inanna myth, on the other hand, indicates that the soul continues to cycle eternally between heaven, earth, and the underworld, obeying the laws of spirit wedded to matter, consciousness embodied in nature. This reflects a matriarchal perspective and spirituality and, it might be argued, a more 'primitive', submerged consciousness.

However, I feel this is only one level of the myth, and there is another deeper and surprisingly sophisticated meaning. It lies again in Geshtinanna's transforming love and compassion. Geshtinanna I see as an early and female symbol of the Boddhisattva; the path of the Boddhisattva is encountered again, and named more than two and a half thousand years later, with the emergence of Mahayana Buddhism. The Boddhisattva is the spiritual aspirant who vows not to seek eternal bliss or *nirvana* for him or herself alone, in a transcendent heavenly sphere of existence. He or she vows to keep returning to help all those who are suffering in the eternal round of *samsara*, whether they be in heaven, on earth, or in the hell of the underworld. The Boddhisattva embodies compassionate action and love for others, and this is, I believe, the hidden aspiration of the myth of Inanna-Ereshkigal-Geshtinanna. The old consciousness, which we tend to think of as more primitive than our own, may have been far more sophisticated and evolved, both psychologically and spiritually, than we imagine. Its wisdom, like Inanna, may have gone underground five thousand years ago.

Today this myth is resonating so strongly with many women because after all these millennia Inanna is finally making her return. During all these ages woman has gone, like Ninshubur, dressed like a beggar, circling the houses of the gods, unable to enter and unable to find the one who could release her queen. Now things are changing. Women are becoming conscious of what they can and must do, and a more receptive masculine consciousness is beginning to emerge, awakening to the cries of the banished Goddess. In the myth of Lilith, the Goddess was exiled, cast out as 'other'; through the myth of Inanna-Ereshkigal-Geshtinanna we see the way to embrace her again as 'self', feminine spirit embodied. Now is the time to stop losing our way in madness or unconsciousness and to open, with courage and strength on this path of suffering, to our capacity for authentic feeling. The greater our capacity for grief, the deeper our love; the deeper the pain, the fuller the joy; the more we feel our fear, that much courage do we have; and the stronger our anger and passion, the more powerfully our compassion may eventually grow.

The Messenger

Soft gold like sunlight filtered
through the quiet lull of afternoon—
a moment's pause between the things of this world and the next.
Wings of finely tempered gold, marked
with velvet brown like deep caves of rest for sorrowing.
As I approach they open wide a heart of scarlet red.

Beauty is a name too common for this noble creature, messenger
who comes into this life for but a passing moment,
bringing gifts from far beyond
her own mysterious appearance,
then departs.

Wounded, the butterfly limps circle-wise,
trailing blood as clear as rain
or tears, shed for the world.
Thinking that I can take her to a safer place of rest,
out of the path of clumsy treading feet,
my hand swoops down like an army from the dark sky
to seize what needs gentle holding,
destroy a life that needs protecting.
My wise messenger withdraws, and I feel the blunt mistake
run through my body like a call to silence.
Time opens to eternity, space filled with quiet listening.
Hand resting by a pale-gold wing of butterfly,
and there is nothing to be done.
We wait, and listen to the silence,
touching lightly to this moment.

She is ready, little friend,
wise warrior friend from other worlds,
and climbs upon my trusting finger, walking firmly,
drops her roots into my hand like earth.
And in that instant we are joined and know each other
perfectly. This knowledge flows between us like a bond
that ties our purpose to the world, each to the other.

A little trembling in her wings, then violent beating,
feet sunk deep into the current of my mind. Will she die here
in my hand? But no, the time for death is past,
and she is healing,
pain beating through her wings. I feel the course
of life and death run through my being. I am being.
There is nothing to be done, no thoughts,
and she is healing as I wait here in the
still and quiet, with the power of the earth
which fills and empties through me
at each trembling. Love is being,
and we heal.

She is ready, little friend, wise warrior friend
from some mysterious beyond.
And now she spreads her velvet wings—
pale gold of the sun, deep dark of night, red like blood
at the heart where they meet.
Flies through an open window, and is gone.
That was our moment — it is past,
yet it is present in the still attentive recesses of being,
where we may fall — in love — into ourselves, and heal.

Did she fly away and live a moment longer,
or fall there through the open window to her death,
wise friend, messenger of my soul?
She went with no assurances, and left behind
only her precious gift for me
to hold and trust
with open hand.

7 The Wounded Healer – Shamanic Initiation

nitiatory death and rebirth, such as the myth of Inanna tells, has been a theme central to the cultural and religious life of pre-modern societies since the beginnings of history, and beyond. The occurrence of initiatory ordeals and rites of passage in every tribe, culture, and religion of antiquity suggests that such rites fulfilled a social, psychological, and spiritual need; the need to symbolically mark, honour, and indeed facilitate significant moments of passage in the course of a human life would appear to be a universal response to growth and change. However, with the exception of a few vestiges of initiatory ritual, such as Christian baptism, holy communion, the marriage ceremony, and circumcision in the Jewish tradition, our modern society is almost totally lacking any meaningful rites of passage. There is little real recognition, understanding, or acknowledgement within our culture or orthodox religion of the initiatory process and the human psyche's need for it.

Of course, along with the loss we may find the question arising: 'Do we as modern men and women, with our developed intellect and culture, still need such rituals of initiation? Were they, and the beliefs that surrounded them, not just the product of a primitive mind which did not understand the scientific workings of the universe, a culture based on naïve superstition and belief in spirits, ghosts, and gods? Haven't we, with our more sophisticated consciousness, simply outgrown such a way of thinking and being in the world?'

The view has already been put forward that, as we approach the end of an age and are in the process of transition towards a new kind of consciousness, we are being challenged to re-embrace and consciously to integrate older modes of thinking and being which we may seem to have outgrown. More 'primitive' modes of consciousness are our psychic foundations and still operate within us, usually unconsciously. This is of course only a point of view; but what I would also like to explore here is a reality that is observable all around us. The fact is that people *are* going through initiatory ordeals, whether or not this is acknowledged and formally ritualised by society, state, and church; that it may be deemed primitive and irrelevant to twentieth century man and woman is a redundant argument in the face of the fact that the initiatory process is actually occurring everywhere, whether people wish to recognise and value it or not. That initiatory rites are not recognised for what they are, and consciously accorded the value that they hold for us unconsciously, may have become a source of intense personal and social conflict today.

Before we explore the way ordeals and rituals of initiation may be unconsciously manifesting today, let us first look at the function and meaning of initiation itself, and how it has been symbolically enacted or represented in cultures for whom initiatory rites are held to be an essential part of individual and collective life. As Mircea Eliade describes, initiation can be grouped into three main categories. The first is 'puberty rites' or 'tribal initiation'. Every member, both male and female, of a community still connected to nature and the old ways, undergoes some kind of ritual which marks their passage from childhood or adolescence into adulthood. These are usually public ceremonies in which the whole community participates in some way, and a group of young girls or boys are often initiated together; male and female rites differ in form, and are usually performed separately, though they are essentially the same in meaning and purpose. In some tribes, a girl's initiation would take place with her first menstruation, and not within a group.

There is far more evidence available concerning male puberty rites than female, and some historians have taken this to imply that the initiation of girls was not so widespread, or of such significance as that of boys. On this point, two facts must be borne in mind; first, members of the opposite sex are usually not allowed to witness the initiation rites, and are not given access to the knowledge that is handed down by the elders to the young. Great secrecy is maintained around the mysteries thus imparted. Most, if not all, early researchers into these communities and their customs were men who were fortunate enough to witness male initiation rites; but as they would be excluded from participation in or knowledge of female rites, these traditions remained shrouded from us in a greater amount of secrecy. As more women become involved in this area of research and experience, more information about specifically female rites is beginning to emerge. The writing of Lynn Andrews, for example, has imaginatively opened our minds to the feminine mystery traditions in native American culture,[2] and Bani Shorter discusses women's initiation within the context of depth psychology.[3]

Secondly, as humankind began to emerge from matriarchal consciousness, the fear of being re-engulfed in the dark womb of unconsciousness led to a fear of the power of woman. Women's own mystical knowledge and rituals would undoubtedly have suffered from patriarchal suppression and control, undermining the power of the female mysteries and initiation rites. Bearing in mind that there are differences in male and female initiation, and that the information I am basing this discussion of puberty rites on comes primarily from a study of male rituals, I would nevertheless like to explore some elements that seem to be common to all rites of initiation.

Through the initiation ceremony, the young person leaves behind the world of childhood and takes his or her place in the adult community; in doing so she or he accepts the responsibilities that this entails, and sometimes receives a new name which symbolises that she is now a different person and of different status. This is the social function of the puberty rites. Initiatory rites also contain a profound psychological and spiritual meaning; they represent not only the end of childhood and the beginning of adulthood, but implicit within this transition is a death to the profane world of childhood, and a spiritual rebirth in a world that is sacred. Towards the sacredness of life, the young person must now accept his or her responsibility. Eliade writes:

> 'Initiation represents one of the most significant spiritual phenomena in the history of humanity. It is an act that involves not only the religious life of the individual, in the modern meaning of the word 'religion'; it involves his *entire* life. It is through initiation that, in primitive and archaic societies, man becomes what he is and what he should be – a being open to the life of the spirit, hence one who participates in the culture into which he was born… *the puberty initiation represents above all the*

revelation of the sacred – and, for the primitive world, the sacred
means not only everything that we now understand by religion, but
also the whole body of the tribe's mythological and cultural
traditions.... . From a certain point of view it could almost be said
that, for the primitive world, it is through initiation that men attain
the status of human beings; before initiation, they do not yet fully
share in the human condition precisely because they do not yet
have access to the religious life. This is why initiation represents
a decisive experience for any individual who is a member of a
premodern society; it is a fundamental existential experience
because through it a man becomes able to assume his mode of
being in its entirety.'[4] (Original italics)

Although the form, content, and mythological symbols of the initiation
rites of different cultures vary greatly, there are several underlying themes
and events that are universal to all. Part of the initiatory process involves
the passing on of traditional knowledge to the neophytes; they learn of the
creation of the world, the stories of their ancestors, the sacred myths of
their people, and they witness secret ceremonies being performed. They
must also learn about their duties as adult members of the community. The
period of transmission of the culture's sacred knowledge by the elders
may take several days, weeks, months, and sometimes as long as a year.
During this period, the initiates often remain in isolation from the rest of
the community, and may be placed under strict taboos, dietary restrictions,
and other hardships. Being instructed in the traditions and beliefs of their
culture opens the young people to the possibility of recognising sacredness
in the world, but it is primarily through the ordeals endured during the
initiatory process that they may have a direct experience, an encounter with
the sacred.

Some form of physical and psychological ordeal is the central and crucial
element of the initiation. The ordeal symbolically represents a death out
of which the initiate then returns, reborn or resurrected, to the world of
the living. In many cultures the ritual death is not only symbolic, but is
intended to evoke an experience of genuine religious awe and terror in the
young novice, through which he or she will be deepened to the presence of
spirit in the world. 'Initiatory death is indispensable for the beginning of
spiritual life,'[5] writes Eliade. As he points out, to the primitive mind an old

state must first be annihilated if it is to be changed; the present condition must die so that there can be a *new beginning*.

Each new beginning also reflects the *original beginning*, the creation of the world; hence the cosmogony, the birth of life out of the primordial chaos, is represented in the symbolism of the initiatory rites. Those to be initiated are returned to the original chaos, the state of death or non-being, in order that being may be created anew. Their experience instils them with awe and respect for the divine. The initiation ceremony may represent a re-enactment of the mythical history of the tribe, which serves to reconnect the individual and the community with the source and the Creator of life. It hence also fulfils the purpose of spiritual regeneration for the whole community.

Death is represented by a period spent in darkness and isolation where the young person is separated from the everyday life of the community, and connection to the past life of childhood is disrupted, severed. This may involve being taken to a forest hut built specially for the purpose, being buried in a cave or hole in the ground, or spending time in an isolated place in the bush, desert, or on a sacred mountain. Or the initiand may be blindfolded for a long period, made to lie on the ground in silence, covered in leaves, as if dead. Symbolically the return to darkness represents death by such means as being swallowed by a sea monster, or buried in the womb of Mother Earth. It is frequently accompanied by harsh physical ordeals and tortures, such as circumcision or scarring; the initiand may have to fast, be prohibited from sleeping for several days and nights, and be 'scared to death' by the prospect of being devoured, dismembered, or killed at the hands of mythical beings or deities.[6] The young person is psychologically changed and spiritually strengthened by these encounters and sufferings; the intensity of the experience brings him or her to a threshold beyond which he or she moves towards maturity. The severity and duration of the ordeals varies considerably from one culture to another, but the meaning is universal.

The initiand may then be symbolically resurrected or reborn. In many cases the state of death is also identified with a return to the womb, a period of gestation where a new life prepares for birth. Much of the imagery associated with initiatory death therefore also reflects a return to an embryonic state. In some male rites, the initiand is forbidden to speak, to feed himself, or walk upright, having instead to crawl on the ground or lie there inert; he may be buried in the womb of Mother Earth or wrapped in skins from which he will later emerge, signifying birth. Rebirth is represented by return to the light of day and the community of the living, but the ritual has served to disrupt life as it was before and the young person returns profoundly changed. The initiated is the 'twice-born', but born this time into a spiritualised state of being.

Today we have, by and large, no formal channels for the ritual of initiation into adulthood, and yet if we look at the mythic imagery and the nature of the ordeals associated with such rites we can find that they are occurring in a whole range of different ways all around us and within us. The mythic journey of initiatory death and rebirth is being re-enacted internally through our inner experiences and externally in society; but because we are usually unconscious of the greater meaning, and have little to guide and orientate us, we flounder and founder, or find ourselves blindly attempting to re-enact our initiatory ordeals again and again in destructive repetition, as we seek for their completion through addictive patterns of behaviour. Psychologists would call this a repetition compulsion.

Depression and chronic or terminal illness bring us psychologically into the dark womb, the chaos of primordial night, the belly of the sea monster which devours us and denies us participation in life, cuts us off from the freedom of innocence and our former state of ignorance. Severe illness, both mental and physical, can reduce us to a helpless foetal-like state, totally vulnerable, dependent, isolated, and 'in the dark'. But there is also an element of 'brutality' in the initiatory process, as represented in many cultures by the physical ordeals and mutilations that the initiands must suffer as they are symbolically torn from their former life and self-identity. When we look at much of the violence in our society today, we see reflections of the initiatory rites attempting to be enacted: bullying, street fighting, gang warfare, juvenile delinquency and crime, and the tortures we hear about in the legendary public boys' school initiatory rituals seem to reflect in many of their details some of the elements of primitive initiation rites. We could see this as bearing witness to a deep-seated need in the psyche of young people to experience ritually the death of their childhood state, and entrance into the community of adults.

Yet today these rites, often extremely cruel, violent, and misdirected, are performed outside of and sometimes against mainstream society, rather than as part of the intrinsic fabric of the culture – outside of an organised system of religious or mythic belief and social structure, without the wisdom and guidance of the elders, but by the young people themselves. Uncontained, the forces that direct the initiatory process may become unmanageable and destructive to both self and others. In an earlier chapter, I mentioned the book *Lord of the Flies*. This story can be seen as just such an initiatory ordeal for the boys involved. Unintended and unguided by the wisdom and experience of their elders, the boys' initiation into manhood evoked savagery and primal forces they could not contain. Such a story suggests that the need for initiatory experience is so strong that the situation where it might occur will be unwittingly created, if it is not consciously provided.

The symbolic wounding may also be turned into violence against one's self — acts of suicide, self-mutilation, poison by drugs, either medical or recreational, alcohol, and 'accident' often reflect graphically elements of the process that is symbolised in ancient initiation rites. They may be attempts by the unconscious psyche to participate in the ritual death that makes possible rebirth into a new way of being. The ultimate punishment of prison also seems not to deter many young offenders; some almost seem to seek out this form of boundary as if in an unconscious attempt to recreate the symbolic space, the place isolated from the world, in which the rites of initiation into adulthood can occur. In some subcultures, a boy is not considered a man by his peer group, until he has spent a period of time in prison.

Too many people today seem to be getting lost in the initiatory process and are literalising what needs to be symbolised and ritualised. The extreme horror of this can be seen in war, where elder statesmen send millions of young men to sacrifice their youth and be initiated into manhood on the battlefield. But this is a gross distortion of the initiatory ritual, one that has lost contact with meaning and religious context, and too many of the deaths end up being not ritual and symbolic, but tragically real. If we could understand the deep significance of, and need for initiatory rituals, then perhaps we might be able to stop much of the needless violence that we are all suffering from and perpetuating today, whether it be violence inflicted upon ourselves or upon others. That doesn't necessarily mean returning to the ancient ritual forms of other cultures; we have to create our own ways of ritualising our passages through life, which reflect the culture we live in today. But we need to become aware of the meaning and significance of initiatory ordeals and rituals, and how the phenomenon of initiation is attempting to come into our consciousness today. We may begin to find new ways to address some of our intractable social problems if the pathology we are witnessing today could be re-evaluated in this light.

Initiation of the Shaman

A second category of initiation in primitive cultures is into secret societies, usually either male or female only, though not always. This type of initiation is not taken by all members of the community, but generally a person can be initiated by request. Again, the motifs of ritual death and rebirth are central to the initiatory rites, which are usually more severe and arduous than the obligatory rites of puberty. Spiritual strength and courage must be cultivated through these ordeals. As with the puberty rites, the novice is initiated into secret knowledge, traditions, and ceremonies to which the uninitiated do not have access, and which bring him or her into closer contact with the sacred. The initiate of a secret society may endure symbolic or ritual death and rebirth not once but many times.

The third category is the initiation of the shaman, 'technician of the sacred' as Jerome Rothenberg describes her. The place and function of the shaman has been central to the society of primitive peoples throughout the world of antiquity, going back to prehistoric times, and the practice of shamanism is still found amongst some cultures today. The shaman is many things; he or she is healer and mystic, artist and poet, psychopomp, visionary, and wise person to her community. She may fulfil the functions of priest and politician as well as master of sacred ritual. Her knowledge encompasses the sacred and the secular; she knows the herbs and plants of the earth, the laws of the cosmos and of the human psyche, the mythic life of her culture. The shaman may possess powers that correspond to those of the magician, sorcerer, and medicine woman, but as Eliade describes, shamanism is essentially a religious phenomenon that embraces but is distinct from the practice of magic and healing.[7]

What distinguishes shamanism is that it is first and foremost a 'technique of ecstasy', to use Eliade's definition. In shamanic cultures, ecstasy is considered to be the essential religious experience, and the shaman is the 'great master of ecstasy'.[8] She is therefore a figure of central importance in the religious as well as social life of the community. Today ecstasy has come to mean 'an overwhelming feeling of joy, rapture',[9] but its root is in the Greek word *ekstasis*, which means 'standing outside oneself'.[10] We may come into a state of ecstasy, be 'beside ourselves', through terror, awe of beauty, pain or grief, rage or unbounded joy and rapture. The shaman is one who can travel to the farthest reaches of such extreme states, who can perceive beyond her ordinary earthly existence and journey 'outside of herself' to the highest realms of heaven and through the gates of the underworld to hell.

In the view of shamanic cultures, the cosmos consisted of three worlds – the middle world, or earthly reality within which we normally live, the celestial realms of heaven, and the underworld of death. At the centre of the world was an opening through which passage may, under certain circumstances, be made between the three worlds. Joan Halifax writes of this:

'The Centre of the World, the *Axis Mundi* or world axis, the "unmoved mover" of Aristotle, is the threshold place between space and spacelessness, between multiplicity and unity, between mortality and immortality. It is said of this cosmic centre that it is everywhere.'[11]

Eliade remarks that:

'The symbolism of the "Center" is not necessarily a cosmological idea. In the beginning, "Center", or site of a possible break-through in plane, was applied to any sacred space, that is, any space that had been the scene of a hierophany and so manifested realities (or forces, figures, etc.) that were not of our world, that came from elsewhere and primarily from the sky. The idea of a "Center" followed from the experience of a sacred space, impregnated by a transhuman presence: at this particular point something from above (or from below) had manifested itself.'[12]

It is at this sacred place, which is both the centre of the world and potentially everywhere at once, that the shaman may descend to the underworld or ascend to the sky and heaven. The *axis mundi* may be the Holy Mountain or World Tree, actual or represented by a pole in the ground, a ladder, or platform for example. The tree and mountain touch both sky and the depths of the earth, intersecting the middle world; by it the shaman can ascend or descend through all the realms. The sacred threshold place may also be found within a plant such as tobacco, or an hallucinogenic substance, which is held sacred when used to stimulate a shamanic trance; or it may be in the drum or other ritual object which carries the shaman on her ecstatic journey. Sometimes the passageway between the worlds is depicted as a doorway that opens and closes very swiftly; passage through it must be made instantly, or not at all.

In some cultures, a belief is held that at one time there was no barrier, no veil separating the three worlds; communication between them was spontaneous and sacredness permeated the whole world. However, through some 'sin' of humankind, the possibility of existing simultaneously in all three worlds was denied to the people. The shaman is the individual with a special ability to maintain contact with the transpersonal realms, and communicate on behalf of the people with the powers beyond.

The powers with which the shaman interacts are the gods and spirits, beings of the other worlds who are non-human or non-corporeal. In the shamanic world-view, everything is connected; spirit lives within matter, within the plants, animals, stones, and earth, and the shaman is one who perceives and participates in this state of unity. The shaman can communicate with the spirits of ancestors, of deceased shamans, and of animals. In her travels to the other worlds she confronts the spirits and demons that cause sickness, learns what a patient needs for healing, offers sacrifices, and receives messages from the gods or Supreme Beings which cause fortune and misfortune to befall. She also escorts the dying in their journey to the underworld, or brings back a soul that has wandered and got lost there. The shaman is one who has died herself and returned to life, and through this she has mastered death; in dying she becomes in a sense immortal and can travel at will between the worlds of the living and the dead, of ordinary and non-ordinary reality, acting as mediator between her people and the powers which bring sickness, life, and death.

The shaman's death is her initiation. Very few become shamans; unlike the tribal or puberty initiations, that of the shaman is individual. Shamanism is a calling that requires special election. In some cultures, the shaman inherits her vocation from a parent or ancestor, and a few seek to become shamans of their own volition; these latter are considered to be lesser shamans. In most cases, the shaman is 'called' to her vocation by the gods and spirits. Not all go willingly, but it is said that refusal to accept the calling can result in incurable illness or death. Initiation occurs through dreams, visions, and physical or mental illness; sometimes ceremonies similar in kind to the puberty rites, but of far greater severity, also form part of the initiatory process, but shamanic initiation can occur wholly in the inner realm of dream and vision.

A direct experience of death is the essential element of initiation, and it may occur through accident, illness, psychological disintegration, dream or vision, and sometimes in the course of the ritual initiation ceremony. The ordeal is of the severest kind, the suffering and terror experienced extreme; the initiand is taken beyond the edge of unbearable pain and fear where all that is known about self and the world dissolves, and the very core of self is broken open. Through such an extreme disruption of normality the shaman's being is reduced to utter nakedness, and thus opened to spirit.

Symbols of the descent may include journeys to the underworld, under the sea, through caves and labyrinths, or into the belly of a monster. The theme of death by dismemberment is most common; the organs may be removed and then replaced by new ones, or by crystals, precious stones, or sacred objects. Often the head is cut off first, so that the initiand may watch her own dismemberment. Or the flesh may be stripped from the body to reduce it to a naked skeleton. Skeletonization:

'...[I]ndicates a passing beyond the profane human condition and, hence, a deliverance from it.... . [D]eliverance from the illusions of the flesh...[is a] recovery of the very source of spiritual existence, which is at once "truth" and "life" '.[13]

Death may also be by fire, sometimes by 'cooking', or by ice. Initiation may also occur through an ascent or flight to the sky and celestial heavens; or descent to the underworld may be followed by a journey of ascent. Possibly, this provides a necessary integrating and unifying experience after the disintegrative process of descent into the lower world.

The shaman experiences all of this subjectively. The patriarchal mind views death in terms of the realms 'beyond' or 'hereafter', hence the exiling of the gods and goddesses associated with death and the dark side of life and human nature; but the shamanic way is to learn to encounter and master death through direct experience. Through this, when actual death eventually comes, she knows the territory and the ways through the underworld, and does not fear it. She has become in a sense immortalised through dying in life.

Instruction into the ways of shamanism always follows or accompanies the initiatory death. This may occur through tuition by elder shamans, or in dreams and visions by gods, animal spirits, the spirits of sickness, and the spirits of dead shamans. Without this instruction, training is not complete, but it is the experience of death and rebirth alone which marks the true shaman; if initiation does not produce a genuine ecstatic experience, then the initiand will not be accepted as shaman. Joan Halifax writes:

'Three days dead, three years dead, like the dark of the moon, is the pause between the personal past and a realized, transtemporal life. Dreams and visions, madness and sickness cause loss of the neophyte's soul. The soul thus freed of the time-governed mortal body is open to instruction and ultimately transformation.'[14]

The person who is to become a shaman is often of a particularly sensitive disposition, and may show signs of disturbed behaviour, often from childhood or adolescence. Frequently the child has lost a parent early in life, or suffered some other shock or unusual event that may have left her particularly sensitive and vulnerable. As was discussed in the chapter on the wounded child, such sensitivity leaves the child and adult especially open to the collective unconscious and to psychic phenomena beyond her own personal and immediate experience. Such a person is potentially more attuned to the collective and transpersonal dimensions if her psychic 'skin' is thin and fragile, her ego boundaries less clearly defined. She is easily 'possessed' by forces that her personal will cannot control, which take her 'out of herself'.

The shaman-to-be is often afflicted by a long period of illness that no kind of medicine or healing can cure. This incurable condition is often of a psychological or psychosomatic nature, involving a partial or complete disintegration of the personality which is death-like in essence, and usually necessitates a prolonged period of withdrawal from normal life. It may be many years from the onset of illness, the visionary experience, or the dream that heralds the shaman's calling, until the time when she is finally healed and can begin to shamanise. But, as Joan Halifax reminds us, time is needed in order that power can be safely manifested:

'The initial call to power takes the shaman to the realm of chaos, the *limen*, where the cosmos is disorderly, where power moves freely – untransformed. The beginning of mastery of that power can be ecstatic. The act of mastery, however, implies that balance and equilibrium have been achieved, creating a right presence of mind. Only the practice of power allows for its mastery; and only through time and experience is the potentially damaging power safely manifested.'[15]

Healing comes when the shaman's profane self is sacrificed, through psychological death, to the sacred vocation to which she has been called. In dying, she sacrifices herself for the benefit of her people, to act as medicine woman, seer, and spiritual leader to them; the shaman's initiation is never only for her own healing, but is in service of others. This points to an important issue concerning the meaning of wounding and sickness, and its sacred purpose for the community; in shamanistic cultures the wounding of the individual is recognised as the opening through which the gift of healing and divine knowledge comes to the people. The sickness of the individual called to be shaman is necessary to ensure the health of the whole community and its right relationship to the cosmos. In the phenomenon of shamanism lies a gift, and this gift may also be a potential within many cases of psychological illness witnessed today. Eliade writes:

'Disintegration of personality and possession are symptoms common to many North American initiations; but when loss of personality and possession occur with exceptional intensity, they are the outstanding syndrome of shamanic vocation.'[16]

'...In Siberia, the youth who is called to be a shaman attracts attention by his strange behaviour; for example, he seeks solitude, becomes absent-minded, loves to roam in the woods or unfrequented places, has visions, and sings in his sleep. In some instances this period of incubation is marked by quite serious symptoms; among the Yakut, the young man sometimes has fits of fury and easily loses consciousness, hides in the forest, feeds on the bark of trees, throws himself into water and fire, cuts himself with knives.'[17]

The symptoms of the future shaman's sickness appear similar to states of acute psychopathology and madness. However, two major factors distinguish the experience of shamanic initiation from mental illness. Firstly, the shaman is one who has cured herself, has suffered a psychological or symbolic death and returned to life healed and reborn into a new state of existence:

'Like the sick man, the religious man is projected onto a vital plane that shows him the fundamental data of human existence, that is, solitude, danger, hostility of the surrounding world. But the primitive magician, the medicine man, or the shaman is not only a sick man; he is, above all, a sick man who has been cured, who has succeeded in curing himself. Often when the shaman's or medicine man's vocation is revealed through an illness or an epileptoid attack, the initiation of the candidate is equivalent to a cure.'[18]

The completion of a process of profound healing must involve a full return to life, a renewal or rebirth; if the process of renewal has not been completed, the sick person may make only a partial return, not healed in the fullest sense, and cannot bring back the gift that was potentially promised. In the case of the shaman, initiation is complete when the gift of shamanising is revealed and the sick person returns to life with something of value to offer to the community. Often the shaman is not cured until she begins to shamanise, at which point her illness may completely disappear. Her initiatory ordeal was not for herself alone, but for the benefit of the people, and she may not be freed of the symptoms of illness until the deeper purpose of the initiation is fulfilled. Because she has intensely participated in the experience of sickness and death, she is now able to commune with the spirits that cause sickness, and with the souls of the dead, and so has gained access to hidden knowledge and the power to heal both body and soul.

Secondly, the shaman's initiatory illness and ordeal follows a pattern that is universally recognisable, and the content of her visionary experiences relate to the specific mythic structures of her culture. The reality that she has encountered on her inner journey into death is not a private one, but is a cultural reflection of a universally perceived reality. Thus she can return to the land of the living with knowledge and wisdom that serve to renew the very foundations of the religious culture in which she participates. The psychotic, on the other hand, is considered to encounter a reality that is divorced from that in which the majority of people live, and hence her experience is thought to have no benefit for either herself or others. However, this is a belief that needs to be more widely explored and seriously questioned. The shamanic, and in general the religious, view shows us that there are other realities as valid as the 'middle world' reality of which we are normally conscious. When we evaluate the psychotic's reality against our own, we are assuming that our consensus reality has some kind of ultimate validity, which in fact it does not. As we explored earlier, there is a madness deep at the heart of the supposed sanity of modern society, and we cannot entirely blame the sensitive individual who is unable to adapt to 'normal' reality *and* maintain her or his inner integrity.

There is today a small but growing movement in psychotherapy and psychiatry, seeded originally by the work of Jung, towards exploring the shamanic view in relation to profoundly disturbed states of consciousness. In his extensive work with altered states of consciousness and the perinatal experience, Stanislav Grof has discovered unquestionable relationships between states of regression in individuals, and spiritual dimensions of their experience, which closely resemble the shamanic journey. He writes:

'The perinatal dynamics seems to represent an intersection or frontier between the personal and the transpersonal; this is reflected in its deep association with birth and death – the beginning and end of individual human existence. The transpersonal phenomena facilitated by holotropic therapy or traditional shamanic methods reveal connections between the individual and the cosmos which are at present beyond comprehension. All we can say is that somewhere in the process of perinatal unfolding, a strange qualitative Mobius-like leap seems to occur in which deep self-exploration of the individual unconscious turns into a process of experiential adventures in the universe-at-large – a process that involves what can best be described as cosmic consciousness or the superconscious mind.'[19]

John W Perry is another psychiatrist who has done much research into this area. Joan Halifax writes of his findings:

'[T]he insights of psychiatrist John Weir Perry into the psycho-symbolic processes of individuals diagnosed as schizophrenic give us important clues about the archetypal nature of the shamanic complex (*The Far Side of Madness*, Perry). Dr. Perry elaborates ten features that characterize the reorganization of the Self... .

'The Renewal of the Self, as Dr. Perry describes this process, has striking parallels in the shamanic complex. Each feature has its counterpart in the psychosymbolism and mythos of the protohistorical world.'[20]

There appears to be an archetypal process at work in the individuation journey, as Perry discovered, which is also reflected in, or a reflection of, the shaman's initiatory ordeals. In the shaman's vision we find a map of the journey of individuation which creates order out of the chaos of intense emotional and psychic experience; and through artistic and poetic creation she gives expression to the most profound human experiences in a language that is transpersonal and mythic.

'The psyche that is emotionally saturated organizes itself by means of mythological conceptions that form an explanatory system which gives significance and direction to human suffering. The seemingly irrational is found to be ordered though paradoxical. The socially unacceptable becomes the stuff of sacred social drama. The extraordinary dangers that are encountered in the psychophysiological adventures of the shaman become at first bearable, and then ultimately heroic.'[21]

During states of psychic disruption and disintegration, a process of deep psychic healing is attempting to occur, for which there is little guidance in our modern culture. Having abandoned belief in gods and spirits, and lost meaningful connection with the mythic patterns that underlie our lives, we are culturally adrift when faced with these depth experiences, with little to orientate or guide us through them. The pattern of shamanic initiation, however, which has persisted since the beginnings of antiquity, may offer such guidance for an experience which is still occurring today, and with increasing frequency, in the midst of modern civilisation. As Melanie Reinhart writes:

> 'Many extra-ordinary states of consciousness which were recognized by shamans to be of potentially healing value if handled correctly are pathologized by us, labelled, suppressed with drugs or negative attitudes, and perhaps somatized into fatal disease.'[22]

The attitudes and interventions of society can be extremely damaging to the course of such a healing process if it is not understood, supported, and guided appropriately. The potential for rebirth can be easily aborted. It may not be only the potential for personal healing that is lost, but the gift that the initiated person might return with may also be a gift that will help others in their own healing and transformatory journeys. Within the extreme reaches of the individuation process, a shamanic initiatory experience may be attempting to unfold.

We might assume that initiation would also represent individuation for the shaman, though it may not necessarily be true that every process of individuation today also results in shamanic vocation. Individuation brings personal healing, but what distinguishes the shaman is the ability to use the power, knowledge, and healing gained through her own death-rebirth experience for the benefit of her community. *And* the shaman dies not once but again and again; as master of the technique of ecstasy, she has the power to leave the ordinary world and travel in other realities. She lives on the threshold between the worlds and can journey at will and consciously. She knows the ways through the underworld and the celestial heavens alike, and so can return, bringing knowledge and wisdom that will benefit and heal. For the shaman, death, renewal, and rebirth is a process with which she engages continually.

'Knowing intimately and personally the realm of sickness, decrepitude, dying and death readies the shaman for his or her actual mission.... . By dying in life, the shaman passes through the gates of fire to the realm of eternally awakened consciousness. Having tasted immortality, the laughter of compassion wells up from the human heart. The suffering that the shaman endures, then, gives rise to the realm of play, for the shaman is both in *and* out of the field of life.

'...[S]hamans are trained in the art of equilibrium, in moving with poise and surety on the threshold of the opposites, in creating cosmos out of chaos. The Middle World, then, is still a dream that can be shaped by the dreamer.'[23]

Shamanism Today

So might personal growth and healing through the individuation process be related to shamanism in modern culture? As the work of Dr Perry and others shows, the process of individuation sometimes takes a person through extreme states of psychosis which very closely resemble in both content and structure the mythic journey of the shaman through initiatory illness and death. As explored in earlier chapters, psychosis is a state that is potentially open to any one of us, and in the present period of social and global turmoil, with its opportunities for awakening consciousness, many people are opening or being opened to deep psychological experience. It is one of the disturbing phenomena of our changing modern world. The disruption of normal life that marks the shaman's initiatory illness traditionally may last for three or seven years; whether these numbers are actual or symbolic, they point to the long period of submersion in the inner psychic process which is required to develop the power and equilibrium needed to master the power that has been accessed. Today we are witnessing an epidemic of long-term and chronic illness, physical and psychological, which appear to defy all cures, both orthodox and alternative. The parallel with shamanic initiatory illness should not be overlooked. Together with this are the seemingly unresolvable problems of our global community in crisis. As Melanie Reinhart writes:

'Today, whole cultures are already in a state of disruption, dissociated from harmony with nature and floundering in a profusion of broken religious, societal and family traditions. We could see in this the symptoms of a *collective* initiatory illness.'[24]

If there is truth in this perspective, then clearly our attitude and approach to the disruptions and illnesses we are experiencing needs to change. Denying feelings with defensive posturing, suppressing symptoms with drugs, misunderstanding and wrongly labelling profound states of consciousness, invalidating potentially transforming experiences with reductive theories, and dealing with social ills through aggression, repression, and judgement are some of the many ways in which we individually and collectively may dismiss or abort potentially healing crises. When someone is in an extreme state of consciousness a safe place is needed to protect her and enable the process of dissolution to occur; as we saw earlier, the 'cocoon' is both an understanding attitude and an actual safe place where the experience can be supported and contained during its extreme stages. When all of one's energy and consciousness is focussed on the mythic and transpersonal dimensions it is difficult, extremely painful, and at times impossible to focus attention on the mundane. The need to be completely absorbed at times in the inner process of spiritual and psychic renewal has been understood by all pre-modern cultures and religions; periods of retreat from ordinary life, whether in the monastic cell, forest, desert, mountain cave, or women's menstruation hut, were considered natural and necessary to religious and spiritual life. We are now sorely in need of finding ways to support the process as it is manifesting today in states of spiritual emergency.

The shaman's potential comes to fruition in large part because there is a cultural context to hold her experience within. She receives support, guidance, and instruction at both an outer social, and an inner psycho-spiritual level. Without a mythic and historical context to orientate and validate her experience, and a tradition of knowledge within which she can learn how to use her gifts, she may become as lost as the chronic schizophrenic. Not only is the shaman's experience, when recognised, given credibility, but it is highly valued; the shaman herself is respected and revered by her community.

A culture that has lost touch with its roots in a living mythology, and even denies the existence of the psychological need for such roots – a culture that has banished the gods and spirits, and dualistically separates the worlds of matter and spirit, of life and death – has nothing by which to hold and guide a person through the initiatiory experience. Processes that may be shamanic in essence can only be labelled, and hence treated, as pathological, when there is no meaningful context for them. In modern society and medicine, the potentially healing crisis is rarely supported in a way that allows it to come to completion. The individual may remain chronically sick, or the symptoms may periodically return without a real healing ever taking place. To heal, to become whole, the experience of death *and* the gift that is found through it must be embraced and integrated into life. Whatever was missing before is found during the initiatory journey, and must now be re-included in the fabric of the individual's life. If the potential that is striving to emerge is continually thwarted, we cannot know whether personal healing might also involve a vocation of service to the community that could be shamanic in essence.

It is neither possible nor desirable for us to go back wholesale to a primitive consciousness and simply embrace the beliefs of another culture, although I do believe we can learn greatly from them, particularly in our present time of global crisis. If shamanism is to exist in modern society, and there is much evidence to show that it is re-emerging, then it must do so in a way that is congruent with the consciousness of the modern world. Healing is most effective when the patient believes in the system being used; a common ground between healer and patient greatly enhances most approaches to medicine and healthcare. The belief systems of our culture may need to shift or even break wide open in order to embrace the perspective of the shamanic view. But consciousness is evolving, and old knowledge and traditions will also be reviewed through the lens of new awareness.

I hope that traditional shamanism will continue to survive in those communities where it is still being practised today, and that western people will continue to be interested in learning from these teachers and their traditions. For some westerners, the practice and even lifestyle of the traditional shaman may feel appropriate, but for most people grown up in modern society this is not really a viable option. We need to be realistic, accept that we are moving forwards not back, and perhaps need at this point to embrace what is relevant and of value in the tradition of shamanism for our world today. Shamanism is the oldest form of religion we know of; it has existed for many millennia, and may continue to exist in some form far into the future. It is not new for shamanic elements to be successfully incorporated into the so-called 'higher' religions, as consciousness and culture develop; elements of the shamanic Bon religion of Tibet, for example, were integrated into Tibetan Buddhism, and there are many aspects of ancient Greek culture and religious rites that have shamanic elements. There are other examples, such as Taoism, and even orthodox Judaism and Christianity retain some relics of shamanic essence, though to a lesser extent and more covertly. Such incorporation of older belief systems and traditions does not need to be viewed as regressive, but can be highly enriching and integrative of otherwise repressed areas of experience. The growing interest of westerners in the teachings of the American Indian medicine wheel, in Taoism, and Tibetan Buddhism, for example, seems to indicate that they offer something highly relevant to us today.

In *The Shaman's Doorway* Stephen Larsen records the account of JB, a young white American, who successfully underwent shamanic initiation with a Dogrib Indian named Adamie. Although he had visions and gained power through his arduous training and initiation ceremonies, he eventually found that he could not remain within the Indian community and adopt the traditional lifestyle and work of the shaman there. It was too alien from his own culture. And yet back at home in Brooklyn he struggled to find a place for himself again; here there was no ear receptive to his song, no context within the culture for him to enact his vision, no easy place for the power he had gained. He speaks of the difficult choice he faced after being initiated into a tradition that was so far removed from that of his own culture:

'I would be a second-rate shaman if I stayed.... A sort of crazy man who hung out in the woods and went down to Edmonton in midwinter, because I wasn't Indian and couldn't stand the barrenness. That's pretty much where I'd be. I would have been between two cultures... .

'It's coming back into the world with a song after having a vision – but then there aren't many people to share it with, not like a primitive tribe where you can come back and say, "Here are my bear's teeth or my vision, this is what my name is, this is the spirit who guides me." I can't really do that here... .

'I felt I had to go back to my own culture, to work things out. I had to somehow take the little I'd mastered back to my own culture, and make it work there. There's no grounding mythology for me here, no strong physical presence of a human guide, but the song remains. The song is always there.'[25]

Rather than attempting to adopt shamanism, its belief systems and culture, we may be in need of integrating something of the essence of shamanism into modern consciousness and culture. If we don't we may be at risk of being overwhelmed by the powers, however we name them, which are calling us individually and collectively to heal through initiatory illness and death. Today we may prefer to call those powers, the gods and spirits of antiquity, by other names; we might understand them as the powerful emotions, psychological complexes, thought-forms, and archetypal powers that live within us. As we come to an understanding that it is forces within us that create the conflicts, the chaos, and sickness we suffer from, we cease to project them outwards, and learn instead to confront the gods and spirits of sickness within us, in whatever powerful and terrifying forms they may take on. The actual *experience* of people today seems to be not so different in essence from the shamanic experience, but we *name* it differently, for the process of individuation exists within a new context of awareness and understanding that is psychological in orientation.

It must be said that there are dimensions of shamanic experience that go beyond the understanding and skill of even the most adventurous and insightful proponents of modern psychology. The shaman is also a mystic and mystery is, and maybe should remain, at the heart of the phenomena. There *is* more than meets the eye. Therapy is the place where a person may seek help when going through what may be an initiatory crisis. However, the therapist may not necessarily be open to such a perspective *and* have the personal experience and capacity to guide someone else through such an initiatory process. Initiation has always been performed by the already initiated, as only they can mediate the powers of the transpersonal dimension. The requirements of whatever power has 'elected' a person for initiation may differ from the projected theories of the therapist about what this client needs psychologically; dealing with the 'calling of the gods' as if it were *only* a personality or character disorder may be disastrous, or at best ineffective therapy. However, the therapist does also need to attend effectively to the sickness or pathology of the client, for it is the way to healing.

There are many potential pitfalls here. We may be playing with fire and not know it. And yet we need to learn how to play with it. Jung was the first modern psychologist to open the doors to the mystery realms of the human psyche. Others who have followed him are further exploring and mapping the paths that may lead us deeper through those doors. The psychotherapist of tomorrow may indeed need to be the one who has travelled 'from the Promethean peaks through the blazing ecstasy of death into caves of remembrance'.[26]

The traditional shaman, as we saw earlier, fulfils many functions – she may be medicine woman, seer, visionary, priestess, artist, and political leader. Society over the ages has moved further and further towards specialisation, and the function of the shaman today has also followed that trend. All of these roles are now rarely taken up by one individual alone, but by several, each expert in their own field. The shaman of today may be a healer, therapist, mystic, artist, writer, teacher, *or* social and political leader, for example. That does not mean that all of these people are also necessarily shamans; the shamanic vocation necessitates a profound experience of death in life, and the mastery of states of ecstasy, the ability to go beyond oneself at will and travel within the inner terrain of altered states of consciousness in order to find wisdom, knowledge, and inspiration. Shamanism is essentially a religious experience which reunites the worlds of the sacred and profane. And yet it could be in any of these specialised areas that we may find the shamanic experience being expressed today. (I wonder, for example, how so many years of incarceration might have affected Nelson Mandela, after he returned to political life, with such dignity, wisdom and inspiratory leadership.)We may also find it attempting to unfold through the visionary experiences of the 'insane', as well as the inner work of the meditator or the client in therapy.

We have looked in previous chapters at how the transition we are facing today is of a movement away from social structures, rules, and values that are God-ordained and fixed, towards the process of individuation through which each person may connect to and learn to live by their own values, conscience, and authority. We are moving towards an age where the voice of each individual in the group seeks to be heard and listened to, and unreceptive hierarchical structures no longer serve as they once did. This also means that the responsibility for our own health, healing, and growth now lies more fully in our own hands than with those who represent authority for us. The 'priests' of the church, of the medical professions, and of the psychoanalytic and psychotherapeutic circles become less god-like and almighty in their power and authority over us, as we as individuals begin to search for wisdom, healing, and inspiration within ourselves.

We are already witnessing today the beginnings of a movement towards personal experience of the sources of healing, life, and spirit. We may in time become less dependent on the 'expert' of religion or medicine to mediate for us with the powers that determine life and death, as we seek more and more within for our own direct experience. In this the function and position of the shaman, as mediator of the worlds of spirit, must also shift. As divinity becomes a matter of personal experience, and wisdom and authority are gradually internalised rather than projected onto others, the emphasis can shift from hierarchical structures where responsibility is taken by the few, to systems of mutually supporting individuals who are able to participate actively and consciously in their own healing and growth, and hence in that of their community. I don't mean we will no longer need teachers and guides – initiation has always involved transmission from a teacher, in some cases directly from the 'gods and spirits', but in most traditions the source of inspiration is represented by a living person who has also been initiated – but our relationship to the outer teacher changes as connection to the inner teacher grows.

Here we come back to the relationship between the individuation process and shamanic vocation. If there is any truth in this vision of the consciousness emerging – and there seems to be much real evidence to suggest that there is – then the potential is that each individual who is able to transform deeply and heal him or herself also participates through this in the growth and transformation of the community of which she is a part. This may happen on a subtle level; we all know of instances in our own experience when something within us has changed, and immediately a change also happens in our outer environment or relationships, which seems to have been spontaneously facilitated by the inner shift. In such moments we realise how connected we all are, and how personal healing can contribute in some small way towards collective healing. But we can also participate more consciously and actively in the growth and healing of our communities when we bring awareness from our inner searchings back into the relationships we have, or renewed creativity and insight into the projects or work through which we contribute to the world. I am suggesting that every individual who is able to transform and heal their own being at a deep level may return, like the shaman, with deepened awareness and 'the ability to transform self, others, and nature'.[27]

The process that Jung called individuation may in fact be one form that shamanic initiation is taking today. When the disturbance has affected the deepest levels of psyche, when psychological death has been suffered and the healing allowed to follow its course to completion, the process may be considered shamanic in its essential content and purpose. If a gift is brought back which serves the community, and the individual has learnt to travel between the worlds with 'poise and surety', can make the journey into the heights and depths of experience again and again to access the wisdom and treasures there, might we not essentially call this shamanism? Ancient traditions may be finding new forms of expression appropriate to our age and culture; the challenge is to keep alive what is of value in the ancient traditions as we search for these. And sometimes it takes no form; there are people who have the ability to transform simply through their presence – being without doing. This may be an evolution of shamanism to which we are aspiring today. It is the essence of Buddha activity.

Stephen Larsen, in his excellent study of the shaman's vision and how it relates to society today, writes;

> 'Our great myths are heaps of broken images, and our spiritual sight seems unable to penetrate beyond the personal level, the little vision. This may indeed be the most basic fact the contemporary spiritual seeker has to take into account. We may be moving, at least for a while, into a time of individual rather than collective mythology. We have been used to myths only of the collective variety, validating the myth of the individual only when it would fit into the larger one of the sociocultural framework. But the changed emphasis we might now have to take into account is on the personal journey. The collective myths are fragmented, dismembered, and the

responsibility for finding a meaningful place within the universe falls back on the individual.

'When the shamans are dismembered, as we now collectively seem to be, they look forward to the prospect of recreation, of being born anew. And it may very well be that like them we will gain the mastery of those same primordial forces that have been devouring us, fragmenting our collective identity, breaking our mythic images. The pieces are, in fact, all around us now, and perhaps our present task is most like that of those spirit healers who reconstitute the shaman; or that of Isis with her helpers, looking for the pieces of her beloved brother-husband Osiris. We may join in the task and find that in the process of helping to reassemble the god we are also recreating ourselves.'[28]

The Myth of Chiron, the Wounded Healer

An exploration of shamanism as it is manifesting today would not be complete without a discussion of Chiron, the image through which the archetype of the Wounded Healer is now expressing itself. Like the phenomenon of shamanism, the meaning of Chiron is complex, and I will only attempt here to give a simplified account of the myth and its significance for us today. I have drawn particularly on the work of Melanie Reinhart, who presents an in-depth look at Chiron from an astrological and psychological perspective in *Chiron and the Healing Journey*. She describes what she understands the planet Chiron to represent as:

'…[A] spirit of philosophical independence, compassion in the face of our suffering, and an ongoing process of learning to trust the Inner Teacher or Guide. The Chironian way of learning is to prepare oneself to listen to the Inner Teacher, whose classroom is no less than our own life experience and whose skills develop over time by allowing meaning to emerge organically.'[29]

Chiron was one of the gods of the ancient Greek pantheon. He was a centaur, half-human and half-horse. In this, he represents the conflict, and also the potential healing of the conflict, between our upper, rational, civilised human nature, and our lower, instinctual, untamed animal nature. Historically the splitting of instinct and passion from reason and the spiritual aspirations of 'civilised' man began with the dawning of the patriarchal age. Chiron, as a symbol for the conflict *and* the potential healing of this split, is significant at this time of transition when the patriarchal age is coming to an end and we are being called to re-embrace archaic modes of consciousness and the more 'primitive' levels of our being. The reintegration of body, mind, and spirit, masculine and feminine, consciousness and feeling, control and passion are central issues in this time of transition, and it is to this that the image of Chiron speaks. Astrologically, Chiron is associated particularly with times of transition, which also hold potential for the healing of old wounds.

In the myth, Chiron was orphaned at birth, rejected by his mother as the offspring of a passionate, instinctual union, and never known by his father. Like many people in our culture today, Chiron was thus wounded early on in life in both his relationship to his parents, a rejecting mother and absent father, and to his own instinctual nature:

> 'When a child has no loving relationship with its parents or guardians, its psyche is left wide open to the imaginal realm, and ego-formation is hindered or prevented altogether. Positively, this can foster in us (just as Chiron was fostered) an early sense of destiny and the urgency to develop our own individuality; negatively, it may drive us to flee from the pain of our wounds into an increasing emphasis on the spiritual in a rarefied and one-sided way, where the instincts are suppressed in order to maintain a false sense of elevated consciousness. Needless to say, the instincts will eventually hit back in order to redress the imbalance, often causing crises of physical or mental illness.'[30]

The orphaned Chiron was fostered by the sun god Apollo, 'god of music, prophecy, poetry and healing, a noble paragon of youth, beauty, wisdom and justice'.[31] Although obviously a gift in many ways, Apollo's civilising and educating influence would also further separate Chiron from his instinctual nature, deepening the wound. Chiron himself became a renowned healer, wise man, prophet, and teacher, but as 'the mediator of Apollonian ideals in a kind of harmony, culture, order and creativity which sets itself *against* the instinctual'.[32] He was teacher to many of the heroes and healers of ancient Greece, but it was by one of his students, Hercules, according to one version of the story, that Chiron himself was wounded. He was struck by an arrow in his leg, a poignant symbol for the woundedness that he, like many of us today, had already suffered to his 'lower', instinctual nature. Chiron, the famous healer, was unable to heal himself. It is said that he suffered so much from the agony of his unhealable wound that he lived a life of retreat in a mountain cave, on the dark side of the mountain where no sunlight fell. Those seeking healing and teaching would come to him there in his wilderness home, but he himself was unable to participate in life as they did.

Chiron, as the Wounded Healer, may represent that which we can do for others but cannot do for ourselves. His woundedness represents our own open wounds which continually bleed and will not heal, but which in fact keep us sensitive to the suffering of others and force us to look deeply within ourselves for the essential nature of healing. Like Chiron, in our search to find relief from our own suffering, we may learn much with which we can help others, but none of it heals our own deep woundedness. This is a situation so many people today in the helping and healing professions know too painfully well. In fact the understanding we gain and the skills we learn through our own search may eventually become obstacles to our own healing, for they can become so many ways of trying to escape from or get rid of the pain of our woundedness, when what is actually needed is acceptance and surrender.

The unhealable wound is what we must face when we descend to the underworld in the depths of an initiatory crisis, for within it lies our healing. Like the shaman, we must encounter the gods and spirits that cause our sickness, sacrifice our flesh and our life to them; only through this will they restore us to life. Each spirit is said to cause a specific illness; the shaman gains the power to heal the illnesses caused by each spirit that has eaten her flesh during the initiatory ordeal. The shaman gains mastery over the spirits of disease not so much through *knowing* them, but through being intimately *known by* them, through surrender and sacrifice to them.

Chiron's own plight shows us that all the methods of healing we have at hand may be of little real benefit when we are confronted with our own deepest wounds:

'...[W]hen a plethora of cures, philosophies and methods of growth continually seduce us into the sneaking feeling that "If I could only just (scream it out, analyse it away, discover the meaning of it, understand the astrology of it,...) then everything would be all right." Chiron's story underlies the need for acceptance of our woundedness as a precondition for any healing that may follow; it also shows how the wisdom of our own psyche may bring us healing in ways that we have difficulty receiving.'[33]

Unable to heal his wound, Chiron is also unable to die, for he is an immortal god; and so he suffers interminably. But eventually he is released in a fateful exchange of places with Prometheus. Prometheus had been punished by Zeus for tricking the gods, not respecting and giving them their due; for his rebellion and his inflated defiance of the gods, Zeus had him chained to a rock where every day his liver would be torn out by a huge griffon. However, it would grow again each night, and so Prometheus was doomed to suffer eternal torture. The one condition for his release was if an immortal would take his place, and in so doing give up his immortality.

Significantly, it was Hercules, the original cause of Chiron's wounding, who petitioned for Chiron to be allowed to take Prometheus' place; from Hercules' action we learn that 'it is *that within us which wounds us* which must repent and come to our aid'.[34] Chiron is thus associated with both shamanic and homoeopathic healing, where 'like cures like'. The exchange was made. Chiron died and was finally released from his suffering. He was later immortalised by Zeus as the constellation Centaurus. Through dying, Chiron's woundedness is healed. He is healed through renouncing his god-like state of immortality, the perfection of culture which cut him off from his physical, instinctual nature; in his dying he becomes mortal and fully human, but paradoxically through it he, like the shaman, also becomes immortalised. He is thus made complete and whole.

Prometheus is essentially connected to the healing of Chiron, and of our own unhealable wounds. Like Chiron, what he represents is of great significance for us today. Melanie Reinhart suggests that:

'The archetypal pattern of the Wounded Healer has constellated, and Prometheus may indeed be seen as a guiding spirit for our age: he represents the clear recognition of the need to uphold our human values whatever the cost, and a parallel warning to give the gods their due. He represents the struggle of individuality emerging from enchainment by the forces of oppression which do not value human life, whether these forces be political or transpersonal.'[35]

The planet Chiron was discovered in 1977. The discovery of a new planet signifies that an archetypal pattern is emerging into the collective consciousness, and it is no coincidence that Chiron, the Wounded Healer, was discovered at this point in time. Poised on the threshold between the old age and the new, we need to re-embrace old forms of consciousness that lie buried within, remarry the parts of ourselves that have grown apart. It is with the wounded and split off instinctual side of our nature, and the conflict of duality between nature and spirit which he embodies, that Chiron is associated:

> '[T]he *reintegration* of mind and body is…one of the major themes associated with the planet Chiron. Centauric consciousness, then, is the capacity for *both/and* – for *both* differentiated rational thought *and* awareness of our connection to the unified force-field which lies beyond what our senses can perceive… .

> 'In psychological terms, Chiron stands at the doorway between the personal and transpersonal realms. He represents the interface between the confines of the ego and the structures of the known world and the vast force-field of archetypal and transpersonal energies that lie beyond, and indeed within, the world of form. Chiron's dimension and way of thinking is that of both/and, rather than either/or.'[36]

This both/and consciousness may emerge when, like the shaman, we have immersed ourself in that which lies beyond, or deeply within, communed with the gods and spirits, surrendered and sacrificed ourself in the primordial womb of life where we die and are reborn. But most importantly it may emerge when we have also *returned* from that experience and can integrate the learning, the 'messages of the gods', into conscious thinking and action; this is the mark of the shaman – the enactment of vision. Not to do so is to remain in a state of regression, submersion in unconscious content, undifferentiated. The shaman lives comfortably and consciously in both worlds. The both/and consciousness which Chiron represents is equivalent to the non-dualistic 'threshold' awareness of the shaman which perceives spirit in matter and matter in spirit; or, in the terminology of Buddhism, emptiness as form and form as emptiness.

Chiron's wounded lower body points to the need, when the separation of our own upper and lower selves has led our instinctual nature to rebel and create illness, to pay attention through the wounded body to what we have denied or rejected within ourselves. The wound calls us home, to be at home in both body and spirit. Our body symptoms, our dreams, and our visions can guide us through the worlds that lie beyond the world of form, to encounter the 'spirits' that are causing our sickness and are also the source of our healing. Chiron reminds us to:

> '...[N]ot seek to rise above or transcend human life, but rather to embrace it, acknowledging both divine immanence and also the reality of the unknowable beyond the forms which our senses perceive and our minds imagine.'[37]

Dance

I will go to the mountains
and dance, where the dance
will be my only witness.

I will be near the sea and there
carve my moving into the wind's sharp edge,
softly roll the sand into its meeting
with the cold shock of wave
upon wave.

I will find a green jewel meadow, grasses
in the sunlight swaying
to my own heart rhythm, dancing
with me.

I will lie on soft brown earth
sweet from sighs of whispering
leaves, like lovers, in the breeze meeting,
touching, parting.

I will go to the mountains
and dance for joy, for I
can feel my soul ride on the circling wind,
can know my body press, fall, fly
into the earth's great arms.

8 The Way of the Artist

Traditionally the work of the shaman embraced the arts of ritual and theatre; she was actor, dancer, poet, musician, and artist for her community, as well as healer, mystic, and visionary. Artistic creativity was in fact inseparable, in the shamanic vocation, from the functions of healing and divination.

The shaman's costume itself was often an extraordinary and elaborate work of art, depicting in symbolic form the myths of the people, the essence of the shaman's initiatory ordeals, and images of the gods, spirits, and animals which were her helpers. The designs of masks, headpieces, drums, and other ritual objects were also rich in symbolic meaning and infused with powers from the gods and spirits of the 'other world'. In the shamanic ceremonies of initiation, healing, and divination, the story of the shaman's flight or descent to other realms would be acted out, sung, or recited in poetry so that those present, the community or family members of the sick person, could witness and participate in the journey.[1] The beat of the drum or rhythm of the chant often transported the shaman on her journey to the other world. There are also many examples of paintings and sculptures representing the shaman at work. There is no doubt that the creative arts were the essential medium through which the shamanic journey was enacted and often induced, and the vision communicated to those concerned.

The earliest forms of artistic activity had their origins in the tradition of shamanism, and the original function of art was both personal and social, but primarily religious. The concept of religion is not so popular with many people today, including many artists, associated as it is with hierarchical authority, dogma, and repression; but I refer here to its original meaning and function as a bonding to something greater than ourselves, a uniting together with, and in reverence of, the intangible powers that underlie our lives. The work of the artist is one important way through which the vocation of the shaman may still express itself today; in essence, the tradition of great art in human culture goes back in an unbroken line right to its source in the shamanic tradition. Great art holds the potential to unite people together in a common feeling of appreciation and awe at the beauty, power, and mystery of the hidden forces of life.

As we noted earlier, in ancient times the role of shaman encompassed many functions – healer, visionary, priest, magician, politician, poet, psychologist, ritual master – whereas today we live in an age of specialisation where it is rare to find one person embodying more than one or two of those functions with any degree of mastery. We are usually identified as a poet *or* a politician, a priest *or* an artist, a healer *or* a dramatist. However, there is still very much in common between these diverse occupations. All are concerned, ultimately, with the healing of souls – the soul of the individual, the soul of the community, the soul of humanity.

Yes, even the function of the politician could, and I believe should, be regarded in this way, although today there may be not so many leaders in positions of power who truly assume the art of healing society as part of their role. And yet what we are in dire need of at the moment is politicians who can lead us through these turbulent times with wisdom and vision. Individually and collectively, we experience being split, fragmented, in conflict within ourselves and with others; both inner and outer relationships are in need of healing. We need leaders in all areas of life who have the power to envision and create a future in which human society is not tearing itself apart at its core, and that means the power to evoke healing in the collective as well as the individual. World-wide, people are suffering so much because we do not have enough people in the positions of greatest power with a genuinely compassionate and inspired vision.

The artist and creative person is one who is connected to and enacts her vision. I will use the general term 'artist' to include those who practise all forms of art, such as music, poetry, writing, acting, dance, as well as the visual arts; much of what is discussed here can also be applied to creative thinkers, philosophers, scientists, as the creative process is similar in essence no matter what our medium of expression. It is the potential of the creative artist as 'visionary' and 'healer of souls' which I now wish to explore.

The Artist as Healer and Visionary

The artist, like the shaman, lives on the threshold. One eye on the world within and the other on the world without, her awareness travels between the two. Her creative imagination is a bridge between tangible, earthly reality and the other world of the gods and spirits. The artist must learn to live with this threshold awareness; she must learn to travel between the worlds, like the shaman, and bring back to ordinary reality her vision of beyond, her experience of non-ordinary states of awareness, giving form to them in the creative act.

The threshold lies between the worlds of dark and light. It is the place where the darkness of the unknown touches the light of possibility, where the past in which we have been bound opens to the vision of that which is our potential. Standing at the threshold, we stand in the present – and present to our past and future also, in touch with our wholeness. Such a vision opens us to mystery; it may give no concrete answers, but its message is recognised by the mind of intuitive knowing. When we open to this level of intuitive mind we can bear to stay with the uncertainty of not knowing, to hold the creative tension until new ideas and solutions emerge, and see that the threshold may be not just a state to transition through. For the artist and the shaman, the threshold is a place to live – a place in which to hold out, often alone, in the face of the unknown. It is not only a border but also a bridge between the worlds. Accepting the nature of the threshold is essential for the artist; both light and dark, known and unknown, are contained within this acceptance, and the present held in eternity. The threshold is the place where we may step beyond dualities, and this is the work of the artist. Marion Woodman writes:

> 'Soul dwells in the intermediary world, in the subtle body.... .
> Journeying between earth and heaven, joining one to the other,
> the soul understands the language of poetry, the language of
> metaphor, which integrates the image with feeling, mind and
> imagination. The metaphor, or the symbol, heals because it speaks
> to the *total* person.'[2]

Engagement in creative activity can be likened to the initiatory ordeals or ecstatic encounters of the shaman. It involves a total entering into threshold awareness, a 'living in the ambiguous not-quite-here-and-not-quite there', writes Keith Thompson. He goes on to say:

'[T]his transition between states of being…is a place of enormous fertility and spacious potential, even though most of us tend to experience openness and receptivity as emptiness and loss. In his classic essay "Betwixt and Between: The Liminal Period in Rites of Passage," Victor Turner writes that the major function of the transition between states is to render the subject invisible. For ceremonial purposes, the neophyte – that is, the one undergoing initiation – is considered structurally "dead". That is, classifiable neither in the old nor in a new way. Invisible – not seen.

'…On the other side of the frustrations of life in the margins lies a perception available to those willing to enter it: not being *able* to classify oneself is also *freedom from having to* cling to a single identity. Living betwixt and between, in the realm of uncertainty and not-knowing, can make possible new insights, new ways of "constructing reality". In this sense the … experience serves as an agent of cultural deconstruction, prodding us to take apart easy ideas about the supposedly interminable gulf between mind and matter, spirit and body, masculine and feminine, nature and culture, and other familiar dichotomies.

'Living in the ambiguities of marginality can be seen in terms of paradise lost, or else as a refreshing freedom from having to keep a particular one-dimensional sense of paradise intact. We can mourn the loss of clear boundaries, of black and white, right and wrong, us and them, or we can willingly enter the marginal, liminal, twilight realms of being, discovering face-to-face our unmet demons and angels – facing them, if we choose, as fiercely as they face us.'[3] (Original italics)

In *Fruits of the Moon Tree*, Alan Bleakley describes two stages of initiation. The first is into memory, a descent into the earth-tomb and primordial womb of consciousness, where we return to our source and origins. We surrender to memory of personal history, and to immersion in the great and timeless mythic processes of death, birth, and creation. In the work of psychotherapy or analysis, this would represent the uncovering and reworking of past personal history and deep psychological processes. For the shaman, it is the mystical flight or the descent, dismemberment, and death at the hands of spirits or demons, the journey to the other world to seek vision and knowledge. In the same way, the artist dives deeply into her unconscious, submerges herself in the realms of living imagination, fantasy, feeling, archaic memory, and collective myth for the vision, the image that will inspire and inform her work. It is the undoing that will eventually release new creative energies and inspiration.

Initiation into Memory is a timeless, wordless process. As with the shaman, it is played out in the inner terrain of deep psychological experience, vision, and dream. The underworld processes are hard to articulate in words, and should not be revealed too soon. There must be a necessary period of incubation, of going inward to the source, allowing time for the creative work to take root and grow in the depths. Disturbance of the process at this stage by premature revelation can dissipate the creative power. Learning to fathom these depths can be difficult and dangerous, and many months or years may be spent in this first stage of initiation until some degree of mastery of the overwhelming forces of the unconscious is achieved. The person who founders here or remains too long and is unable to return with the gift, the created work of art, risks, like the shaman, becoming lost in the world of psychosis or depressive illness. But once the art of travelling between the worlds is mastered, the artist repeatedly engages with other dimensions of consciousness, rooting her creativity within her depths and drawing from this source for inspiration and guidance.

This is not always a comfortable or easy process. In order to draw creative power from her depths the artist must confront the gods and spirits or, in our modern day terms, 'deep psychological needs, spiritual energies, healing powers, archetypal fears, prophetic dreams, forces of nature, and the souls of the dead'[4]; in other words, all that is normally inaccessible to consciousness. The artist, by the very nature of her work, is in contact with a depth and intensity of feeling and experience that most people touch only a few times in their life. Learning to master these deep realms of experience means learning to embrace the darkness, the loss, the failures, the death, and woundedness within her, as well as her brilliance and power, as a natural part of the changing process of life. She may go through many crises before she is able to enter consciously the experience and safely, successfully channel the energies evoked into creative work. But this is part of mastering the art of living or travelling between the worlds, and creative strength and insight can be gained from even the failed attempts. In another context, this could be likened to Psyche's path of trials, or Inanna's passing through the seven gates of the underworld; such processes always take time, and go in stages. As with the shaman, it can take many years to master the skill of passage between the worlds.

The creative process, like the shaman's initiatory journey, also reflects the original creation of Being out of the cosmic Void. The artist's work is, in a very real way, god-like. It creates a connection back to the sources of life. The forms and images that the artist creates can help us to perceive anew our place in the universe by drawing out of the unformed and terrifying chaos an order that is aesthetic and pleasing to our senses, our heart, and our mind alike. Her creative work may be fuelled by the energy of her own rage, passion, fear, love, or grief, but if her work speaks to the hearts of others it is because she has accessed levels of collective experience that embrace but go beyond her own personal reality. The artist mediates these extreme states for us in fathoming the depths of human experience and creating form out of chaos. The artist's creation potentially has the power to awaken in us an intuited sense of the meaning of our existence, as it reconnects us to the roots and origins of our being. It brings the power of the darkness into conscious light.

The second initiation, says Bleakley, is of Intelligence. For the person undergoing it, it is:

> '...[A] second Initiation, of putting Memory to use, an initiation of Intelligence, where memory raised to consciousness is then concretised in creative *act*. For the second initiation he becomes as the Hanged Man of the Tarot, who hangs by one leg from a T-shaped tree, as immersion in symbolic life, to return with a gift. The one-eyed then becomes the one-legged too.'[5]

The image of the Hanged Man is an apt one for the artist engaged in creative work. He is suspended, tied to the tree, symbol of the *axis mundi*, the place of passage between heaven and the depths of the underworld. One eye looks down into the earth from whence he has now returned, fixed on the realm of Memory whose depths yield the source of his creative vision. He is now no longer submerged in the other-worldly encounter; consciousness has returned to ordinary reality. Yet he cannot move, cannot participate fully in life.

This image represents the artist engaged in the work of bringing into form and into life, of realising or enacting her vision in the everyday material world. The actual giving form or expression through the creative *act* to the vision, dream, idea, feeling, or inspiration, encountered during the initiation into Memory, is the second initiation into Intelligence. It can be, for the artist, as much of a trial and ordeal as the first initiation, though it may be as full of joy as of hardship. Like the first initiation, it demands her whole attention, energy, and commitment; during such periods of creative activity most artists find themselves, like the Hanged Man, unable and often unwilling to engage in the affairs of normal social life. This is an active rather than receptive phase of the creative process, but equally absorbing. The artist's whole being is engaged in the creative act; awareness is stretched between the worlds of material form and the elusive realms of the imaginal, and body is immobilised, suspended between the two. There is, though, a greater degree of distance and discrimination between herself and the very subjective and emotional experience of the initial encounter; a little more objectivity may enter as the Hanged Man looks down upon the territory of inner experience and works the ideas, feelings, and images into tangible and communicable form.

The act of bringing intelligence to bear is the artist's actual work of creating forms that will embody and communicate the elusive, inarticulate experiences accessed in the depths. The soul speaks to all of us in images and symbols, through our dreams, visions, and reveries. The artist concretises these images in forms that can be perceived and shared by others. As with the shaman, what distinguishes the visionary experience of a gifted artist is the ability to bring back to the world something of beauty, of usefulness, or meaning – something that awakens our awareness and communicates to us in a way that is comprehensible within our own realm of experience and perception of reality. In this, the artist contributes to the culture of her community. But she does much more than this.

Today the work of the artist is no longer looked upon as sacred, except perhaps in some rare circumstances. The connection of the creative arts with the shamanic religious vocation has largely been lost, and would probably be denied by many. However, as Brian Bates argues in *The Way of the Actor*, the essence of the shamanic tradition is still undoubtedly to be found in the work of some actors and, I would add, also in the work of artists of all kinds. Though we may call it by other names, the sacred tradition lives on through the work and lives of gifted artists of all media, some famous and some totally unknown.

Here is one small example. Last night I found myself compelled to watch a repeat showing of a film made by journalist Danziger in Afghanistan. I had seen the film once before. It is a moving documentary of his encounter with a war-torn community, and his successful attempt to set up a home for a group of healthy children, 'imprisoned' in a mental asylum with no proper care or prospects of a normal life.

What compelled me to watch this programme again was the image of one young boy that had stayed in my memory. He had been wounded and taken to the local hospital. The rest of his family had been killed in a rocket attack, and he had remained with his dead relatives for some time before help came. As well as suffering severe physical injuries the boy was, understandably, mentally disturbed, and his condition was deteriorating rapidly. He was filmed on what was thought by all to be his last night; it was a tragic moment. But it was not the tragedy of his story that stayed in my mind so much as the incredible light that radiated from this dying boy. At times he would pull himself up in bed and, his whole face radiant and beaming, he would call to everyone, '...I am going to sing. I feel a song coming on.' He would sing and the whole ward would listen, laugh, enjoy, whether it was a raunchy love song or a song of longing for home and times gone by.

Miraculously the boy didn't die that night; he returned from the edge of death and began slowly to recover. An unforgettable light radiated from this child. His horrendous experience, his encounter with death, and the song that welled up from deep inside him show the mark of the true shamanic artist. It was the light that shone from him and the power of his song that I remembered and was so deeply touched by. Joan Halifax describes the shaman's song thus:

'Like seeds buried in the earth or bubbles in the sea's depths, song seems to emerge from the shaman only in a special season. The pain of the body and loneliness of the soul can decay the husk protecting the song within the singer. At that moment when the shaman is most profoundly enmeshed in the experience of suffering or joy, at the moment of ecstasy when he or she is transported to a place that is beyond mortality, the poetry breaks forth to overwhelm, a potent and aesthetic resolution.'[6]

Bates also records numerous examples amongst modern actors, of both screen and stage, of experiences that are, in essence, shamanic. However, as he tells, the actor of today is no longer held with the same kind of respect, or given the same social prestige as in traditional societies. The work of the actor, and the artist generally, used to be considered sacred. Today it has by and large been reduced at best to sophisticated entertainment, and at worst to use for commercial or political ends in manipulating the public, as in advertising and propaganda. Of the demise in status of the theatrical arts, Bates writes:

'Traditional societies today, as were western societies before the first millennium, are crowded with spirits. These pervasive beings co-exist with the material world and are a manifestation of the forces of life and death. They give identity and form to many phenomena for which we have only general terms because they fall outside the understanding of science: deep psychological needs, spiritual energies, healing powers, archetypal fears, prophetic dreams, forces of nature, and the souls of the dead. The spirits represent wisdom: knowledge from the other world.

'These spirits are invisible. Invisible, that is, until the actor incarnates them, is possessed by them, and brings them into the presence of the public through his performance as a human medium...

'...The spirit, through the actor, gives access to visions, voices, mysteries and deep truths. The actor in performance dips into the timeless ocean of human concerns, and intervenes in the conduct of life by incarnating the spirits and their wisdom. The actors and audience know why they are there. They are witnessing, participating in, a sacred ritual.

'So what happened to sacred actors? Religion. A rival religion.

'The world of spirits belonged to pre-Christian spirituality and fell outside the jurisdiction of the Christian Church. Spirits were agents of folk religion, attacked by the Church as "paganism". And actors, as spirits made manifest in performance, were therefore enemies of the new orthodoxy. In its missionary capacity, the Church had to remove actors from the religious "stage" in order to convince the heathen populace of Europe that the spiritual forces of life were expressed not by actors but rather through the intercession of ministers of the Church.

'The Christian missionary campaign in Europe was quickly allied to the political and military authorities, and repressive measures instituted against actors. Performances were restricted and banned. Actors were declared from the pulpit as outcasts. They were described as being possessed not by "spirits", but by "devils and demons". Actors tumbled from their position as high status "performing mystics", interpreting the knowledge and power of the spirit world.'[7]

Not all religious developments have treated their actors and other artists in this way. All over India and Indonesia, dance and music are still performed as sacred art forms; here both 'high art' and 'high religion' blend exquisitely together. The practices of Tibetan Buddhism abound in elaborate ritual, and dramatisations of mythic and spiritual themes are enacted by dancers, actors, and musicians at public ceremonies; their temples are filled with beautiful Thangka and Mandala paintings that have often taken years of meditative work to create. In the Noh theatre of Japan, masks are still believed to embody the power of specific spirits that the actor incarnates when wearing the mask; the putting on of a mask is a ceremonial ritual in itself, with obvious shamanic roots. These are but a few examples of how the sacred traditions of the arts are still being practised in certain societies today. But despite the interest and sometimes even reverence with which western society has begun to accord these traditional art forms, the status of most of our own contemporary artists still suffers from the profanation and commercialisation of art itself. Those who do succeed and receive wide acclaim may be treated as if they truly were gods, but personally they may still be viewed by public and media alike with a certain amount of suspicion.

Artists are frequently still treated, however subtly, as outcasts, and this is in no small way because they are no longer respected as mediators or technicians of the sacred. The undoing of the arts and their mediating function by the Church still lingers on in society's unconscious attitudes towards the artist. Even the most famous and most beloved of our stars, whom we may in fact unconsciously treat like gods and goddesses, can feel like outcasts and are aware that the public may love them but also fears and despises them at the same time. Some of the actors interviewed by Bates know that one fatal slip and the audience, the media, and the public at large wait like vultures to topple them gleefully from the pedestal on which they have been placed. This ambivalent attitude reflects the deep-seated needs the actor or artist fulfils for us, but also the fear we have of the power to transform that they embody. However, an outcast is not necessarily the same as an outsider, and the artist is necessarily an outsider in certain ways.

The artist is primarily an agent of transformation whose function is often to unsettle the status quo, not to confirm it, and this is something we both long for and fear. For this reason, the artist must inevitably be to some extent an outsider, free of certain controls and restrictions imposed by the need to conform. The artist is sensitive both to what is happening culturally and to the spiritual meaning of the times. She perceives the larger picture of the society in which she lives, and reflects issues of current concern in her work; she is also instinctively attuned to the movements of the collective unconscious which underlie the fabric of society, and it is her task to speak of this. She intuitively sees beneath the surface of things to what is real. The vision that her work expresses is not always popular with those who are invested in maintaining order and control. Rollo May writes of this:

'Stanley Kunitz believes the poet is inevitably the adversary of the state. The poet, he says, is a witness to the possibility of revelation. This the politically rigid cannot stand.

'Dogmatists of all kinds – scientific, economic, moral, as well as political – are threatened by the creative freedom of the artist. This is necessarily and inevitably so. We cannot escape our anxiety over the fact that the artists together with creative persons of all sorts, are the possible destroyers of our nicely ordered systems. For the creative impulse is the speaking of the voice and the expressing of forms of the pre-conscious and unconscious; and this is, by its very nature, a threat to rationality and external control.'[8]

Hence the artist must be in some measure an outsider; but she must also be inside, participating deeply in life and in her world if her art is to speak to the reality of others in that world. This is part of the bridging function of the artist; to live in both worlds at once, with an eye to the social context of the times, and an ear to the unconscious tides that will carry us into the future – or in the terms of the shaman, knowledge of both the sickness and of the spirits that caused it, and hence of what is needed to rebalance and heal. Through her awareness and sensitivity to these tides, the artist intuitively reflects the present social and cultural trends, even as she also envisions the potential future, and communicates the essence of this vision through her work. In this, the artist also creates the conscience of the race, as May writes:

'The artist is not a moralist by conscious intention, but is concerned only with hearing and expressing the vision within his or her own being. But out of the symbols the artist sees and creates – as Giotto created the forms of the Renaissance – there is later hewn the ethical structure of society.'[9]

And in doing this, May continues, the artist rebels, as did the saints who:

'...[R]ebelled against an outmoded and inadequate form of God on the basis of their new insights into divinity.... They rebelled ... against God in the name of the God beyond God. The continuous emergence of the God beyond God is the mark of creative courage in the religious sphere.

'Whatever sphere we may be in, there is a profound joy in the realization that we are helping to form the structure of the new world.'[10]

This is both the responsibility and the great joy inherent in the work of the artist.

The sacred and healing function of the artist is connected to the creative process itself as much as to the power that the created work of art conveys. Within the creative process, we should also include the experience of witnessing the work of art; this is also a creative act, an active engagement in which something new and original may awaken in the awareness of the audience, something which was not there before. The process of creating unites opposites and takes us beyond duality. It creates a moment of alignment and integration which can be felt as joyful, exhilarating, liberating, and releases energy that has been bound by a too narrow appreciation of reality. Like the dream image, the creation of the artist originates in the deeper levels of the psyche and brings those unconscious depths to light. Like the dream, it balances what was out of balance, completes what was only partially formed, and thus offers a symbol of, or a way towards, wholeness. Having its source in the depths of the artist's being, where the wholeness beyond duality may be intuited, the created image also has the power to touch that place in the audience, evoking in them the response that will rebalance and realign.

Ritual, like art, serves to contain the paradoxes of life, acting as a bridge between disparate areas of experience. In creating and enacting rituals, we build a vessel that can hold what is both known and unknown, what is complete and incomplete, a sense of wholeness and of woundedness together. The invisible is made visible, the unformed given form, and the successes and failures of life are both held within the mandala that the ritual creates. The artist creates rituals that are both sacred and profane; the smoking of the cigarette, the cup of coffee, the wearing of special clothes perhaps, taking a walk, lighting a fire, listening to music, meditating or praying – these are all rituals that help to create a special time and place set aside from everyday life, within which the creative work can unfold. Within the sacred space that her personal rituals create, the artist can come face to face with the eternal contradictions of human nature and life, and give expression to the wisdom of paradox in her art.

The artist is a juggler, a balancer; she lives at the personal and collective edge of consciousness, and balances awareness of both worlds. For an age that has placed so much importance on the reality of the material world, the work of the artist is essential medicine for our collective ills. It is not only a luxury, enriching the 'quality of life' for the privileged; it is a necessity for the well-being of us all. During the worst times of crisis, whether personal or collective, people will turn to the arts to express their deepest anguish, fears, hopes, and aspirations. In traditional societies people dance and sing at funerals, and also during wars; performances of music and drama were also a highlight for soldiers and civilians of our own society during World War II, for example, necessary food to sustain their spirits through the endless horrors of war.

During times of collective crisis or grieving, people have a strong need to come together and share their experience with others through the medium of music, dance, drama, or ritual; participation in some kind of creative expression is needed, to make bearable and meaningful the unbearable experiences of life. During turbulent times, such as we are in today, when people feel alienated and insecure, they look to the images created by the artist, whether it be in the theatre, gallery, on the street, the cinema, or on TV, for solace, a sense of belonging, and clues as to what is happening to their world. Being sensitive to the collective unconscious and the tides of change, the artist intuits what is about to emerge before it appears to our senses and our conscious mind. Like a sensitive antenna of the collective psyche, she can bring awareness to a situation when her experience and her perceptions are acknowledged. In this, she still has an important role to play in society. We need authentic artists who can touch us deeply, and in such a way that we feel our connectedness to others, our shared humanity; and we also need our own artist within, who reconnects us to our own source when the trials of life have pulled us too far away from it.

When we create art, we draw upon many levels of our awareness and being, and are bringing into dialogue and balancing these often opposing functions. Alan Bleakley's description of the two stages of initiation is a helpful way of looking at this. Essentially the first initiation into Memory is a connection with the deep psyche – all that is normally beyond the everyday realm of consciousness and experience, such as archetypal images and fears, spiritual and healing powers, deep psychological processes, repressed feelings and memories, and altered states of consciousness. The second initiation into Intelligence demands conscious thought, creative activity, sifting, sorting, discriminating, ordering, crafting of the raw material accessed in the depths into formed images. Within these two aspects of the creative process, we see a reflection of the fundamental polarity of receptive and active, yin and yang, feminine and masculine, dark and light. We could also describe it as intuitive, process-oriented, cyclical, 'right-brained' thinking and rational, product-oriented, linear, 'left-brained' thinking. The artist draws upon both aspects of the mind, and in doing so creates connections that help to integrate their functions – building bridges between the worlds.

This duality could also be seen in terms of unconscious psyche and the conscious mind or ego. Let us, for just a moment, give them names; let's call them Ereshkigal and Dumuzi. In this naming, Inanna-Geshtinanna would represent the integrating or synthesising element in this dialogue. The myth of Inanna describes the cyclical process of creativity: Inanna's descent into the unconscious and encounter with the Goddess of the Underworld; the return, where Inanna enacts the power and wisdom she has accessed there in relation to Dumuzi, bringing new consciousness into life; then the completion of one cycle and the beginning of the next turn of the spiral in Dumuzi's descent. Through the transformation of Inanna-Geshtinanna, the opposites have been united in the cycle of eternal creation. Heaven and the underworld are brought into relation through the earthly love of Geshtinanna and the awakening of Inanna's compassion – that is, within the human heart.

This is also the work of the artist – through her own experience of life, of human love, joy, and suffering, she acts as a bridge between the worlds, keeping the circle ever connected. When we are deeply connected in this way we may feel confidence in our power and pride in our humanity, without being taken over by the dangers of inflation and the abuses which this brings; at the same time as recognising our power, we are also humbled by knowledge of the great forces of life and our own place in the universe. The artist may be proud of her creation, but also shy to show to the world a work that touches on things of greatness, yet is at the same time so relatively small and insignificant. At the level of personality, the artist often shows a peculiar combination of confidence and shyness, of personal power and invisibility, which can result from inhabiting the liminal margins of consciousness. The experience and the work of the artist, as well as her own personality, is full of paradox.

The Wilderness as Sacred Space

Every creative person recognises the need for periods of reflection during which time the creative work begins to form. But as well as conscious reflection, there must also be a letting go, a time of doing nothing, of letting the process go unconscious and continue underground. Each artist, in fact each individual piece of work finds its own rhythm, a balanced movement between conscious thought and activity, and a letting-go and surrendering of the work to unconscious processes. To the modern western mind this emptying process, which is so necessary to creativity, has become almost taboo. Day-dreaming is seen as wasting time, and someone spending too much time alone, or in prolonged periods of reverie, is likely to be told to 'snap out of it'. There is a deep fear in our culture of allowing the mind to open to the boundlessness of the unconscious, and yet we all do it because there is just as deep and as natural a need.

The ancient Chinese have long understood this process as a natural part of the cycle of change, which is creativity itself. In modern western thinking, decay and destruction are viewed as the antithesis of progress and creativity, and stillness or inertia is the opposite of movement and growth. To our way of thinking, change and movement are virtually synonymous, while the stopping of movement is felt as a negative condition, a death-like threat, to be manically fought against or avoided at all costs. To the Chinese, however, decay, destruction, and motionlessness are all part of the cycle of change. The opposite of change would be any attempt to stop or interfere with this natural cycle, to try to hold onto either the movement or the stillness beyond its natural course. This results in stagnation that can eventually lead to disintegration, in the Chinese view.

Not accepting or allowing for periods of decay and destruction, as well as stillness and silence, amounts to such an attempt. To keep moving and doing, when we need stillness and just *being*, disallows the natural process of change and interferes with the movement of the creative cycle. In fact the moment of stillness is crucial to the activity of the return journey, the productive part of the cycle, Inanna's initiation. When we deny death, stillness, and the empty space of non-doing, we freeze our life force and creative energies. To release them, we must accept the feelings of loss, pain, and suffering that are inherent in the downward arc of the cycle, and allow the momentum of activity and stillness to flow on.

The artist and creative person intuitively knows this, but because of this knowledge she often finds her instincts in conflict with the acceptable standards of 'normal' behaviour. She may not always find it easy to cope with the manic pace of life today where she finds herself struggling to find the space to be still and silent. The artist has to 'waste time' in order to ground herself and her work within a deeper source of being, and today she must also develop the strength to resist the criticisms of popular opinion for doing this. Without an ongoing renewal of contact with this source, her work will lack genuine power, or she will eventually 'burn out'.

It is to the wilderness that mystics, visionaries, and healers, as well as artists of all times have retreated in order to seek guidance, wisdom, healing, and inspiration. The wilderness is a place of solitude and isolation, of silence and stillness, arid, alien, forbidding, a place where it is hard to sustain life at all. However, it is also the creative ground of transformation. To enter with purpose is to seek wisdom, knowledge, and power. Joan Halifax quotes an Eskimo shaman, Igjugarjuk, as saying:

'True wisdom is only to be found far away from people, out in the great solitude, and it is not found in play but only through suffering. Solitude and suffering open the human mind, and therefore a shaman must seek his wisdom there.'[11]

Jesus spent forty days and nights in the desert. The Buddha spent many years immersed in ascetic spiritual practices, before his final enlightenment. For native Americans, a time spent in the wilderness on a 'vision quest' is essential to initiation. All religions and traditional societies recognise periods of retreat from the everyday world as necessary to gaining spiritual experience and insight, and the mountain cave, the forest hut, or monastic cell provide an experience of the wilderness, a safe place of exile from society for this very purpose. The outer wilderness functions like the cocoon that protects the chrysalis during its process of dissolution; it allows the initiatory process to occur in a way that is protected by social and religious tradition.

The wilderness is sacred space to those who understand the deep need we all have for it. But for most people today, the wilderness is experienced primarily as an inner, psychological state that, when not consciously accepted, can be one of alienation, an existence empty of nourishment, meaning, purpose, or joy. In our depressions, despair, and sickness we may in fact be seeking for this opportunity to retreat from the world for a while, into the empty spaces of the wilderness within which vision may be sought. Illness may signify an attempt by the wise psyche to create the alchemical vessel that will contain the process of inner transformation. Perera writes:

> 'When entered consciously and willingly by a shaman-healer or prophet, the wilderness experience can convey special vitality, special powers and authority; and those powers and the consciousness gained from the transpersonal source can be brought back to enrich the collective. When entered unwillingly as a condemned alien, like Cain or Ishmael or the scapegoat, the desert is a curse.'[12]

The artist enters the wilderness experience in states of absorption, reverie, intense emotion, or ecstasy, through often prolonged periods of solitude. This is essential if inspiration and insight is to flow from the creative source and carry power from those depths. It is not a sign of pathology if she seeks solitude, or often appears 'out of touch' with ordinary reality. It is more closely akin to the meditative states of the mystics, or the wilderness experience of all those who seek vision. The creation of a safe and sacred space is essential both for the artist, healer, and visionary, and for the individual facing a deep healing crisis; it enables the process of transformation, the *undoing* and *recreation* of being, to take place safely.

During extreme states of dissolution, the individual is psychically undefended against the collective unconscious, and requires a safe holding environment. Perry describes the provision of such places in a clinical setting, when extreme processes have led to temporary psychotic episodes:

> 'Because the renewal process causes considerable disruption of the ordinary conscious mind by robbing its energy, favorable conditions are required in which to handle this transition during its progress of several weeks.

'The psyche seeks its own privacy by withdrawal. Psychiatrists generally disapprove, yet ritual procedures included establishing sacred enclosures for renewal processes to allow a clear differentiation between sacred and secular; what transpired in such a sanctuary had different rules. Perhaps the term "retreat" is more fitting than "withdrawal". One good reason for such safe asylum is that the activity of the mundane world is positively painful to people in this state of high arousal. Such activity can also be confusing since one is dwelling at this time in a mythic world totally alien to the mundane. This experience was overt and conscious to people in the ancient cultures of five thousand years ago, but today it is deeply unconscious and misunderstood.'[13]

A renewed understanding and recognition of the need of the spirit for the wilderness experience is called for. The creation of sacred space is a necessity not only for the person engaged in formal spiritual practice, but also for the artist, the healer, and all those seeking personal transformation.

It is in the wilderness that we each face our greatest test and trial. It is a place of death, but it is also a place of potential where, with patient waiting and heightened awareness, we can fathom our depths to find new insight and create the forms that will give expression to the knowledge and wisdom gathered there. The wilderness is transformed, through this awareness, into a garden rich with life, and this life is brought back to enrich and heal the collective. The wilderness within and without asks to be reclaimed. It is our original home.

The Artist in Society

The artist's place in society today is a precarious one. She has been stripped of her function as mediator of the sacred, and the needs and behaviour of the person with artistic or shamanic temperament tend to run counter to the trends and demands of mainstream modern society. This means she is often viewed with a certain amount of suspicion, if not outright resentment or antagonism. The artist, even the successful one, therefore finds herself somewhat on the fringes; if she feels she belongs anywhere, it is usually to a fringe sub-culture, an outsiders group. This can be both a blessing and a curse. All of us have a need to be accepted, respected, to feel we belong somewhere, even if we also have a need to stand apart, alone, not to have our individuality subsumed by a collective whose values are not our own. The artist also stands on the threshold between belonging and not-belonging, and this is not an easy position to hold.

In our society, there is a tendency to view the artist as emotionally unstable, more than usually neurotic, or mentally disturbed in some way. Certainly, the lives and characters of many creative people could seem to offer grounds for this kind of view, but it is a very limited and ill-informed perception. The artist has a particular sensitivity to what is unconscious to most of us most of the time: to deep feelings, intuitive perceptions and prophetic visions, collective psychic energies and archetypal patterns. Her boundaries to the collective unconscious are, like the shaman's, especially permeable and finely tuned. This means that she intuitively experiences and brings to consciousness what most people are subject to but unaware of. Sometimes she reflects what other people would rather not be aware of; the messages of the gods, as Esther Harding reminds us, are not always welcomed by the people.

When the artist reflects something that we do not like about ourselves, our lives, or our social values, something we cannot accept, do not want to look at or own, the artist can become a target for the projection of what is unacceptable within us. In traditional societies, the states and emotions the artist represented were understood to be expressions of the gods and spirits, and hence the audience or observer was challenged to look directly into their own heart to find the meaning that the messages of the gods held for them personally. Today the artist's work has lost this reference point and source of inspiration, which means that it may be the artist herself who comes under scrutiny, as a means for the audience to avoid confronting themselves. The artist who pleases us becomes a star, an idol, a cultural heroine, and her person itself may be worshipped, rather than the powers she embodies for us; but if the artist displeases us we feel quite justified in crucifying her. This is a distortion of the original function of the artist.

When a person is especially in touch with the collective unconscious, through an openness to her own vulnerability, grief, fear, rage, or despair, whether she expresses it in works of art or not, others sense it. And if they fear it, people will shun this individual like a leper, projecting their unowned feelings onto her. The sensitive and unprotected person may pick up these unowned feelings of others like a 'psychic sponge', and if she is not able to deal with the projection of such energies consciously it may eventually create sickness. The person with a 'shamanic disposition' may not be able to defend herself against collective energies. Sensitivity is an essential aspect of her nature, yet it is also her gift, and should not be reduced to merely a symptom of an inadequately developed ego.

The shaman has learnt to deal with these energies consciously and for the purpose of healing, but today we largely lack the understanding of how to deal with such processes safely. The vulnerable and sensitive person becomes the 'carrier' of the ills of those around her, and if living in a psychologically unhealthy environment she may be particularly susceptible to negative effects. She experiences the collective energies subjectively and must, if she is to protect herself from illness, transform these energies in some form of creative activity. Like the shaman who will remain sick if she does not shamanise, the artist may suffer illness and die to her true self if she does not enact her vision through creative work.

I remember a renowned healer, Bob Moore, saying that the best form of protection is expression. This is what the artist does, and she does it both for herself and for society. She consciously experiences and feels for the collective, and transforms what is too big, too painful, too dangerous or awesome for us to experience directly, into symbols and images which we can encounter safely. In this way, the raw material of the unconscious can be more easily accepted and assimilated; through creative transformation, what was harmful in its raw state becomes a source of beauty, inspiration, transformation, and healing. It may still be shocking; art is meant to awaken us, and we need to be woken up in many different ways. But this can initiate transformation and healing too.

The question of the artist's sanity, the closeness of genius to madness, is an issue that has long intrigued people, particularly psychologists, and stimulated much debate and writing. In the traditional psychoanalytic view first put forward by Freud, the creative impulse has been largely reduced to a means of compensating for failures in early development, which have resulted in an inability to adapt to life and society in a 'normal' way – that is, in the way in which Freud and the psychoanalysts believe she should adapt. For example, the fact that some, though by no means all, creative people do not have so-called 'normal' and stable heterosexual relationships and families, and often live alone, has been regarded as a sign of an inability to form such relationships; the fact that the artist may choose and require a different kind of life style and relationship is not seen as the positive choice that in fact it may well be. Nor is it acknowledged in this view that the *capacity* to be alone and to use solitude in a creative way is an ability that not many possess, and which in fact requires a high degree of ego-development and personal integrity to sustain. Where prolonged solitude causes most people to fall into debilitating depression, anxiety, or addictive behaviours, the artist is one who can use it creatively. Anthony Storr discusses this issue in depth in his book *Solitude*.

The attitude that creative activity is a purely regressive process is a gross misunderstanding of the function of artistic creativity, in my view, and reflects a very pessimistic view of the human condition. I agree that an important function of art and the creative process is to help us to adapt – to our own inner impulses, to the requirements of interpersonal and social relationships, to the environment we live in, and to the many dimensions of the universe in which we exist. The shaman, too, facilitates the community's and the individual's adaptation to the 'will of the divine'. However, if we view the function of creativity as *only* adaptive, we are reducing humanity and all of its creative endeavours to the position of victim to life itself. If this were the case then we are doomed forever to the endless treadmill of adapting as best we can to the inevitable sufferings of life. There is no way out of this cycle, no window that will shed a little light and offer another more optimistic and forward looking perspective. There is a risk that a person may spend as much as ten or twenty years in psychoanalysis, digging into the endless problems and failures of their personal history, without making any real or significant changes.

It is here that Jung and the transpersonal psychologists have contributed important insights and perspectives, bringing the dimensions of spirituality and sacredness back into exploration of the human condition. Our problems, anxieties, and fears seen in the light of a spiritual context, automatically take on a different meaning, a different kind of importance, and a sense of the purpose of human existence or of direction in life may be restored. The place and function of creativity also takes on a different meaning. Jung did much to restore to our awareness the value of creativity for healing and as a way of experiencing the sacred. Of course this healing can still be viewed as adaptation to the forces of life, and to the condition of being divided within and without; but the 'adaptation only' view denies the mystery of life and of the creative spirit which exists in all life, and expresses itself most originally through human thought and activity. As Rollo May writes:

> 'Symbol and myth do bring into awareness infantile, archaic dreads, unconscious longings, and similar primitive psychic content. This is their *regressive* aspect. But they also bring out new meaning, new forms, and disclose a reality that was literally not present before, a reality that is not merely subjective but has a second pole which is outside ourselves. This is the *progressive* side of symbol and myth. This aspect points ahead. It is integrative. It is a progressive revealing of structure in our relation to nature and our own existence, as the French philosopher Paul Ricoeur so well states. It is a road to universals beyond discrete personal experience. It is this *progressive* aspect of symbols and myths that is almost completely omitted in the traditional Freudian psychoanalytic approach.'[14]

We can give no concrete scientific evidence for this mysterious creative spirit which integrates and reveals the way ahead; it can only be felt, experienced directly. And it is for this very reason that going further along the route of analytical thinking may never lead us to a radically new perspective, no matter how far along the road we travel. At some point in the study of creativity and the psychology of the artist we must step off this well-beaten track and turn our thinking around. If not, we risk reducing some of the greatest and most creative people – artists, scientists, and thinkers of all ages – to neurotic and disturbed, albeit talented, individuals attempting to work out their personal and sexual hang-ups on the public stage. I think nothing could be more misguided, or more demeaning of the creative spirit in all of us.

It is not difficult to see why such views have arisen. Many artists' lives are unconventional and their characters often seem unstable. Before pursuing this discussion further, let us note that not all artists could be considered more unstable than the average person, nor are all mentally or emotionally unstable people necessarily gifted artists. But there are a number of circumstances that contribute to this popular view. Firstly, as we discussed earlier, the artist has lost her formerly respected place in society as mediator of the sacred. Loss of status inevitably influences the artist's own feelings of security, as well as the attitudes society has towards her. At a practical level, as Bates has pointed out with respect to the profession of the modern-day actor, the majority of artists have little or no financial security. Few ever receive a regular income for more than a few months at a time, or have the luxury of knowing that they will have enough work to live by for any period of time. He remarks that at any one time ninety per cent of actors are out of work – not because of laziness or lack of talent, but simply because of the way the profession is organised in our society. This inevitably creates a greater measure of insecurity than most working people experience, or could probably tolerate, and must greatly contribute to the artist's reputation of being a financial liability, unreliable and irresponsible. Living with insecurity is an inevitable result of living close to the edges of consciousness and of society too.[15]

Studies have shown that in fact the artist can tolerate a greater degree of insecurity, anxiety, and chaos than most people are able to. Living with uncertainty, with the unformed potential of threshold awareness, is necessary to maintaining the creative tension required for the artist's work. The popular belief, which has certainly been reinforced by the psychoanalytic view, that the artist has a weak ego, an underdeveloped self-identity, has also been shown to be erroneous in a number of studies of creative people. To bring to completion works of art the creative person needs, as well as artistic talent, a strongly focussed will, determination, and perseverance in the face of inner doubt and outer criticism. The person with a weak or undeveloped ego does not have these qualities, and is unlikely to be able to bring to completion creative work of any real substance.

Yet the sometimes unpredictable behaviour of the artist can be misleading if it is not understood. Again, Bleakley's description of the two initiatory processes can offer a helpful model. The first initiation involves some degree of dissolution of personal ego boundaries and absorption in the collective unconscious. Of course total dissolution can lead to psychosis; but the artist's skill, like the shaman's, is to master, not be mastered by the unconscious, and there is a very great difference between the two. Like Inanna with her servant Ninshubur, the artist has some knowledge of the world in which she travels, and its dangers, and maintains a connection with the 'upper worldly' ego consciousness. The second initiation can be likened to a reforming, a reconstituting not only of the raw material of the unconscious into artistic form, but of the personal self or ego of the artist herself. She undergoes the initiatory process of dismemberment, death, and renewal, a rebirth of her self, each time she creates.

Self-realisation is not a once-and-for-all achievement for the artist, but a process of continual challenge, renewal, and growth. This means that the artist's personality may undergo quite profound changes during the creative cycle, which to the observer may look like inconsistency and lack of a clearly defined sense of identity; artists frequently experience profoundly altered states of consciousness, and may go through deep crises during stages of their creative work, which are in many ways parallel to the shaman's mystical flight or descent to the 'other world'. The artist's personality and attitude to life is kept flexible and open to change through this process. Openness, curiosity, a willingness to learn, and mental flexibility are personal qualities found in very many creative people. However it is expressed, such openness and fluidity of character is not necessarily a sign of an undeveloped sense of self; it can indicate a person sensitive to the subtler levels of reality and responsive to the changes going on around and within her. Rigidity of attitude and behaviour is usually a sign of loss of contact with one's creative source.

The artist tends to have a greater awareness than the more pragmatic character of the insubstantiality of matter and form, of the impermanence of structures of any kind. She is accustomed to witnessing and participating in the creation and dissolution of boundaries, of images and forms. She knows that the boundary between the worlds of spirit and matter is immaterial, that only the mind creates the separation and the imagination can restore the link. Poetic meaning runs through the tangible world and the world of dreams like an unbroken thread. The artist knows both existence and non-existence, and her work is to restore unity to such dualities. Experiencing non-existence, or emptiness, necessitates also affirming existence by creating form, or the artist intuitively knows she will face annihilation. This is a source of the deeper anxiety that the artist inevitably lives with. Many people prefer to remain unaware of this level of reality that the artist continually faces in her work. To confront deeper levels of reality, and to grapple with the emergence of new forms which this necessitates, inevitably engenders anxiety and also feelings of guilt in the creative person, as May describes:

'A dynamic struggle goes on within a person between what he or she consciously thinks on the one hand and, on the other, some insight, some perspective that is struggling to be born. The insight is then born with anxiety, guilt, and the joy and gratification that is inseparable from the actualizing of a new idea or vision.

'The guilt that is present when this breakthrough occurs has its source in the fact that the insight must destroy something ... . Whenever there is a breakthrough of a significant idea in science or a significant new form in art, the new idea will destroy what a lot of people believe is essential to the survival of their intellectual and spiritual world.'[16]

He goes on to say that in the creative encounter:

'Our sense of identity is threatened; the world is not as we experienced it before, and since self and world are always correlated, *we* no longer are what we were before. Past, present and future form a new Gestalt... . The anxiety we feel is temporary rootlessness, disorientation; it is the anxiety of nothingness.

'Creative people...can live with anxiety, even though a high price may be paid in terms of insecurity, sensitivity, and defencelessness for the gift of "divine madness"... . They do not run away from non-being, but by encountering and wrestling with it, force it to produce being. They knock on silence for an answering music; they pursue meaninglessness until they can force it to mean.'[17]

The openness and sensitivity of the artistic temperament may also require the creation of defensive patterns within the personality – neurotic behaviours, addictions, and so on – which serve to protect the vulnerable core. Certainly some artists find it difficult to cope with everyday life, particularly whilst immersed in the depth of the process, or committed to the act of putting into form. There may be little energy or attention available for everyday life and social relationships, because the creative process can be so intense and deeply absorbing. And defensive mechanisms may be needed to protect the artist's extreme sensitivity and her vulnerability during 'dissolution' phases of the creative process.

At one time the attitudes of society, and the special status accorded to the artist, provided such protection, but now the artist must do it for herself. And of course, if we don't value the work of the artist we will inevitably ask the question, 'why should the artist's irritating ways be given special consideration?', and perhaps think of her as childishly needy or irresponsible. In fact, most artists show an extraordinary degree of responsibility, commitment, and dedication, only not to the same principles as those of mainstream society. Part of the artist's function is to bring us back into balance, so she will always seem to be a little off-kilter to the rest of us if she embodies in her life what she seeks to bring back into collective awareness. Yet, I would disagree with the view that such extreme sensitivity is necessarily pathological. Rather than asking 'is creativity a result of, or a compensation for pathology?', we may need to recognise that what is often viewed as pathological is in fact the psychic opening which allows new insight and awareness to enter into the collective.

A sensitive disposition may be not only a result of the failures of early holding; it may also be the case that the disposition of the child causes her to experience her early environment in a certain way, and the child's innate disposition is as much a causative factor in her development as is her early environment. This view makes the child less a passive victim of circumstances and more a creative force in her own life. Thus the creative person does not become an artist because she has been wounded and cannot cope with life by any other means; we have all been wounded deeply in some way. Rather she is an artist because she has an awareness of and sensitivity to her own and others woundedness – as well as to the aspirations and potential of humanity. The openings in her psychic armouring are not so well defended. She slips easily through the cracks in consciousness which others would side-step.

What I am suggesting here – as with the shaman and also the awakening consciousness of the wounded child and the feminine – is that collectively we need those cracks and we need people who can slip through them: that this should not be looked upon as pathological, but as an essential path towards collective growth and healing. This is not to deny that the artist takes great risks, and sometimes comes adrift in these deep waters. As R D Laing has written:

'Sanity today appears to rest very largely on a capacity to adapt to the external world – the interpersonal world, and the realm of human collectivities.

'As this external human world is almost completely and totally estranged from the inner, any personal direct awareness of the inner world already entails grave risks.

'But since society, without knowing it, is *starving* for the inner, the demands on people to evoke its presence in a "safe" way, in a way that need not be taken seriously, is tremendous – while the ambivalence is equally intense. Small wonder that the list of artists in, say, the last 150 years, who have become shipwrecked on these reefs is so long – Holderlin, John Clare, Rimbaud, Van Gogh, Nietzsche, Antonin Artaud, Strindberg, Munch, Bartok, Schumann, Buchner, Ezra Pound...

'Those who survived have had exceptional qualities – a capacity for secrecy, slyness, cunning – a thoroughly realistic appraisal of the risks they run, not only from the spiritual realms that they frequent, but from the hatred of their fellows for anyone engaged in this pursuit.'[18]

In his study of *The Dynamics of Creation*, psychiatrist and analyst Anthony Storr discusses several famous artists, giving analytical interpretations of what appear to be pathological traits in these creative people. Storr does, however, hold that the Freudian view is only partially valid, and in this and his later work, *Solitude*, he goes a long way towards showing that creativity may be not merely a compensation for a pathological condition, or a form of wish-fulfilment or sublimation of sexual and aggressive drives. Storr explores the psychology of the artist through the ideas of Freud, Jung, and other renowned psychologists, and brings more balance to the question of the artist's motivation to create. He discusses the various arguments as to whether the artist creates out of her unhappiness and neurosis in order to adapt, or compensate for some inner weakness or loss; or whether her creative ability is an inherent gift that may or may not be set into motion by some suffering or loss in her life. His work is well researched and informative, and is an invaluable account of the development of psychological thinking on this fascinating subject. Yet, it stops just short of the point where we need to turn right around and cut through the whole argument.

What is needed is to restore to the role and function of the authentic artist a dignity and respected status in society; and to do this we must begin by acknowledging the importance and even necessity, psychologically and spiritually, but also socially, of the artist for human culture. We need to honour both her creative talents and her sensitive woundedness, which is the gateway to the inner world. It is, after all, primarily through the great works of art that human culture is expressed and the history of humankind recorded. Art expresses what is greatest in human nature, and reflects our perception and experience of the qualities we most aspire to, such as beauty, harmony, love, truth, sacredness. We would be greatly impoverished, psychologically and spiritually, without it. Today, people are undoubtedly fascinated not only by the process of creativity, but also by the state of the mental health of the artist herself. However, this interest borders on an intrusive invasion of the artist's person; nobody studies the psychopathology of the businessman, the lawyer, the politician, or the priest, for example, in such an in-depth or irreverential way. This must be because unconsciously we recognise the sacred power of the artist and the deep significance she has for us. But unless this is made conscious, the artist's role and function will continue to be undervalued and misunderstood, and she will continue to be made to carry the projections of what we dare not own for ourselves. Thus the artist is made scapegoat.

Discussing the scapegoat complex, Perera writes:

'Scapegoat-identified individuals have been devoted to a transpersonal role and carry transpersonal intensities. If they are to serve that role without identifying with its misery and grandiosity, they need other channels into which the released energies can flow. Clinical experience shows that these channels take primarily one of two forms: creative expression into some vessel of art, or initiation into a healing discipline. Both channels permit working at the edge of the collective in order to process the intensities most people cannot bear; and both permit the transpersonal waters to flow in individual patterns.... . These expressions serve the collective by mediating what it needs and can bear to see of itself.... . They serve through dealing with the damaged and diseased aspects of individuals and collectives.... .

'...Exiled scapegoats can, thus, return to serve the collective as agents of its deepest and most difficult needs. They serve by mediating the libido necessary to collective and individual life. But they are also a community unto themselves...they form a loose society of nonconformists. It is one devoted to the transpersonal processes underlying individuality and the secular collectives. Those in this society listen for the guidance that comes from the intersection of life and death, joy and pain, love and wounding. They are more or less willing to feel its paradoxical and raw nature. Since they struggle continually to accept that intersection in their own hearts, they can work with inevitable shadow projections, not as a prelude to scapegoating and splitting in order to attack, but as a means of lifelong personal growth and ethical actions.'[19]

Thus the artist and wounded healer, initiated in the work of transforming collective unconscious processes, engage with the shamanic work of mediating between the worlds of spirit and form, light and shadow, sickness and health, consciousness and the undertow of collective unconscious energies. They are empowered to facilitate renewal and healing for others who seek transformation.

As well as restoring the sacred function of the artist, we also need to honour the artist within ourselves. Most of us may not have the talent to create great works of art, but we all have to some measure the ability and also the need to create. The writing of a poem or painting of a picture, done privately for ourselves alone, can evoke an integrating and healing experience for each of us, just as it can for the artist of great genius. Some form of artistic or creative expression is also necessary to the resolution or completion of a therapeutic process. Natalie Goldberg states this very simply. 'Art goes beyond therapy,' she writes.[20] I believe this is true; art, both the creating and the witnessing of it, takes us out of ourselves, carries us beyond our normal awareness, and thus enables us to experience for a moment the wholeness which lies beyond duality and the states of fragmentation we find ourselves in. Without the greater perspective, the expanded awareness which such experiences can give us, the healing moments of the therapeutic process may elude us.

In his wonderful book on the subject of creativity, Rollo May describes how the creative process is a heightening of awareness, or intensifying of consciousness which:

> '[D]oes not at all mean increased self-consciousness. It is rather correlated with abandon and absorption, and it involves a heightening of awareness in the whole personality.'[21]

May describes how this absorption is truly 'ecstatic', in the sense of being free from the dualistic split between subject and object which is the condition of ordinary consciousness. It brings into relationship the principles of Apollo and Dionysus, achieving 'a union of *form and passion* with *order and vitality*':

> '*Ecstasy* is the accurate term for the intensity of consciousness that occurs in the creative act. But it is not to be thought of merely as a Bacchic "letting go"; it involves the total person, with the subconscious and the unconscious acting in unity with the conscious. It is not, thus, *irrational*; it is, rather, suprarational. It brings intellectual, volitional, and emotional functions into play all together.'[22]

In bringing together the cultured and refined aspirations of the Apollonian principle, with the earthy passions and abandonment of Dionysus, the ecstatic process of creative activity is also closely connected to the myth of Chiron and Prometheus, and hence to the crucial issues of this transitional time in history. Prometheus is an apt symbol for the artist; he embodies god-like consciousness in humanity, and balances the impersonal will of the gods with the personal needs of human nature. In releasing Chiron from his immortal suffering, Prometheus effects the healing of the split between the instinctual-physical and mental-spiritual aspects of his being. This is also, in essence, the sacred and healing work of the artist.

All Goddesses' Eve

Surprising us, behind a tree she glides discreetly
where the thick leaved branches part,
barely seen. Her light in fragments, patched with ever-green,
yet shining still; her wisdom, veiled and partial,
still holds, even as it hides. Golden moon tonight, queen
of All Goddesses' Eve. She seems to sleep, in lofty boughs,
untouchable and tamed of night-deep passions;
her hand, concealed in roundness, searches deep
for fire and purpose
in her slowly cycling womb. But she is only waiting
for the passing of the dusk dark shadowy forms
that shroud her face; pausing
as they bow apart before her solemn
patient smile and soft ploughing through the nightly sky,
before she leaps in joy — so slow and strong, her motion,
to be felt by quiet watchful hearts alone—
into her own.

She rides now the space of sky, her queendom,
treading dusk until the night comes down
to reveal her in her pride and shining, to give honour
to the Goddess light, seen and not seen,
untouched and never used or held, but touching always
to the trail of sky and filling earth with beauty.

See her mystery in the coming and the going
of eternity. Watch her as she draws the empty sky
into her, like a lover
hungry for her radiant form.
She conceives the world this night,
and births her daughters to the souls
who weep and laugh and cry, all in her name,
and sing her name. Luce. Luce. Her name. Her name.

9 Guidance on the Path

When we embark upon the journey of deepening soul and renewing spirit we are required to go beyond the boundaries of what we know. The cutting edge at which we work is the border of consciousness, the limits of what we know and believe about ourselves and our world. In this, we need something to orientate and guide us — a map, a teacher, a philosophy, a theory or principle that speaks to our unfolding experiences. Humankind has always felt a need to make sense of experience by creating systems of thought that contain it; diverse philosophies and mythologies have developed out of this need. We perceive principles and laws by which things work, and create rituals and theoretical maps to contain and express our knowledge and experience of the world. The maps and rituals change as consciousness evolves.

In the crisis of soul and spirit which the modern world is now facing we have, for the most part, lost connection with the guidance that our own western traditions once provided. We find ourselves walking on uncertain ground, swimming though uncharted waters as we step out on the journey that this time of necessary change is requiring us to make.

The consciousness which is emerging in our times needs a holding structure which is both psychological and spiritual in nature, a guiding map that speaks to both the search for personal meaning and freedom, and the universal presence and purpose of spirit. We are evolving beyond the tribal and group consciousness which has dominated the matriarchal and patriarchal ages, where identity was defined through membership of the family or tribe and a God-given place in society. We live in an age of emerging individuality, but with that comes the threat of isolation. As we go through the lonely process of individuation, we experience an intense need to feel our spiritual connectedness with humanity, to become a member of the whole human family. So the process of psychological growth and the evolution of individual consciousness necessitates a renewed connection to spiritual life and values. Without this, the individuation process may turn in on itself to become only another ego-centred quest.

The interface of psychology with spiritual practice is an important one for seekers in the west. It is only in recent times that the science of psychology has been so thoroughly divorced from the paths of spiritual mysticism. Ancient traditions, both eastern and western, were based on a holistic view of the human being where psychological work was at the core of spiritual practice. Before the scientific revolution and the emergence of the materialistic and mechanistic world-view that it engendered, the psychological and spiritual aspects of the human being were seen, and therefore also experienced, as integrally connected. Modern western thought, in separating science from mysticism, has created a gulf between psychological understanding and spiritual experience. Furthermore, religion has replaced the processes of psycho-spiritual transformation, central to ancient mystical traditions, with a morality based on faith and obedience to an external authority.[1]

Our modern culture has lost connection to its spiritual roots, and the traditional doctrines of the church no longer bring meaning and fulfilment to many people. There is a need to reconnect to the teachings of tradition in a way that has personal meaning and value, through our own inner experience and understanding; and there is also a need to restore to life a sense of sacredness, in order to bring together again the disparate parts of ourselves. We are seeking not only maps that will orientate us in the realms of psyche and spirit, but means of reuniting these intrinsically related areas of experience.

Mainstream psychology of the twentieth century developed out of the scientific approach. It provided many helpful models and theories of psychological development and pathology. The fundamental aim of this research and practice was the healing of the personality and the restoration of a well-adapted ego that would enable the individual to relate more creatively to others and to society. Psychology provides the logos – the word of reason and understanding – of the psyche. As such, it addresses all that is essentially knowable and nameable within our experience at any particular time. Modern depth, transpersonal, and sacred psychologies recognise that there is also something within the psyche, or soul, that is mysterious, intangible, indefinable, and in this they offer a bridge between the known areas of psychological study, and the elusive and hard-to-speak-about experiences of spirit. These psychologies include in their explorations the subtleties of transpersonal experience and the worlds of archetype and myth, the dimension of the collective unconscious where the deeply personal meets the universal in the symbols and stories that have unfolded through the lives of humankind throughout all times.

My own path led me to pursue Buddhist spiritual practice and the transpersonal psychology of psychosynthesis. I found myself travelling two paths that were distinct, yet seemed to have many points of meeting. Within this meeting of ways, I felt the possibility of making a deeply personal connection to universal truths, and seeing the personal within a larger context of spiritual meaning and unfoldment.

The initial and preparatory practices of Buddhism, and all well-founded spiritual traditions, have as a primary purpose the development of a healthy and strong vehicle for the consciousness later to be encountered in more advanced practice. This vehicle is a well-integrated bodymind, a stable enough ego, and a compassionate and realistic attitude towards life. To build a secure foundation, we must create a healthy sense of self, and a loving, respectful attitude towards all life. In this the teaching begins with understanding our own psychological nature, and gradually learning the art of mindful and compassionate living and relating. Gradually, with the guidance of the teacher, we create a vessel that will be worthy of the teachings we may be given, a vessel that will not crack and leak the precious energy away.

This process is quite different from the typical ego-building of our culture, which has as its primary objective the maintenance of the ego's own self-centredness. Such a vessel may be too tightly closed to allow in higher and more inclusive states of awareness, or too brittle to contain them. The vessel that we strive to create through spiritual practice is both flexible and strong, but permeable. It develops from a growing sense of the authentic nature of our being, the value of life, and a confidence in our own basic goodness. As we build up, so too do we gradually strip away all that obstructs the clear experience and expression of our hearts, our inner good nature. A kind and compassionate attitude towards all life needs to be cultivated, so the power that grows from spiritual practice will be directed towards positive ends and not used to harm others.

Today ancient spiritual traditions are emerging from the mountain caves and monastic cells, into the heart of western culture. But they emerge into a culture that is based upon a different psychological foundation and belief system from those in which they originally evolved. The western and modern mind, with its roots buried deep in dualistic, materialistic, and individualistic thinking, does not necessarily understand and assimilate the teachings in the way that eastern and ancient cultures were conditioned to do. We may have lost faith in our old God, yet the guilts, fears, and scapegoating practices which centuries of God-fearing religion have instilled in us still survive in our unconscious mind and may subtly affect the way in which we adopt a new religious or spiritual attitude.[2] The lives of our ancestors may live on within us, and our personal and collective history is one of the threads we must observe in our quest for spiritual freedom. The work of therapy can potentially help us to recognise and cut ourselves free from the powerful hold that these unconscious forces exert on us, and deepen us to the level of being where they do not hold sway.

However, it is a limitation of mainstream psychotherapy and analysis that they base their theory and practice on models of sickness, not health. The therapeutic process can be limited by a too-narrow approach that does not offer adequate methods to free ourselves from suffering at the deepest levels. Here the eastern view can help; the philosophy of Buddhism, for example, is based upon belief in the inherent good nature of every living being, and practice focuses on revealing the 'basic sanity' (Trungpa) which underlies our neuroses, and is in fact our true nature. John Welwood writes:

'Western theories of personality and mental health have mostly focused on the causes and symptoms of neurosis and psychosis, while rarely spelling out what healthy human functioning consists of. The Eastern traditions, on the other hand, have emphasized states of optimal health and expanded being, rather than focusing on disease or psychopathology. An East/West approach to psychotherapy needs to bring a larger understanding of human well-being into the healing process...

'...The process of meditation reveals a deeper core of well-being beyond ego strength in the therapeutic sense of a well-adjusted, functioning personality structure. If psychotherapy can heal the self-defeating splits between different parts *within ourselves*, meditation allows us to go one step further, by starting to dissolve the fortress of "I", and heal *our split from life as a whole*.'³

But Welwood goes on to wisely caution us:

'The Eastern teachings assume that a person already has a healthy self-structure. However in modern society it may be dangerous to make such an assumption. The breakdown of family, tradition, and community has undermined the whole fabric of meaning and supports that help people develop a realistic sense of themselves, their possibilities and limitations.'⁴

As we descend into deeper levels of experience, there can be dangers and pitfalls. As Mokusen Miyuki describes, the western ego-structure is different from that of the east; in the east the individual ego is closely identified with the family or collective ego, and it tends to operate in harmony with the collective conscious and unconscious. The western ego, on the other hand, is individual, separated, and less closely related to the personal and collective unconscious.⁵ This may be a reason why the ego-structure of the westerner can be particularly vulnerable to disintegration when deep states of consciousness are evoked through intensive meditation practice, or other methods.

It must be remembered that casualties on the spiritual path are not a recent phenomenon; the occurrence of *kriyas* has long been recognised by ancient traditions as a risk inherent in intensive spiritual practice. There may be a particular danger in those approaches which aim to deny, suppress, or halt the movement of emotions, desires, and instinctive energies that surface through practice. The same danger is inherent in some transpersonal therapies that also stimulate these energies to arise but may not adequately address them, focussing instead on a transcendent pseudo-spirituality. As Stephen Larsen writes:

'It is generally recognized that in the practice of asceticism (*tapas*) and continuous concentration (*ekagrata*), by forcing back the natural flow of energy, which travels from the unconscious sources within to interact with the forms without, an artificial situation is created not unlike the damming up of water behind a barrier or the sealing of a pressure cooker. And as with the pressure cooker, while the goal of intensifying the process within the vessel is served, there is simultaneously the danger of the process getting out of control, or explosion.

'…[T]his deeper engagement is not to be taken lightly, for one has activated the entire realm of the mythological within, demons as well as gods, hell as well as heaven… . …[B]ecause of the intensity of concentration, psychosis may be the result rather than enlightenment.'[6]

A grounded psychotherapy might help avoid or heal such effects, and fruitfully complement spiritual practice, providing its place and purpose on the psycho-spiritual path is properly understood. A therapeutic approach, if skilfully applied, may help to reintegrate the damaged core when powerful psychological energies from the unconscious have overwhelmed the self. As Charles Tart writes:

'…[T]here may be some psychological structures in the personality that have so much charge, so much energy, that specific therapeutic techniques are required to dismantle them, otherwise they have too much ability to distort one's attempt at mindfulness whenever one gets into that content area.'[7]

Trust and Betrayal

Spiritual practice entails learning true surrender – surrender of our inherent sense of badness, of a mistaken conception of ourselves, of self-cherishing and attachment to personal opinions, and surrender of personal will. Surrender of our personal will can be an act of great power when we are ready for such an act, for we are letting go of our attachment to a limited sense of self and opening to something greater. In the *ultimate* view of Buddhism, there is no surrender of the self, for the self as we conceive it has no inherent reality – when we realise this, there is in fact nothing to surrender. But from the *relative* psychological perspective, we form an identification with an experience which we call 'I', 'my self'. From this relative standpoint, we find there are times when we are called to give up our attachment to this limited identification and embrace more of who we are.

To do this we need to be held by something, and it is to this holding power that we surrender. For this, we need trust. It is to the path of our own soul, to our own enlightened mind and heart, and to the spiritual purpose of our life that we must ultimately surrender our personal will. But most of us need intermediaries in this process, someone or something that represents and embodies for us the wisest and most loving aspect of our being. We are called to trust that the one we surrender to is in fact worthy of our trust, and able to hold and guide us as we let go. We may call this God, Christ, Buddha, the Divine Self, the Beloved, or the Enlightened Mind and Heart of the Teacher who embodies the path for us. If we will, we can take refuge in the protection of the teacher's compassion, and surrender to the guidance of her wisdom as we commit ourselves to the unknown territories of our path.

For most of our lives we have been surrendering to false gods – to parents, lovers, teachers, ideals, causes, giving away ourselves to that which cannot truly hold us. We will always be hurt, betrayed, abandoned in this, for the holding we seek is beyond ordinary human powers – but we have not yet looked high and deep enough. To face that which truly holds us means to face ourselves in our own 'godliness', to realise our own 'Buddha-nature', the essence of spirit within us, but it is not easy to accept and realise this within ourselves. The Beloved to whom we surrender is the one who will hold this image for us, until we are able to reclaim the face in the mirror as our own true nature, the Spirit, God-Goddess, or Buddha within.

In the enlightened teacher, we can find such a mirror. The genuine teacher is one whose mirror is clear. She can reflect back to us our own image without distortion because she has realised the inherent emptiness and clarity of her own mind. Her perception of us is not clouded by her own projections, and her actions do not come from motives of self-interest. The genuine spiritual teacher acts selflessly and compassionately towards her student. If we place such a deep level of trust in another human being, it is essential that he or she can respond to us in this way. In trusting and surrendering, we make ourselves vulnerable; we potentially give the other person power and control over us, and open ourselves to the possibility of that power being abused. Trust comes from the heart; when trust is betrayed the heart is broken. It is one of the deepest wounds we may experience.

The same applies to religious or philosophical systems of belief, doctrines, theories, causes, and so on. Sometimes we put our faith and trust not in a person, but in a principle or system of belief. We will only be held to the depth that the system can embrace, and may be let down by an ill-founded ideal or concept just as surely as by an unqualified teacher. When looking for guidance on the spiritual path we need to seek a teacher who has achieved genuine spiritual realisation, and a teaching based upon authentic experience or tested tradition.

Science has become the new religion of the modern world. We have come to worship the supremacy of man's reason and intellect above all else, and the ego orientation of the west does not easily lend itself to the practice of devotion to the guru or submission to the teachings of tradition. Some believe, in these days of proliferate and powerful techniques of transformation, that we need no other guide than ourselves on the spiritual path. At the deepest level, this is true, for we are ultimately seeking the wisdom that lies within us. But most of us need instruction, guidance, and protection at times. We also need the mirror that will reflect our image back to us; without this mirror it is almost impossible to recognise and cut through the subtlest operations of the ego, for the ego will always resist giving up control by cutting through itself.

However, the ego of modern man and woman is often reluctant to accept the guidance of a spiritual teacher or tradition. Deeply conditioned by the presence of the all-powerful, demanding, and punishing authority of the old patriarchal God-religion, and eager to be independent of it, the western mind fears that involvement with a spiritual teacher will require us to give up our own inner authority, integrity, and freedom. It is true that this sometimes does happen, as we have all been deeply conditioned into accepting external authority over our own; this conditioning will affect our relationships to those we see as teachers so long as it remains unconscious.

As a reaction to this, and perhaps as a protection from it, the ego has now grown up to be an authority unto itself, and may judge acceptance of a teacher to be a childish dependency. This is in fact far from the truth; the genuine teacher encourages us to grow up and take responsibility for ourselves to a depth that few of us would have the courage to do without her constant prodding. It is true that the ego has to give up its control to a greater authority, but it is to our own genuine spiritual authority that the clinging ego must eventually surrender. But the ego doesn't very much like being prodded, and it doesn't like surrendering its power. The proud ego wants dominion and readily jumps in at any opportunity to claim whatever power and understanding we have accessed in the genuine search of our depths, allowing us to say, 'I can do it all myself, I don't need anyone to tell me.' Any movement towards genuine spiritual authority is lost, as these statements are spoken from the wrong place, from the place of the usurper of power, the ego inflated with an authority which does not belong to it. We are in fact in some ways utterly helpless to begin the process of freeing ourselves from our conditioned habits without some genuine and trustworthy guidance.

Knowing who or what is a trustworthy guide is a difficult question for a westerner today. The modern psyche is complex, and we have been exposed to so much more intellectual, moral, and spiritual choice than previous generations. There certainly are enough ill-qualified and self-appointed 'gurus' around today to warrant some caution, and also some therapists who overstep the boundaries of their role by inappropriately interfering in their clients' spiritual life. No one should attempt to impose, overtly or covertly, their own spiritual beliefs, attitudes, or judgements onto another; to do so is to override the other's own authority and integrity. If someone in a position of authority, such as a teacher or therapist, attempts to do this to a student or client, it is an abuse of the power that their role lends them. This kind of behaviour is a use of spiritual authority by the ego, and the effect of the ego charged with such power is control and manipulation of the other at the deepest level. Loss of integrity at this level can be dangerous, for we lose our essential ground. When we can allow the power to simply *be*, where it belongs, in our depths, then the gentleness of our inner heart will ensure that we never wrong another with it, never judge, manipulate or make claims over them.

Today, as many people are turning away from the church and orthodox religion, and even the gods of rationality and science are beginning to fade in the light of new understanding, therapy is taking the place of religion for many, consciously or unconsciously. This is understandable, as psychotherapy speaks to the process of individuation, and so to the challenge of the development of consciousness which is now facing us. It is also potentially in tune with those ancient traditions that did not separate psyche from spirit, as we have come to do. But psychotherapists are not necessarily trained and qualified to work with the spiritual dimension of a client's psyche.

When therapy takes on a pseudo-religious function there is a danger of the therapist unconsciously 'playing God'. Transpersonal therapists may be particularly susceptible to this, as these therapies work directly with the spiritual dimension, and offer means to systematically open to transpersonal powers. A therapist must be able to work with great integrity to avoid misappropriating the power evoked through such methods. In the therapeutic interaction, the spiritual authority and power within a client's projections belong to the client, not the therapist. The person in a role that carries authority must always guard against their own ego appropriating such power.

We are inevitably in some way like trusting children if we open to the potential healing that therapy may bring us. There must be an openness to trust and love if we are to redeem our old hurts in the light of a new experience within the therapeutic relationship. But the therapist may be seduced by the trust placed in her, and become inflated with the positive regard of her clients. In the role of therapist or teacher the trap of inflation is one that must be guarded against. Inflation occurs when the therapist's ego takes on power which belongs at another level of the psyche. This misappropriation of power by the ego can be avoided when the teacher or therapist is in relationship to a greater spiritual authority to which she can refer the projected power. Those who work directly or indirectly with the spiritual dimension of their client's psyche need to be in relation to such a spiritual principle or authority.

Psychotherapy cannot work effectively and wholesomely without humility, honesty, and authenticity on the part of the therapist; the pride and arrogance of inflation corrupt the therapeutic vessel and interfere with the natural processes of healing. Pride, arrogance, and inflation in a therapist can be, in my own experience, of far more danger to the client than lack of skill or technique. Similarly, a false 'guru', inflated by the power projected onto her, can also cause great harm to a trusting student when that power is abused.

The attitudes, beliefs, and theories held by those guiding others through deep psychological and spiritual processes, and the kind of guidance or treatment they offer, can greatly influence the way the process unfolds, and sometimes its eventual outcome. A particular theory, practice, and practitioner or teacher can facilitate transformation and healing, but also has the power to misdirect, undermine, and even abort the process altogether. This can be a matter of life and death, sometimes even literal as well as metaphoric death. At the same time, healing through such ordeals is ultimately dependent upon the will, motivation, and courage of the person in crisis; even when damage is wrought by inappropriate or abusive treatment, and all attempts to heal seem to fail, the individual who is determined and committed to her recovery and growth can always find a way through. As Jean Houston assures us, when we have travelled so far along the road, already suffered so much, the gods will not let us be forgotten.[8]

Of course, sometimes in life we do suffer from the mistakes and betrayals of others, but there can still be growth and learning in the experience. We are forced to delve far deeper within ourselves than we have ever gone before. It is when we reach the furthest extremes of disintegration and despair that we must reach further than we know towards the inner source of our healing, and to those enlightened ones who hold and mirror that source of healing for us. When we finally recognise our false gods and accept that they cannot help us, we may begin to truly surrender to the ones that can. In the depths of disintegration we come to understand how it is Love which holds all things together. Loss of the connection to the source that is Love leads to fragmentation and destructive chaos. The 'BA', the term given by the Egyptians to this unifying principle, is described by Bika Reed thus:

> 'Basically a symbol of cohesion, BA represents the unity which mystically links the apparent opposites of life... .

> '...[T]he simultaneous presence in the world and in human beings of both inner conflict and the unity within which it operates, the BA.'[9]

The irony of the situation is that when we are most helpless and in pain, most vulnerable and in need of loving protection and guidance, is when we are in fact most held, most in touch with the Love within and around us. But we may not be able to feel it in our pain and loneliness. There is a Sufi story that tells of a woman who was walking on a sandy beach with God, talking with him. She came to a dark time in her life when she suffered deeply and felt terribly alone. When she later looked back to where she had walked, she saw only one set of footprints in the sand. She cried to God, why had he deserted her in her time of greatest need? He told her that at this time he had been carrying her, and so she saw only one set of footprints where they had walked.

When we travel the path of the heart, it sometimes feels like open-heart surgery, without an anaesthetic. The body feels this, as does the mind. The teacher or therapist may act as doctor and healer in this painful operation; the skilful healer knows exactly when and where to cut, and how deeply. The knife goes in cleanly, and the heart is opened, tender, bleeding from its wounds. We feel its life, the warmth of the blood, and the pain of the cutting knife, but we accept it because we know it will also heal us. If we cut away too many layers at once the pain becomes too great, and our heart feels vulnerable, unprotected; but we are not insane – just a little crazy with the pain we feel. And slowly, slowly as we shed the tears we have held in there throughout the ages, our heart begins to empty out its grief and shed the fear that binds it.

On this path, we are seeking to uncover the 'awakened heart'. In Chogyam Trungpa's words:

> 'If you search for awakened heart, if you put your hand through your rib cage and feel for it, there is nothing there except for tenderness. You feel sore and soft, and if you open your eyes to the rest of the world, you feel tremendous sadness. This kind of sadness doesn't come from being mistreated. You don't feel sad because someone has insulted you or because you feel impoverished. Rather, this experience of sadness is unconditioned. It occurs because your heart is completely exposed. There is no skin or tissue covering it; it is pure raw meat. Even if a tiny mosquito lands on it, you feel so touched. Your experience is raw and tender and so personal.'[10]

The true teacher, and also the good and trustworthy therapist, is the one who can guide us through this awakening of the heart with skill, compassion, and an uncompromising understanding of what we need. The trustworthy guide reflects back to us our inner experience, and holds us through the difficult times, until we are ready to hold ourselves. She mirrors back to us our own beautiful and good nature, but never interferes with it. She can do this because she has travelled the path before us, and therefore does not fear to embrace whatever it may entail.

In ancient Greece the *therapeutae* were the servants who waited on and prepared the initiate for the *sacred dream*; they were the attendants of the gods.[11] The role of the therapist, or healer, was a humble one; he or she did not participate in the sacred dream, but merely served the initiate in whatever way was needed. The experiences of the sacred world of spirit are intensely personal and private. The ancient Greeks understood that the attendant could not enter into the initiate's *sacred dream*, witness and share in the other's revelation and healing, but only assist in the preparations. Therapists today could well heed this simple and humble attitude, and recognise that the spiritual life of those under their care is sacred and deeply personal. When a client opens her heart to the therapist, she is revealing sacred ground that must not be touched or trodden on with carelessness or arrogance. The healing that the *sacred dream* may bring is not something that the servant can participate in, or claim for herself. However, when she acts in a selfless way, fulfils her role with honesty and humility, she will also be serving her own *sacred dream*, fulfilling the purpose of her own soul. Through the activity of genuine service, she expresses and lives her path; this is the path of the Boddhisattva, whose life is dedicated to the service of others.

Emptiness and the Naming of Woman's Experience

Writing this book has been a process of discovering what I know and feel and value, and I have often been surprised by what emerged, surprised to learn what I really know and feel when I open to what is within me and try to name that experience. It is with the naming of experience that I am concerned here, and in particular the naming of women's experience as we go through the birth pains of emergence from the invisibility and oppression that has been the lot of women in a patriarchal society. As Carol Christ writes:

> 'Women's stories have not been told. And without stories there
> is no articulation of experience. Without stories a woman is lost
> when she comes to make the important decisions of her life. She

does not learn to value her struggles, to celebrate her strengths, to comprehend her pain. Without stories she cannot understand herself. Without stories she is alienated from those deeper experiences of self and world that have been called spiritual or religious. She is closed in silence. The expression of women's spiritual quest is integrally related to the telling of women's stories. If women's stories are not told, the depth of women's souls will not be known.[12]

'...Women have lived in the interstices between their own vaguely understood experience and the shapings given to experience by the stories of men. The dialectic between experience and shaping experience through storytelling has not been in women's hands. Instead of recognising their own experiences, giving names to their feelings, and celebrating their perceptions of the world, women have often suppressed or denied them. When the stories a woman reads or hears do not validate what she feels or thinks, she is confused. She may wonder if her feelings are wrong. She may even deny to herself that she feels what she feels.[13]

'...Without stories there is a sense in which a woman is not alive. Continually trying to fit her possibilities into stories where her reality is not acknowledged, a woman experiences nothingness, and perhaps even contemplates suicide.'[14]

It was through my experience in therapy that I became truly conscious of the 'interstices' between my own 'experience and the shapings given to experience by the stories of men'. The therapy I engaged in was founded in patriarchal culture and ideals, and tended to promote a transcendental approach to spirituality – a sense that spiritual realisation was to be accessed through an ascent to higher states of consciousness. This approach did not adequately support a more feminine and embodied approach to spirituality, and risked the dangers of inflation, dualistic denial, and dissociation.[15] Being wounded by this situation initiated the journey by which I could become more fully conscious of deep-rooted patterns of oppression, abuse, and victimisation of the feminine, in both my personal history and that of the collective. My experience as a woman in therapy with a male therapist, inflated by his own sense of power and influence, and not conscious enough of his own shadow, became my guide and teacher.

Therapy sometimes works by the principles of homoeopathic medicine. Like cures like; a very small and carefully prescribed dose of the appropriate 'poison' effects the cure. In therapy, an early wounding situation is often re-evoked by the relationship with the therapist, and if awareness is skilfully brought to bear on the dynamics of this relationship, healing may occur. However, if the dose of medicine is too strong or unskilfully applied, the sickness may deepen. Melanie Reinhart describes this, in relation to Chiron the Wounded Healer:

> 'Thus Chiron is associated with the principle of homoeopathic healing, where "like cures like"... . In psychological terms we can liken this to the "repetition compulsion". The memory of a painful feeling, stored in the unconscious, will tend to attract to it situations in the present which repeat the same ingredients and thus reactivate the old wound. However, these cycles of repetition occur because a wound is still seeking healing, and/or because some change of attitude or expansion of consciousness is trying to occur. At these times healing is possible, but if the dose of repetition becomes too large, the person may be overwhelmed, and the wound may deepen instead or turn into a fatal illness.'[16]

Collectively we are at just such an edge where healing is needed, and a change of attitude and expansion of consciousness is trying to emerge. To facilitate this change, we are each being challenged to face our inner wounding and the wounding we may inflict outwards on the world and our fellow beings as a result of this. Healing is possible through this time of crisis, but so too is a deepening of the sickness if the dose of medicine is too strong. A deepening of awareness is necessary if we are not to fall into a deepening of the woundedness.

The naming and the voicing of the experience of women are vital to this collective healing process, because women are amongst those who have suffered most acutely from the oppressive and abusive shadow of the patriarchy. The quest of women today is both social and spiritual. For many women, despite a century of social and political action that has resulted in many changes and new opportunities, the word 'equality' still has a rather empty ring about it. And although many women are now reconnecting to the qualities of power and awareness particular to the feminine, it still lies largely underground, not yet fully visible or truly effective within the social and political spheres. Overall, the way of the conscious feminine is still not held in equal value to that of the heroic masculine.

Carol Christ, discussing the work of women writers whose work has a social and spiritual dimension, says:

> 'It reflects both women's struggles to create new ways of living in the world *and* a new naming of the great powers that provide orientation in the world. In order to call attention to the spiritual dimension of women's quest, which is sometimes overlooked in the urgency of the struggle for new social roles, I have made a distinction between the spiritual and social quests. In making this distinction, I do not intend to separate reality into the spiritual and the mundane, as has been typical in Western philosophy. Rather, I believe *women's quest seeks a wholeness that unites the dualisms of spirit and body, rational and irrational, nature and freedom, spiritual and social, life and death, which have plagued Western consciousness* ... . I believe that women's spiritual and social quests are two dimensions of a single struggle and it is important for women to become aware of the ways in which spirituality can support and undergird women's quest for social equality.'[17] (Author's italics)

She goes on to say that the woman who rejects the conventional roles and definitions which have been imposed upon her by society:

> '...[O]pens herself to the radically new – possibly to the revelation of powers or forces of being larger than herself that can ground her in a new understanding of herself and her position in the world.'[18]

When a woman connects to these powers, however she chooses to name them, she grounds her being and her experience as a woman in her own depths. This deepened sense of being connects her to a source of inner strength and confidence, which supports her expression of herself in the world and in relationship.[19] Without this inner connectedness to the power of *being*, our attempts to shape the world, according to our experience and values as women, are not well supported and grounded. To find the power to be genuinely creative and effective in the social and political spheres we need to be grounded in love for ourselves, valuing and cherishing our creative feminine spirits, our women's bodies, our instinctive female nature. Until we are grounded in our own being-ness, we are still at risk of betraying our selves for the love or protection of another, usually a man.

The strength and power of a woman who has been hurt, betrayed, oppressed, or scapegoated by family or society, is rooted in her sensitivity and vulnerability, her woundedness, her ability to feel, to empathise, to be consciously aware, and to feel compassion for others. She finds her power through accepting her suffering and vulnerability, through facing her pain and becoming empowered in her aloneness. In the search for her authentic spiritual being, she must face her deepest fears, her guilt and shame, her despair, her rage, her grief and pain, and the madness that torments her from within. In this quest, she will sometimes be called to face and embrace the deepest and darkest recesses of her being.

To enable her to pass from powerlessness and misery to power and compassionate action in the world a woman in the critical stages of this process needs to be held within an attitude of understanding and acceptance, and a personal relationship that is genuinely loving and caring. This helps to create the *containment* that will enable her to surrender to the necessities of her soul and spirit on this journey.

In order to encounter her depths with safety there must also be personal readiness. She must have developed an inner *foundation* through being embodied, grounded in her root chakra, and her ego must be stable enough to support the encounter. In well-founded psychological and spiritual traditions, the building of good foundations is a necessary prerequisite to enduring the intensity of depth processes. Good foundations are built in the world through relating to the reality of one's life as it is, and through this developing a clear sense of self.

On this quest, we also need *guidance*. Wrong guidance will lead us astray as surely as lack of foundations will leave us adrift in the uncharted waters. We need a source of guidance that will both understand our own psychological qualities, limitations, needs, and obstacles, and also orientate us in the unknown depths. Guidance is grounded in a spiritual or philosophical system, the 'tower' of Psyche's story, and may be represented by an inner or outer teacher or guiding figure. We must be able to recognise authentic and trustworthy guidance. We must also be willing, able, humble, and courageous enough to follow it. Guidance also comes through the myths and stories that speak to our innermost experience.

To come through the experience of the descent to the underworld, we must be able to return, bringing back to the world the inspiration, the power, the wisdom, or healing which we have accessed in our depths. We have not fully returned until we begin to express our gift, to use it, like the shaman, for whatever benefit it is intended. The experience and awareness that has been gained through the journey must be grounded in life, the sense of deepened connection to being grounded in conscious activity and relationship. This is the process of *integration*. Through it, we begin to recreate ourselves and our world out of a renewed vision and a restored sense of values. When our deepest experiences can be consciously felt, accepted, understood, contained, and contextualised, we may find meaning and value in our suffering.

On this inner journey, we are called to embrace our personal history and wounds, recognise the archetypal patterns, the myths that guide us, and open ourselves to the presence of spirit. Spiritual awareness grounds and inspires the personal quest, and infuses our personal and collective stories with sacredness; it is the greater context, the embracing attitude, which accepts everything, just as it is.

Vajrayana Buddhism, for me, seems to offer a philosophical framework that supports this multi-layered encounter with our depths. At the personal level, there is relationship to a wise and compassionate teacher, a spiritual friend who has travelled the path before us. Within the archetypal dimension there are spiritual practices that enable us to systematically engage with and transform the energies arising from our depths, skilful methods that guide us towards an experience of ultimate reality. And the philosophical ground of Buddhism offers an understanding within which all of our life experiences can be held, accepted without judgement, and eventually liberated.

Buddhism teaches that all phenomena, although existing in the ordinary relative sense, ultimately have no inherent and lasting existence; the essential nature of reality is *emptiness*. This view can provide us with a philosophical context when faced with the existential void within the depths of our experience. When we are immersed in the chaotic depths of the psyche, the mind needs to find a place to rest, to be still. Meditation techniques based on an understanding of emptiness can guide us to find such a resting place for the mind. A genuine understanding and experience of emptiness does not come easily, especially for us as westerners conditioned by a dualistic and materialistic way of thinking. It is a process that necessitates much study, practice, and time. When the experience of emptiness cannot be realised, then the gods and demons arising from our depths may take on a too-substantial sense of reality and overwhelm the personality. Whether they are evoked by the rigour and discipline of intensive meditation practice, or the probing techniques of psychotherapy, the result is much the same.

Without an understanding of emptiness, our thoughts, feelings, perceptions, and experiences tend to take on a heavy and solid sense of reality. Weighed down by this fixed and too rigid way of being, we miss the ever-present moment that is now. Attachment to the sense of rigidity that we hold about our experiences clouds over the natural flow of mind. Meditation teaches us to dance with the momentary interplay of existence and non-existence. This is also the play of the artist, though in a different way. The artist's work is to catch the elusive moment of awareness and bring it into form, thus resolving and releasing it. The meditator's way is to continually let it go, allowing each thought, feeling, and perception to dissolve back into the emptiness from which it arose.

The self, too, is ultimately empty of any inherent existence, according to the Buddhist view. H H Drukchen Rinpoche, an eminent Tibetan Buddhist teacher, has used the analogy of a bamboo stick to describe the nature of self. The bamboo is clearly there in a tangible way, but, if we cut through it, we find it is empty inside. We don't need to cut through it at every point, but simply to cut in one place, in order to discover the empty nature of the bamboo. So too with the self; we don't need to cut it to pieces and destroy it to understand its nature, but simply cut clearly through at one point to see what is actually there. When we do so, we find it is empty of inherent existence. It is the task of the teacher to determine at which point the self, and our attachment to it, can most effectively be cut through, so that we can realise the true nature of our mind.

To extend this analogy a little further, it would not help us to understand anything by hacking the whole bamboo to pieces; it needs to be intact in order for us to see clearly what is at its core – empty space. Were the bamboo to disintegrate there would simply be undifferentiated space, and we could not clearly recognise the nature of the bamboo itself. This is relevant to the need for an integrated sense of self, discussed earlier, and is also especially relevant to the psychology of women in patriarchal culture. Women often tend, by nature or nurture, and perhaps both, to have a less clearly defined sense of self. Their boundaries may be permeable, transparent, often damaged; the distinctions between their own life flow and feelings, and those of others are often not clear. Women easily attune to the energies of the collective flowing through them. This is a great strength, but it can also be a hindrance if a woman cannot also relate to her world as an individual with a clear and boundaried sense of self. Such a woman may find it difficult to achieve real power in the world and, not feeling herself clearly, may feel only emptiness within. Christ writes that:

'Women's spiritual quest…begins in an experience of *nothingness*. Women experience emptiness in their own lives – in self-hatred, in self-negation, and in being a victim; in relationships with men; and in the values that have shaped their lives.'[20]

'The experience of nothingness often has a different quality for women than for men. Men are not conditioned to think of themselves as worthless. For them, the experience of nothingness often comes after they have taken their place in the world of male power and joined the traditional hierarchies that support men's dominance in family and society. After achieving power and respect, men may come to experience their power as illusory. They may then open themselves to a deeper experience of power "not as the world knows it". As literatures of both East and West indicate, the male mystic's quest is arduous and difficult. Men have often found it difficult to give up conventional power and ego gratification to open themselves to union with the powers of being. Women, in contrast, live in a male-defined world in which culture has, for the most part, denied them access to power. The ordinary experience of women in patriarchy is akin to the experience of nothingness. Women never have what male mystics must strive to give up.'[21]

Women's experience of nothingness, as Christ is talking about it here, is of course not the same as a conscious awareness of the empty nature of reality, as described in mystical literature. But what Christ suggests is that the experience of psychological and social negation that women must often endure, and a woman's less defined, more permeable sense of self, may make mystical experiences of emptiness more accessible. It may also indicate that a different path to realising that state is required for a woman. She goes on to say that:

> ' "Awakening" is perhaps a more appropriate term than "conversion" for describing women's mystical experience, because "awakening" suggests that the self needs only to notice what is already there. Awakening implies that the ability to see or to know is within the self, once the sleeping draft is refused. Conversion often seems to imply that one has turned from one source of authority to another, for example, from materialism to God. It seems to be characteristic of women's awakening that the great powers, while larger than the self, are within as well as without.

> 'Awakening also takes a distinctive form in women's experience. As we have seen, "conversion", for men, means giving up conventional, worldly, egocentric notions of power, and trusting that genuine power is rooted in union with the powers of being. For women, awakening is not so much a giving up as a gaining of power. Women often describe their awakening as a coming to self, rather than a giving up of self, as a grounding of selfhood in the powers of being, rather than a surrender of self to the powers of being.'[22]

The awakening she describes here is in tune with the Buddhist view, which has a strong orientation towards feminine values and consciousness in its essential philosophy and practice. (Rita Gross eloquently argues this point, and thus the need for women to have equal status alongside men if Buddhism itself is to realise its full potential and essential wholeness.[23]) However, Buddhism is, like all mainstream religions of the last few millennia, highly patriarchal in its structure and organisation. As in

Christianity, most important texts have been written by men, and there are relatively few stories of enlightened women in the Buddhist tradition. There have been few famous women teachers, and few women hold places of authority within the spiritual and political hierarchies.[24]

A woman of the modern world who feels attuned to the basic teachings of Buddhism, may also feel that certain areas of her experience are not so clearly charted. So long as we have to deal with the relative realities of our individual psychology and conditioning (which we must until we are wholly aware of our true nature, completely enlightened), then the difference in our experience does matter and needs to be accounted for. Just as westerners do not approach the teachings from the same standpoint as easterners, so too is there a difference between the approach of men and women. Because most of the literature of all mainstream religions is written, or rewritten, from a male perspective, it may not be such a straightforward task for a woman to orientate herself by it:

> '...[W]omen must even read themselves sideways into analyses of the experience of nothingness. Women need a literature that names their pain and allows them to use the emptiness in their lives as an occasion for insight rather than as one more indication of their worthlessness. Women need stories that will tell them that their ability to face the darkness in their lives is an indication of strength, not weakness.'[25]

As the social and political situation of women in the modern western world is slowly changing, we are beginning to see more women actively involved in the spiritual field also. Women teachers, clergy, and writers are taking positions of responsibility and emerging as leaders. I believe this movement will grow as gradually we come to rebalance our one-sided focus on masculine values. It will grow the more the way of women, and of the feminine, is acknowledged, understood, and named. I also believe it must grow; the world needs enlightened women and female teachers to stand alongside men, embodying in living human form the positive values of the creative feminine spirit which we are so in need of reconnecting to. Women alone may not be able to change the world, but I believe that the world will not change towards a truly healthy and creative direction unless the true voice of woman is heard, respected, and attended to. Until feminine awareness and values, as expressed through women, are accorded equal place to those of the masculine, in all spheres of life, we will not find the renewal and change we seek.

In the journey of descent into the deep feminine, our woundedness opens us to suffer consciously our pain, confusion, fear, and the existential suffering of human life. But through this, through consciously facing and accepting our darkness, our loss and brokenness, we come closer to that within us which is indestructible — to the ground of being, of pure awareness. Each time we descend consciously into the darkness and embrace a little more of our pain and suffering, we come closer to realising our true nature and embodying the loving and healing power of it in our life. When we begin to touch to this level, we begin to feel acceptance — acceptance of what is, just as it is. And the hurt and pain and anger can finally be expressed as a heartfelt care and concern for the suffering we see around us. Buddhism teaches that our basic nature is good, loving, and wise. The journey of the feminine is to travel inwards, deeper into who we are; through opening to our pain and darkness, consciously facing, understanding, and accepting it, we travel deeper to discover our basic good nature, awaken to the power of being within us, and ground ourselves in that source.

And so it is that, through honouring our experiences of loss, of emptiness, and suffering; through courageously entering into them, in full consciousness, as we embark upon the journey through the dark realms within; and through naming our pain and sharing our stories with others on this path, we may begin to develop an inner sureness that will support and empower us as we seek to express our own unique qualities, offering the gifts of our learning to the world.

Epilogue

There is a wild piece of coastland in north Norfolk that I sometimes visit. Pine woods and dunes eventually give way to a vast expanse of deserted beach. The sea is always a long way out. It is the same sea that took my friend's life, though a different part of the country, and it became a special place for me during the time when I was learning to come to terms with my loss and my grief, healing the wound, and writing this book.

The first summer I made a small shrine, a grave for his wandering soul, hidden beneath bushes and overlooking the sea. There I placed shells, leaves, wild flowers, and said all the things I had not had the opportunity to say to him. When I returned the next year the shrine was still there, with the remnants of my offerings. I offered again, and prayed for him, wherever his soul was now. Being in that place made me feel quiet and at peace. He had been cremated; there had been no grave to sit by, and I had needed one.

When I returned the third summer, it was different. Before searching through the woodlands for the shrine, I picked some wild flowers and walked down to the sea. I had no clear idea of what I was going to do that day. I walked a mile or two to the point where the river intersects the beach. As I walked, I saw a black head in the water, bobbing up and down as it swam along beside me. Soon I saw it was rising and falling too slowly to be a human swimmer, and taking far too long a stroke. It was a seal, and I imagined it was following me. It filled me with joy to have a companion on my walk.

This time I felt the urge to give my offering to the sea, and threw the small cluster of wild flowers I had gathered into the water, at the place where the sea and river meet. I stood for a long time watching the flowers as they were slowly carried out, following the currents back and forth along their turbulent path where the river forged its way into the oncoming waves. The seal seemed to be swimming on strongly past the mouth of the river.

A seagull overhead caught my attention for a moment. When I looked back to the water, both seal and flowers had disappeared, and I saw neither of them again. I was filled with a feeling of certainty that my offering had been accepted by the spirits of the sea. And I was glad.

Later I went to find the leafy alcove where I had been the last two years, following the now familiar signs of tree branch and bush and winding paths. But this time it became immediately clear to me that things had changed. Instead of offering my thoughts and prayers, I was surprised to find myself asking for help. Not for anything in particular, but I had the sense that I would need it soon. And with my request, again came the certainty that the powers that were present had felt my wordless prayer and would be guiding me in whatever was to come. I knew at that moment that I had finally laid Dave to rest, and the place that he had left had become sacred ground, filled with a power that embraced me now. What he had come to represent for me was now a part of myself. My heart was at peace. Again I was glad, and felt a strength and calm pour into me.

That night I slept on the beach. I had not intended to, but could not find a guest-house and was too tired to make the long drive home. So back along through the woods and sand dunes I walked, coming out of the darkness of the trees into the moonlit expanse of beach. It was pure magic. A clear night, full moon, sky littered with stars, and no one around for miles but the night animals and me. I sat for some time on the edge of the dunes drinking in the wilderness.

I couldn't sleep at all. It was really a waste of time trying, and I should have spent the night moon-gazing and listening to the distant waves on the beach. I had no proper bedding with me and soon my little sandy nook became hard, damp, and very lumpy. Every half hour or so I would awake and, gazing up into the sky, see a shooting star! I saw six or more that night, before I eventually gave up my attempts to sleep. At about half-past four in the morning I decided nature had rewarded me enough with this beautiful night vision, and I felt deeply affirmed. So, still half asleep, I trudged back along the beach to find my car.

Three times nature had blessed me, and I knew that something inside me had healed.

A year and one month later, I was fulfilling a dream to visit Tibet. After seven long years in the underworld within, I was finally crossing those extraordinary snow mountains, harsh, rugged, and towering miles into the sky, to find a beautiful and powerful land where my heart felt perfectly at home. I wept at the beauty of the wilderness I witnessed beyond the forbidding mountains.

From the depths of the darkness to the snowy peaks of the roof of the world I came, as I had known I must from the very beginning, to complete this part of my life's journey. And I knew I had been helped and guided there.

'When in your death you died to all that was outside of me,
vanishing from the thousand things of the world,
to be fully reborn in my sorrow,
I felt that my life had grown perfect,
the man and the woman becoming one in me forever.'

Rabindranath Tagore, Lover's Gift

References

Introduction

1 Stanislav Grof and Christina Grof, editors, *Spiritual Emergency*.
2 Bika Reed, *Rebel in the Soul*, p89.
3 See Judith Plaskow and Carol P Christ, editors, *Weaving the Visions: New Patterns in Feminist Spirituality*.
4 Chani Smith, 'The Symbol of the Shekhinah – the Feminine Side of God', in *The Absent Mother*, edited by Alix Pirani, p11.
5 Esther Harding, *Psychic Energy*, p320.

Chapter One

1 Stephen Levine, *Who Dies?*, p87-8.
2 Irina Tweedie, *The Chasm of Fire*, Dedication page.
3 Marion Woodman, *The Ravaged Bridegroom*, p214-5.
4 C G Jung, *The Psychology of Transference*, quoted in Marion Woodman, *The Ravaged Bridegroom*, p214.
5 Stanley Keleman, *Living Your Dying*.
6 Steve Smith, in the preface to *Everyday Zen*, by Charlotte Joko Beck, pvi.
7 Andrew Harvey, *A Journey in Ladakh*, p218-9.
8 James Hillman, *The Dream and the Underworld*, p38.
9 Bessel A van der Kolk, MD, *The Body Keeps the Score: Memory and the Evolving Psychobiology of Posttraumatic Stress*, Harvard Medical School Publications, p253.
10 James Hillman, *Suicide and the Soul*, p88.

11 James Hillman, Lecture given at Regents College, London, for the London Convivium for Archetypal Studies, 1988.

12 Marion Woodman, *The Ravaged Bridegroom*, p70.

Chapter Two

1 James Hillman. Lecture given at Regents College, London, for the London Convivium for Archetypal Studies, 1988.

2 Marion Woodman, *The Ravaged Bridegroom*, p18.

3 Keith Thompson, 'The UFO Encounter as a Crisis of Transformation', in *Spiritual Emergency*, edited by Stanislav and Christina Grof, p134.

4 Marie-Louise von Franz, 'Lectures on Jung's Typology', Spring Publications Inc, reprinted in *Caduceus*, Issue 13, Spring 1991.

5 Arnold Mindell, *Working with the Dreaming Body*, p76 and p81.

6 Alexander Lowen, MD, *Narcissism – Denial of the True Self*, pix-x.

7 I am here using the terms 'authentic', or 'true', and 'false self' in the sense defined by Winnicott; he defined the 'true self' as 'the summation of sensori-motor aliveness'. This is basically a psycho-somatic orientation; the notion of 'self' in a psycho-spiritual context will be touched on later, though a detailed exploration is beyond the scope and purpose of this book.

8 Lowen, *Narcissism – Denial of the True Self* pxi.

9 Alix Pirani, *The Absent Father*, p23.

10 Madeleine Davis and David Wallbridge, *Boundary and Space*, p58.

11 John W Perry has written at length on the relationship between psychosis and the individuation process, in *The Self in Psychotic Process*.

12 M Scott Peck, MD, *The Road Less Travelled*, p282.

13 'Self' and 'ego' are often used interchangeably in the translation of Buddhist teachings; in western psychology there are many different definitions of both terms, and they are not necessarily synonymous within the different psychological schools.

14 John Weir Perry, 'Spiritual Emergence and Renewal', in *Spiritual Emergency*, p72.

15 Chogyam Trungpa, *Shambhala – The Sacred Path of the Warrior*, p47.

Chapter Three

1 C G Jung, *Modern Man in Search of a Soul*, p92.
2 Stanislav Grof, *Beyond the Brain*.
3 Alessandra Piontelli, *From Fetus to Child – An Observational and Psychoanalytic Study*.
4 Marion Woodman, *The Ravaged Bridegroom*, p43.
5 *Ibid*, p40.
6 *Ibid*, p74.
7 *Ibid*, p167.
8 Jean Liedloff, *The Continuum Concept*.
9 Woodman, *The Ravaged Bridegroom*, p43.
10 D W Winnicott, lecture notes, quoted in Madeleine Davis & David Wallbridge, *Boundary and Space*, p50.
11 Madeleine Davis & David Wallbridge, *Boundary and Space*, p50.
12 Winnicott, quoted in *Boundary and Space*, p60-61.
13 Melanie Klein, 'Mourning and its Relation to Manic-Depressive States', in *The Selected Melanie Klein*, edited by Juliet Mitchell, p148.
14 Ken Wilber, *The Atman Project* and *No Boundary*.
15 See particularly Alex Pirani, *The Absent Father*.
16 Linda Schierse Leonard, *The Wounded Woman*.
17 Chani Smith, 'The Symbol of the Shekhinah – The Feminine Side of God', in *The Absent Mother* edited by Alix Pirani, p12.
18 Of course the father may also take on some or even all of the mothering function, and vice versa.
19 Edward C Whitmont, *Return of the Goddess*, p42.
20 *Ibid*, p43.
21 *Ibid*, p71.

Chapter Four

1 C A Meier, *Healing Dream and Ritual*, piv.
2 James Shultz, 'Growing up in Adulthood: Stages on the Buddhist Path', in *Reflections of Mind*, edited by Tarthang Tulku, p171.
3 See Jean Hardy, *A Psychology with a Soul*.
4 James Hillman, *The Dream and the Underworld*, p107.
5 James Hillman, *Suicide and the Soul*, p71.

6 See Arnold Mindell, *Working with the Dreaming Body*, and other books by this author.

7 James Hillman, *Suicide and the Soul*, p68.

8 Lewis E Mehl, 'Modern Shamanism: Integration of Biomedicine with Traditional World Views', in *Shaman's Path*, edited by Gary Doore, p137.

9 Richard Moss, MD, *The Black Butterfly*, pp138-146.

10 Caroline Myss, *Anatomy of the Spirit*, p106.

11 See James Lovelock, *Gaia*; and Peter Russell, *The Awakening Earth*.

12 Linda Hartley, *Wisdom of the Body Moving*, Chapter One.

13 Alix Pirani, 'The Kabbalistic Tree of Life: The Goddess's Perspectives', in *The Absent Mother*, edited by Alix Pirani, p227.

14 Hillman, *Suicide and the Soul*, p80.

15 Alice Miller, *Thou shalt not be aware*, p200.

Chapter Five

1 Stephen Larsen, *The Shaman's Doorway*, p37.

2 *Ibid*, p7.

3 Wang Tsung-yueh, 'T'ai Chi Ch'uan Lun', in *The Essence of T'ai Chi Ch'uan*, Benjamin Lo, Martin Inn, Robert Amacker, Susan Foe, p31 and p100.

4 Rita M Gross, in *Buddhism After Patriarchy*, presents an in-depth study of women and the feminine in Buddhism, past, present, and future, and shows that in essence Buddhist philosophy supports gender equality.

5 Tsultrim Allione, *Women of Wisdom*, pp21-22, and quoting Chogyam Trungpa, 'Feminity', in *Maitreya*, pp23-24.

6 Roger Horrocks, 'The Divine Woman in Christianity', in *The Absent Mother*, edited by Alix Pirani, p110.

7 *Ibid*, p127.

8 *Ibid*, pp128-9.

9 See Ean Begg, *The Cult of the Black Virgin*.

10 Asphodel P Long, 'The Goddess in Judaism – A Historical Perspective', in *The Absent Mother*, edited by Alix Pirani, p47.

11 See Barbara Black Koltuv, *The Book of Lilith*.

12 Long, 'The Goddess in Judaism – A Historical Perspective', p38.

13 Marge Piercy, 'For strong women', in *Eight Chambers of the Heart: Selected Poems*.

14 Joseph Chilton Pearce, *Magical Child*, p43.

15 *Ibid*, p95.

16 Jean Shinoda Bolen, *Goddesses in Everywoman*.

17 Alix Pirani, 'The Kabbalistic Tree of Life: The Goddess's Perspectives', in *The Absent Mother*, edited by Alix Pirani, p230.

18 Maureen Murdock, *The Heroine's Journey*, p3.

19 Bika Reed, *Rebel in the Soul*, pp118-9.

20 Larsen, *The Shaman's Doorway*, p12.

21 *Ibid*, pp 12-13.

22 Robert A Johnson, *She*, Chapter Two.

23 Jean Houston, *The Search for the Beloved*, p152.

24 *Ibid*, p158.

25 Johnson, *She*, p65.

26 *Ibid*, p65.

27 Larsen, *The Shaman's Doorway*, p152.

28 Houston, *The Search for the Beloved*, pp167-8.

Chapter Six

1 Diane Wolkstein and Samuel Noah Kramer, 'The Courtship of Inanna and Dumuzi' in *Inanna — Queen of Heaven and Earth: Her Stories and Hymns from Sumer*, pp29-49.

2 *Ibid*, 'Inanna and the God of Wisdom', pp11-27.

3 Sylvia Brinton Perera, *Descent to the Goddess*, p21.

4 Wolkstein and Kramer, *Inanna*, p55.

5 Perera, *Descent to the Goddess*, p51.

6 Kramer, *From the Poetry of Sumer*, p92.

7 Perera, *Descent to the Goddess*, p19.

8 *Ibid*, p61.

9 Wolkstein and Kramer, *Inanna*, p59.

10 *Ibid*, p60.

11 Perera, *Descent to the Goddess*, p63.

12 Wolkstein and Kramer, *Inanna*, p61.

13 Perera, *Descent to the Goddess*, p67.

14 Wolkstein and Kramer, *Inanna*, p64.

15 *Ibid*, p68.

16 Marion Woodman, *The Ravaged Bridegroom*, p117.

17 Marie-Louise von Franz, *Shadow and Evil in Fairytales*.

18 Wolkstein and Kramer, *Inanna*, p71.

19 Stephen Larsen, *The Shaman's Doorway*, p211.

20 Wolkstein and Kramer, *Inanna*, p75.

21 *Ibid*, p89.

Chapter Seven

1 Mircea Eliade, *Rites and Symbols of Initiation*, p2.

2 See Lynne V Andrews, for example, *Star Woman* and *Flight of the Seventh Moon*.

3 Bani Shorter, *An Image Darkly Forming*.

4 Eliade, *Rites and Symbols of Initiation*, p3.

5 *Ibid*, pxiv.

6 See Eliade, *Rites and Symbols of Initiation*.

7 Eliade, *Shamanism – Archaic Techniques of Ecstasy*, p4.

8 *Ibid*, p4.

9 *The Oxford Reference Dictionary*.

10 *Ibid*.

11 Joan Halifax, *Shaman – The Wounded Healer*, p84.

12 Eliade, *Shamanism*, pp259-60.

13 *Ibid*, pp63-4.

14 Halifax, *Shaman – The Wounded Healer*, p13.

15 *Ibid*, p9.

16 Eliade, *Rites and Symbols of Initiation*, p72.

17 *Ibid*, pp87-8.

18 Eliade, *Shamanism*, p27.

19 Stanislav Grof, 'The Shamanic Journey: Observations from Holotropic Therapy', in *Shaman's Path*, edited by Gary Doore, p173.

20 Halifax, *Shaman – The Wounded Healer*, p7.

21 *Ibid*, p19.

22 Melanie Reinhart, *Chiron and the Healing Journey*, p15.

23 Halifax, *Shaman – The Wounded Healer*, pp92, p94.

24 Reinhart, *Chiron and the Healing Journey*, p33.

25 J B, quoted by Stephen Larsen in *The Shaman's Doorway*, pp198-9.

26 Rowena Pattee, 'Ecstasy and Sacrifice' in *Shaman's Path*, edited by Gary Doore, p26.

27 Halifax, *Shaman – The Wounded Healer*, p92.

28. Larsen, *The Shaman's Doorway*, pp159-60.

29 Reinhart, *Chiron and the Healing Journey*, p6.

30 *Ibid*, p21.

31 *Ibid*, p21.

32 *Ibid*, p22.

33 *Ibid*, p28.

34 *Ibid*, p28.

35 *Ibid*, p31.

36 *Ibid*, pp36, p58.

37 *Ibid*, p39.

Chapter Eight

1 One notable contemporary example of this is the enactment of Black Elk's great vision, recounted by John Neihardt in *Black Elk Speaks*.

2 Marion Woodman, *The Ravaged Bridegroom*, p27.

3 Keith Thompson, 'The UFO Encounter Experience as a Crisis of Transformation', in *Spiritual Emergency*, edited by Stanislav and Christina Grof, pp128-31.

4 Brian Bates, *The Way of the Actor*, p22.

5 Alan Bleakley, *Fruits of the Moon Tree*, p75.

6 Joan Halifax, *Shamanic Voices*, pp30-31.

7 Bates, *The Way of the Actor*, pp22-3.

8 Rollo May, *The Courage to Create*, pp84-5.

9 *Ibid*, p21.

10 *Ibid*, p32.

11 Joan Halifax, *Shamanic Voices*, p69.

12 Sylvia Brinton Perera, *The Scapegoat Complex*, p26.

13 John Weir Perry, 'Spiritual Emergence and Renewal', in *Spiritual Emergency*, edited by Stanislav and Christina Grof.

14 May, *The Courage to Create*, p105.

15 Bates, *The Way of the Actor*, Chapter Four.

16 May, *The Courage to Create*, pp62-3.

17 *Ibid*, pp107-8.

18 R D Laing, 'Transcendental Experience in Relation to Religion and Psychosis', in *Spiritual Emergency*, edited by Stanislav and Christina Grof.

19 Perera, *The Scapegoat Complex*, pp87-8.

20 Natalie Goldberg, *Writing Down the Bones*.

21 May, *The Courage to Create*, p46.

22 *Ibid*, pp48-9.

Chapter Nine

1 See Jean Hardy, *A Psychology with a Soul*, Chapter Eight.

2 See Edward C Whitmont, *Return of the Goddess*.

3 John Welwood, 'On Psychotherapy and Meditation', in *Awakening the Heart*, edited by John Welwood, pp57, p47.

4 *Ibid*, p52.

5 Mokusen Miyuki, 'Psychological Adjustment is not Liberation', in *Awakening the Heart*, p40.

6 Stephen Larsen, *The Shaman's Doorway*, pp147-8.

7 Charles Tart, 'Samsara: A Psychological View', in *Reflections of Mind*, edited by Tarthang Tulku, p68.

8 Jean Houston, *The Search for the Beloved*.

9 Bika Reed, *Rebel in the Soul*, p93, p95.

10 Chogyam Trungpa, *Shambhala: The Sacred Path of the Warrior*, p45.

11 C A Meier, *Healing Dream and Ritual*, pp1, 55-6, 107, 127.

12 Carol P Christ, *Diving Deep and Surfacing*, p1.

13 *Ibid*, p5.

14 *Ibid*, pp6-7.

15 See John Firman, *"I" and Self – ReVisioning Psychosynthesis*.

16 Melanie Reinhart, *Chiron and the Healing Journey*, pp23-4.

17 Christ, *Diving Deep and Surfacing*, pp7-8.

18 *Ibid*, p9.

19 In *Meeting the Great Bliss Queen*, Anne Carolyn Klein discusses how the practice of Buddhism can empower modern women.

20 Christ, *Diving Deep and Surfacing*, p13.

21 *Ibid*, pp17-18.

22 *Ibid*, pp18-19.

23 See *Buddhism After Patriarchy* by Rita M Gross, for an in-depth discussion of the place of women and the feminine principle in Buddhist philosophy and practice.

24 Tsultrim Allione, *Women of Wisdom*, pp146-9. See also *Passionate Enlightenment*, by Miranda Shaw, for a historical re-evaluation of women's place and influence in Tantric Buddhism.

25 Christ, *Diving Deep and Surfacing*, p17.

Bibliography

Allione, Tsultrim, *Women of Wisdom*, Routledge & Kegan Paul, London & Boston, 1984.

Andrews, Lynne V, *Flight of the Seventh Moon*, Harper & Row, New York, 1985.

Star Woman, Warner Books, Inc, New York, 1986.

Assagioli, Roberto, *Psychosynthesis*, Turnstone Press Ltd, Wellingborough, Northants, 1975.

The Act of Will, Turnstone Press Ltd, Wellingborough, Northants, 1984.

Bates, Brian, *The Way of the Actor*, Shambhala, Boston. 1987.

Beck, Charlotte Joko, *Everyday Zen*, Harper San Francisco, 1989.

Begg, Ean, *The Cult of the Black Virgin*, Penguin, USA, new edition 1997.

Bleakley, Alan, *Fruits of the Moon Tree*, Gateway Books, Bath, 1984.

Bolen, Jean Shinoda, MD, *Goddesses in Everywoman*, Harper Perennial, New York, 1984.

Christ, Carol P, *Diving Deep and Surfacing*, Beacon Press, Boston, 1980.

Davis, Madeleine, and David Wallbridge, *Boundary and Space*, Penguin UK, 1981.

Doore, Gary, *Shaman's Path*, Shambhala, Boston & London, 1988.

Eichenbaum, Luise, and Susie Orbach, *Between Women*, Viking Penguin Inc, New York, 1988.

Eliade, Mircea, *Shamanism: Archaic Techniques of Ecstasy*, Bollingen Series, Princeton University Press, 1972.

Rites and Symbols of Initiation, Harper & Row, New York, 1975.

Estes, Clarissa Pinkola, *Women Who Run with the Wolves*, Rider, London, 1992.

Firman, John, *'I' and Self – Re-Visioning Psychosynthesis*, John Firman, Palo Alto, CA, 1991.

Franz, Marie-Louise von, *Lectures on Jung's Typology*, Spring Publications Inc, Woodstock, CT, 1971
  Shadow and Evil in Fairytales, Spring Publications, Zurich, 1974.

Goldberg, Natalie, *Writing Down the Bones*, Shambhala, Boston & London, 1986.

Golding, William, *Lord of the Flies*, Faber & Faber, London, 1954.

Grof, Stanislav, *Beyond the Brain*, SUNY, New York, 1985.

Grof, Stanislav and Christina Grof, editors, *Spiritual Emergency*, Jeremy P Tarcher, Inc, Los Angeles. 1989.

Gross, Rita M, *Buddhism After Patriarchy*, SUNY Press, Albany, New York, 1993.

Halifax, Joan, *Shaman – The Wounded Healer*, Thames & Hudson, London, 1982.
  Shamanic Voices, Penguin Arkana, New York, 1991.

Harding, Esther, *Psychic Energy*, Bollingen Series X, Princeton University Press, 1973.

Hardy, Jean, *A Psychology with a Soul*, Penguin Arkana, UK, 1989.

Hartley, Linda, *Wisdom of the Body Moving*, North Atlantic Books, Berkeley, CA, 1995.

Harvey, Andrew, *A Journey in Ladakh*, Flamingo, London, 1984.

Hillman, James, *Suicide and the Soul*, Spring Publications, Inc, Woodstock, CT, 1985
  The Dream and the Underworld, Harper & Row, New York, 1979

Houston, Jean, *The Search for the Beloved*, Jeremy P Tarcher, Inc, Los Angeles, 1987.

Johnson, Robert A, *She – Understanding Feminine Psychology*, Harper & Row, New York, 1977.

Jung, C G, *Modern Man in Search of a Soul*, Ark, Routledge, London, 1984.
  The Psychology of Transference, Routledge, London, 1983

Keleman, Stanley, *Living Your Dying*, Center Press, Berkeley, CA, 1974.

Klein, Anne Carolyn, *Meeting the Great Bliss Queen*, Beacon Press, Boston, 1995.

Kolk, Bessel A van der, MD, *The Body Keeps the Score: Memory and the Evolving Psychobiology of Posttraumatic Stress*, Trauma Clinic, Harvard Medical School, Boston, 1994.

Koltuv, Barbara Black, PhD, *The Book of Lilith*, Nicolas-Hays, Inc, York Beach, Maine, 1986

Kramer, Samuel Noah, *From the Poetry of Sumer: Creation, Glorification, Adoration*, University of California Press, Berkeley, 1979.

Larsen, Stephen, *The Shaman's Doorway*, Station Hill Press, Barrytown, New York, 1988.

Leonard, Linda Schierse, *The Wounded Woman*, Shambhala, Boston & London, 1982.

Levine, Stephen, *Who Dies?* Doubleday, New York & London, 1982.

Lhalungpa, Lobsang P, translator, *The Life of Milarepa*, Shambhala, Boston & London, 1985.

Liedloff, Jean, *The Continuum Concept*, Penguin UK, 1986.

Lo, Benjamin Pang Jeng, Martin Inn, Robert Amacker, Susan Foe, *The Essence of T'ai Chi Ch'uan*, North Atlantic Books, Berkeley, CA, 1979.

Lovelock, James, *Gaia – The practical science of planetary medicine*, Gaia Books Ltd, London, 1991.

Lowen, Alexander, MD, *Narcissism – Denial of the True Self*, Collier Books, New York, 1985.

Macintyre, Dr. Anne, *M.E. – Post-Viral Fatigue Syndrome*, Unwin Paperbacks, London, 1989.

Maslow, Abraham H, *The Farther Reaches of Human Nature*, Penguin USA, 1976.

Masson, Jeffrey, *Against Therapy*, Fontana, London, 1990.
Final Analysis, Fontana, London, 1992.

May, Rollo, *The Courage to Create*, Bantam Books, New York, 1976.

Meier, C A, *Healing Dream and Ritual*, Daimon Verlag, Einsiedeln, Switzerland, 1989.

Miller, Alice, *Thou Shalt Not Be Aware: Society's Betrayal of the Child*, Meridian, New York, 1984.
The Drama of Being a Child, Virago, London, 1987.
For Your Own Good, Virago, London, 1987.

Mindell, Arnold, *Working with the Dreaming Body*, Penguin Arkana, UK, 1989.

Mitchell, Juliet, editor, *The Selected Melanie Klein*, Penguin UK, 1986.

Moss, Richard, MD, *The Black Butterfly*, Celestial Arts, Berkeley, CA, 1986.

Murdock, Maureen, *The Heroine's Journey*, Shambhala, Boston & London, 1990.

Myss, Caroline, PhD, *Anatomy of the Spirit*, Bantam Books, New York & London, 1997.

Neihardt, John G, *Black Elk Speaks*, University of Nebraska Press, Lincoln, NA, 1961.

Pearce, Joseph Chilton, *Magical Child*, Bantam Books Inc, New York, 1980.

Peck, M Scott, MD, *The Road Less Travelled*, Simon & Schuster Inc, New York, 1978.

Perera, Sylvia Brinton, *Descent to the Goddess*, Inner City Books, Toronto, 1981.

The Scapegoat Complex, Inner City Books, Toronto, 1986.

Perry, John Weir, *The Self in Psychotic Process*, University of California Press, Berkeley, 1953.

Piercy, Marge, *Eight Chambers of the Heart: Selected Poems*, Penguin UK, 1995.

Piontelli, Alessandra, *From Fetus to Child – An Observational and Psychoanalytic Study*, Tavistock/Routledge, London & New York, 1992.

Pirani, Alix, *The Absent Father*, Penguin Arkana, UK 1989.

editor, *The Absent Mother*, Mandala, HarperCollins, London, 1991.

Plaskow, Judith and Carol P Christ, editors, *Weaving the Visions: New Patterns in Feminist Spirituality*, Harper San Francisco, 1989.

Reed, Bika, *Rebel in the Soul*, Inner Traditions International, Rochester, Vermont, 1988

Reinhart, Melanie, *Chiron and the Healing Journey*, Penguin Arkana, London, 1989.

Rilke, Rainer Maria, *Duino Elegies*, translated by Stephen Cohn, Carcanet Press Ltd, Manchester, 1989

Russell, Peter, *The Awakening Earth*, Routledge and Kegan Paul, London, 1982.

Rutter, Peter, MD, *Sex in the Forbidden Zone*, Unwin Paperbacks, London, 1990.

Shaw, Miranda, *Passionate Enlightenment*, Princeton University Press, 1994.

Shorter, Bani, *An Image Darkly Forming*, Routledge & Kegan Paul, London, 1987.

Smith, Fritz Frederick, MD, *Inner Bridges*, Humanics New Age, Atlanta, Georgia, 1986.

Storr, Anthony, *The Dynamics of Creation*, Penguin UK, 1976.

Solitude, Flamingo/Fontana, London, 1989.

Tagore, Rabindranath, *Lovers Gift*, anthology compiled by David Loring, Yelf Bros Ltd, Newport, Isle Of Wight.

Trungpa, Chögyam, *Shambhala – The Sacred Path of the Warrior*, Shambhala Publications Inc, Boulder & London, 1984.

Meditation in Action, Shambhala Publications Inc, Berkeley, CA, 1969.

Glimpses of Abhidharma, Shambhala, Boston & London, 1987.

Crazy Wisdom, Shambhala, Boston & London, 1991.

'Femininity', *Maitreya IV*, Shambhala, Berkeley, 1973

Tulku, Tarthang, editor, *Reflections of Mind*, Dharma Publishing, Emeryville, CA, 1975.

Tweedie, Irina, *The Chasm of Fire*, Element Books, Shaftesbury, Dorset, 1979.

Welwood, John, editor, *Awakening the Heart*, Shambhala, Boston & London, 1983.

Whitmont, Edward C, *Return of the Goddess*, Penguin Arkana, UK, 1983.

Wilber, Ken, *The Atman Project*, Theosophical Publishing House, Wheaton, Illinois, 1980.

No Boundary, Shambhala, Boston & London, 1979.

Wolkstein, Diane, and Samuel Noah Kramer, *Inanna – Queen of Heaven and Earth: Her Stories and Hymns from Sumer*, Harper & Row, New York, 1983.

Woodman, Marion, *The Ravaged Bridegroom*, Inner City Books, Toronto, 1990.

Addiction to Perfection, Inner City Books, Toronto, 1982.

The Pregnant Virgin, Inner City Books, Toronto, 1985.